Issues in Higher Education

Titles include:

Jürgen Enders and Egbert de Weert (*editors*)
THE CHANGING FACE OF ACADEMIC LIFE
Analytical and Comparative Perspectives

John Harpur
INNOVATION, PROFIT AND THE COMMON GOOD IN HIGHER EDUCATION
The New Alchemy

Tamsin Hinton-Smith
WIDENING PARTICIPATION IN HIGHER EDUCATION
Casting the Net Wide?

V. Lynn Meek
HIGHER EDUCATION, RESEARCH, AND KNOWLEDGE IN THE ASIA-PACIFIC REGION

Guy Neave
THE EUROPEAN RESEARCH UNIVERSITY

Guy Neave
THE EVALUATIVE STATE, INSTITUTIONAL AUTONOMY AND RE-ENGINEERING
HIGHER EDUCATION IN WESTERN EUROPE
The Prince and His Pleasure

Maria João Rosa and Alberto Amaral (*editors*)
QUALITY ASSURANCE IN HIGHER EDUCATION
Contemporary Debates

Mary Ann Danowitz Sagaria
WOMEN, UNIVERSITIES, AND CHANGE

Snejana Slantcheva
PRIVATE HIGHER EDUCATION IN POST-COMMUNIST EUROPE

Sverker Sörlin
KNOWLEDGE SOCIETY VS. KNOWLEDGE ECONOMY

Bøjrn Stensaker, Jussi Välimaa and Clàudia Sarrico (*editors*)
MANAGING REFORM IN UNIVERSITIES
The Dynamics of Culture, Identity and Organisational Change

Voldemar Tomusk
THE OPEN WORLD AND CLOSED SOCIETIES

Teresa Carvalho and Rui Santiago
PROFESSIONALISM, MANAGERIALISM AND REFORM IN HIGHER EDUCATION AND
THE HEALTH SERVICES
The European Welfare State and the Rise of the Knowledge Society

Issues in Higher Education
Series Standing Order ISBN 978–0–230–57816–6 (hardback)
(*outside North America only*)

You can receive future titles in this series as they are published by placing a standing order. Please contact your bookseller or, in case of difficulty, write to us at the address below with your name and address, the title of the series and the ISBN quoted above.

Customer Services Department, Macmillan Distribution Ltd, Houndmills, Basingstoke, Hampshire RG21 6XS, England

Previous books by the authors:

T. Carvalho, T. Caria & R. Santiago (eds.) (2012). *Grupos Profissionais, Profissionalismo e Sociedade do Conhecimento: Tendências, Problemas e Perspectivas* [*Professional Groups, Professionalism and Knowledge Society: Trends, Problems and Prospects*]. Porto. Edições Afrontamento (ISBN: 978-972-36-1212-7).

L. Meek, L. Goedegebuure, R. Santiago & T. Carvalho (eds.) (2010). *The Changing Dynamics of Higher Education Middle Management*. Springer (ISBN 978-90-481-9162-8).

T. Carvalho (2009). *Nova Gestão Pública e Reformas da Saúde. O profissionalismo numa encruzilhada* [*New Public Management and Health Reform: Professionalism at the Crossroad*] Lisbon. Edições Sílabo (ISBN 978-972-618-546-8).

J. S. Taylor, J. Ferreira, M. L. Machado & R. A. Santiago (eds.) (2008). *The Development of Non-University Higher Education in Europe: Critical View of Ten Countries*. Dordrecht/London/Boston. Springer, Vol. 23 (Higher Education Dynamics Series) (ISBN 978-1-4020-8334-1).

R. Santiago, A. Magalhães & T. Carvalho (2005). *O surgimento do managerialismo no sistema de Ensino Superior Português* [*The Emergence of Managerialism in Portuguese Higher Education System*]. Coimbra. FUP (ISBN 972-98848-9-7).

Professionalism, Managerialism and Reform in Higher Education and the Health Services

The European Welfare State and the Rise of the Knowledge Society

Edited by

Teresa Carvalho and Rui Santiago
University of Aveiro and CIPES, Portugal

Selection, introduction, conclusion and editorial matter © Teresa Carvalho and Rui Santiago 2015
Individual chapters © Respective authors 2015

All rights reserved. No reproduction, copy or transmission of this publication may be made without written permission.

No portion of this publication may be reproduced, copied or transmitted save with written permission or in accordance with the provisions of the Copyright, Designs and Patents Act 1988, or under the terms of any licence permitting limited copying issued by the Copyright Licensing Agency, Saffron House, 6–10 Kirby Street, London EC1N 8TS.

Any person who does any unauthorized act in relation to this publication may be liable to criminal prosecution and civil claims for damages.

The authors have asserted their rights to be identified as the authors of this work in accordance with the Copyright, Designs and Patents Act 1988.

First published 2015 by
PALGRAVE MACMILLAN

Palgrave Macmillan in the UK is an imprint of Macmillan Publishers Limited, registered in England, company number 785998, of Houndmills, Basingstoke, Hampshire RG21 6XS.

Palgrave Macmillan in the US is a division of St Martin's Press LLC, 175 Fifth Avenue, New York, NY 10010.

Palgrave Macmillan is the global academic imprint of the above companies and has companies and representatives throughout the world.

Palgrave® and Macmillan® are registered trademarks in the United States, the United Kingdom, Europe and other countries.

ISBN 978–1–137–48699–8

This book is printed on paper suitable for recycling and made from fully managed and sustained forest sources. Logging, pulping and manufacturing processes are expected to conform to the environmental regulations of the country of origin.

A catalogue record for this book is available from the British Library.

A catalog record for this book is available from the Library of Congress.

Contents

List of Tables vii

Acknowledgements viii

Notes on Contributors ix

Introduction
Towards Changes in Professions and Professionalism:
Academics, Doctors and Nurses 1
Rui Santiago and Teresa Carvalho

Part I Professionals in Higher Education

1 The State of the Academic Estate 15
  Guy Neave

2 Professional Autonomy in a Comparative Perspective 30
  Teresa Carvalho and Rui Santiago

3 The Finnish Academic Profession in Health-Related
  Sciences and Social Services 64
  Timo Aarrevaara

Part II Professionals in Health

4 Reconstructing Care Professionalism in Finland 81
  Helena Hirvonen

5 Beyond the Portuguese Nursing Labour Market: Towards a
  Crisis of Professionalism? 102
  Joana Sousa Ribeiro

6 Managing the Medics in Britain 119
  Mike Dent

7 The Changing Medical Profession in England 135
  Mike Saks

8 The State and Medicine in the Governance of Health Care
   in Portugal   151
   Tiago Correia, Graça Carapinheiro and Helena Serra

Conclusions
Cross-Country and Inter-Professional Convergences and
Divergences in Changes in Professions and Professionalism   172
Teresa Carvalho and Rui Santiago

Index   181

List of Tables

3.1 Respondents according to disciplines, in the CAP survey and EUROAC interviews in Finland 68
3.2 Teaching activities of the respondents according to the discipline (per cent of named activities). Question: During the current (or previous) academic year, have you been involved in any of the following teaching activities? 75
5.1 Number of foreign nurses and total of foreign human resources in the NHS, by country groups, 2004 to 2013 107

Acknowledgements

This work is funded by the Fundo Europeu de Desenvolvimento Regional (FEDER) funds through the Operational Programme for Competitiveness Factors – COMPETE and national funds through the FCT – Foundation for Science and Technology – under the projects 'PTDC/CPE-PEC/104759/2008' and EXCL/IVC-PEC/0789/2012.

We would like to express our very great appreciation to Professor Alberto Amaral for his valuable and constructive suggestions during the planning and development of this book. His willingness to give his time so generously has been very much appreciated.

Contributors

Timo Aarrevaara is Professor of Higher Education Administration, Organisation and Management at the University of Helsinki, Finland. He has participated in and conducted several evaluating and auditing projects and has acted as the principal investigator of a number of projects, including 'The Changing Academic Profession Survey in Finland' (CAP), 'The Changing Academic Profession: The Impact of Globalisation, Diversification and Institutional Reorganisation on Academic Work and Employment Conditions in Finland' (EUROAC-FIN) and 'Public Engagement Innovations for Horizon 2020' (PE2020).

Graça Carapinheiro develops research activities in the fields of sociology of health, illness and medicine and in sociology of health professions for the Centre for Research and Studies in Sociology (CIES/ISCTE), Lisbon University Institute, Portugal. She is considered the founder of the Sociology of Health in Portugal. Her PhD thesis 'Knowledge and Power in the Hospital. A Sociology of Hospital Wards', was published in book form in 1993, which has, to date, been reissued five times.

Teresa Carvalho holds a PhD in Social Sciences. She is a senior researcher at the Centre for Research in Higher Education Policies (CIPES) and an assistant professor in the Department of Social, Political and Territorial Sciences, University of Aveiro, Portugal, where she is a member of the executive committee. She focuses on developing research into public reforms, and she has a special interest in issues related to the role of professionals in formulating and implementing public policies. She has been a coordinator of the European Sociological Association (ESA) network of the Sociology of Professions (RN19) since 2013. She has published research on the new public management sociology of professions and academic careers, both in book chapters and in journals such as *Minerva*, *Higher Education Quarterly*, *Higher Education Policy* and *Professions and Organization*. She is also co-editor of *The Changing Dynamics of Higher Education Middle Management* (2010).

Tiago Correia is Professor of Sociology and a research fellow at the ISCTE, Lisbon University Institute, Portugal; his previous appointment

x Notes on Contributors

was at the University of Montreal. His interests have been related to medical sociology and to the sociology of organisations and professions with a particular focus on the health-care sector. He has been engaged in several scientific communities and has chaired and organised encounters. He has edited books and published in a number of journals including *Health Sociology Review* and *BMC Health Services Research*.

Mike Dent is Professor of Health Care Organisation at the Faculty of Health Sciences, Staffordshire University, UK. He is an organisational sociologist who has been researching, writing and publishing on the comparative organisation of health care and on the professions of medicine and nursing for more than two decades. More recently, he has extended this interest to include user involvement in health and social care services and has been involved in research into e-health aspects of care pathways.

Helena Hirvonen holds a PhD in Social Sciences. She is a post-doctoral researcher and university teacher of Social and Public Policy at the Department of Social Sciences and Philosophy, University of Jyväskylä, Finland. Her research areas include the welfare state and welfare-state restructuring, and gendered structures and organisational practices in the labour market. Her journal articles have appeared in *Gender, Work & Organization, Social Policy & Administration* and *Time & Society*, and she has worked in projects 'FLOWS – Impact of Local Welfare Systems and Culture on Female Labour Force Participation' (FP7) and 'Violence, Professional Practices and Occupational Health in Social and Health Care Sector' (Emil Aaltonen Foundation).

Guy Neave is Emeritus Professor of Comparative Higher Education Policy Studies. He has been Director of Research for the International Association of Universities (IAU) in Paris since 1990 and was elected as Foreign Associate of the US National Academy of Education in 1998. He is one of the world's foremost scholars and writers in the field of higher education policy studies. He joined CIPES part-time in 2007. He has been active as a higher education consultant, most notably for the Council of Europe, the Commission of the European Communities and the World Bank and has been an adviser to numerous governments, foundations and organisations.

Joana Sousa Ribeiro is a researcher at the Centre for Social Studies (CES-UC) and a PhD candidate at the School of Economics,

University of Coimbra, Portugal. Her main research interests include socio-professional mobility and migration, longitudinal studies, citizenship studies and global health. In 2008, she published 'Migration and "occupational integration": Foreign health professionals in Portugal', in M. Saks and E. Kuhlmann (eds.), *Rethinking Professional Governance: International Directions in Health Care*; and, in 2007, 'Gendering migration flows: Physicians and nurses in Portugal', *Equal Opportunities International*, Vol. 27, 1. Moreover, she is co-author of 'Health professionals moving to and out of Portugal: A typical case?', *Health Policy*, Vol. 114, No. 2–3, February 2014, 97–108.

Mike Saks is an international research professor at the University Campus Suffolk (UCS), UK. Previously he was Provost at UCS, Deputy Vice Chancellor at the University of Lincoln and Dean of the Faculty of Health and Community Studies, De Montfort University, UK. He is the former president (and now Vice President) of the International Sociological Research Committee (RC52) on Professional Groups. He has published over a dozen books on professions, including health, conducted funded research projects and acted as a policy adviser to government and professional bodies.

Rui Santiago holds a PhD in Education. He is an associate professor and Head of the Department of Social, Political and Territorial Sciences, University of Aveiro, Portugal. He is also a senior researcher at the Centre for Research in Higher Education Policies (CIPES) and Vice President of the Portuguese Society of Education Sciences. His main research interests are public reforms, higher education governance and management and the academic profession. He has published diverse book chapters and articles in journals such as *Higher Education, Minerva, Higher Education Quarterly, Higher Education Policy* and *Análise Social*. He is also co-editor of *The Changing Dynamics of Higher Education Middle Management* (2010) and *Non-University Higher Education in Europe* (2008).

Helena Serra is Associate Professor of Sociology at the Faculty of Social Sciences and Humanities, Universidade Nova de Lisboa (FCSH-UNL), Portugal. She has published on health-care research and organisations and given several keynote presentations at international conferences. She is a member of the ESA Executive Committee and of the ESA RN 19 'Sociology of Professions' and a board member of the ISA RC 52 'Sociology of Professional Groups'.

Introduction

Towards Changes in Professions and Professionalism: Academics, Doctors and Nurses

Rui Santiago and Teresa Carvalho

Introduction

The profession concept is a social construct, the outcome of the intersection between different but interrelated elements. It is widely recognised in the literature that the possession of a formal body of abstract knowledge, certified by academic and professional credentials, is assuredly a key device for imposing social closure and exercising monopoly over specific jurisdictional areas within the social division of labour (Johnson 1972; Abbott 1988; Brint 1994; Freidson 2001; Larson 2013). Accordingly, the internal dynamics that professional groups develop to uphold their social and cultural status as a profession relates to two institutions which are external to them: higher education (HE) and bureaucracies. In addition, the need to acquire and update scientific knowledge is equally fundamental in maintaining professional autonomy. Such autonomy is evident not only at the level of practice often expressed in terms of discretionary power (Freidson 2001; Evetts 2006) or prudential practices (Champy 2009, 2011), but is also related to organisational structures and decision-making. Historically, this linkage has allowed the institutionalisation and stabilisation of the traditional professions, as well as the emergence of new occupational groups seeking political and social legitimacy for their professionalisation project (Larson 2013).

Autonomy has also enabled the construction of a system of professionalism values and of decision-making in relative independence from market demands, management and hierarchy control, particularly in the public systems. In fact, it is important to highlight that, in diverse national public systems, particularly in the health and HE sectors, bureaucracy was, and still is in some cases, characterised by a singular feature: its structures and processes appear as an outcome of reciprocal influences between the organisation logic and the professionalism logic. Weber (1995) recognised this special character of some bureaucracies, although he has identified them as having archaic forms of organisation and decision-making, as opposed to more rational, industrial-like ones. In more recent times, other authors contend that these organisational forms can be classified as professional bureaucracies (Mintzberg 1979) or professional organisations (Greenwood & Lachman 1996). Independently from the terms used to categorise these distinctive organisational configurations, their principal features show an intersection of bureaucratic and professionalism co-determination mechanisms, which enabled a sort of parallel co-evolution of these two logics (Bleiklie & Michelsen 2008).

Since the beginning of the 1980s, changes in both the public and private sectors, as a result of the development of organisation logic instead of professionalism logic, have, potentially, reduced the control and regulatory power of professional groups over the terms of their employment. And can, eventually, also contribute to break down the professionals' technical autonomy and protection of their working processes against the interference of organisational hierarchy. Actually, the reconfiguration of professional bureaucracies, which, to an increasing degree, are today aligned around priorities, practices and norms derived from managerialism and entrepreneurial models and priorities, also represents a potential threat to professional groups. Introducing competition and the enterprise principles (Foucault 2004) as the central governing and management mode of the systems and organisations is expected to redefine both the internal power relations between professionals and bureaucratic authority while externally readjusting the balance of power between professionals and citizens, the latter redefined as consumers.

Changes in the professional group's landscape

Since the beginning of the 1980s the professions have been the subject of contradictory forces and political pressures that, more than in previous periods, are making their traditional jurisdictions more fluid and ambiguous. The complex political, social and economic dynamics currently shaping the professions pluralise and fragment them as a field of study. As a consequence, it is difficult to construct a global and unified theory on what is a profession, the *locus* of professions in the social stratification and social hierarchy, and how professions deal with transformations in advanced capitalist societies.

Within this framework, contemporary theorisations and empirical analyses on professions and professionalism cannot be done without taking into consideration changes in the political, economic and social environments which are expected to transform the structural, institutional and organisational position of the professions in societies. The reconceptualisation of the welfare state roles in respect to social areas traditionally under its jurisdiction – the extension of economic and market rationality logic to all social areas; the surfacing of new control and regulation modes applied to organisations and professional work; the increasing hegemony of the knowledge society and knowledge economy as a recipe for the crises affecting the (post-)industrial society and financial capitalism; and the ascendency of the technical and cognitive/instrumental rationality on knowledge production, dissemination and use – all of these aspects are present in contemporary developed societies as demanding challenges to traditional and more recent groups of professionals.

However, these challenges entail a paradox. On the one hand, changes in the formation and implementation of public policies are supported on the assumption that the self and corporatist interests of professional groups guide their behaviour, creating an obstacle to the achievement of social and economic efficiency and effectiveness. On the other hand, these changes, entailing a complex and multifaceted nature, require the expertise of professionals to have any chance of success. The emergence of competitive games in the national and economic globalisation arena, and the expected alignment of organisational and professional practices with the knowledge society and knowledge economy logics, require a strong involvement of professionals in their accomplishment and the mobilisation of the ideology of professionalism.

In this respect, recent studies (Fournier 1999; Evetts 2002, 2006) have demonstrated that professionalism, reconceptualised under the lens of the new technologies of governance and management, was redirected to discipline professionals in organisations. The symbolic capital historically embedded in professionalism is exploited by organisations to reach two main goals: the respecification of professionals to become symbiotically connected with the managerial and economic rationality underlying the new organisational structures and processes; and the inducement of transformations in professionals' subjectivity towards a market (or quasi-market) self-discipline and values, which is expected to promote a collective and individual straight commitment (and submission) to the organisational logic. A new space of autonomy is created for professionals, but under managerial and economic rationality guidance

(Foucault 2004). In the end, on behalf of an organisation's legitimacy and success, as well as with regard to financial imperatives, professionals are stimulated to consent to the transfer of their power to external control and regulation systems, and to open their fields of expertise (Rose 1996) to the technologies of micro-control (Reed 2002, 2007), which will then frame their organisational and professional practices.

Taken together, all these measures to create a new social order at institutional and organisational levels, appear, potentially, as being able to induce a process of de-professionalisation; or, at very least, to dissolve the strength of professionalism as both an identity and an ethic of work, as signified, for instance, by Freidson's (2001) third logic ideal type. Professional groups are confronted with less favourable conditions regarding working conditions and security of employment. Despite these adverse circumstances, and perhaps due to them, two important social phenomena are still on the ground in respect to threats coming from the extension of the new market and economic logics to professional fields. On the one hand, the traditional professions seem to develop new political, social and organisational strategies aiming at defending the stabilisation, or even the expansion, of their professional jurisdictions. For instance, some studies suggest that professionals have been able to elaborate active strategies to deal with and/or to meet the new challenges (Kirkpatrick et al. 2005; Kuhlmann & Saks 2008; Carvalho & Santiago 2010b; Carvalho 2012). On the other hand, existent occupational groups are increasingly searching for a confirmation of their professionalisation projects, based on claims of ownership of specialised knowledge and expert skills, which they expect to enable them to obtain the profession statute (Larson 2013).

Towards cross-professional groups and cross-country comparison in Europe

The set of issues discussed in the previous section are part of the research agenda on professions, professionalism and professionalisation processes. As a result, there are a great number of ongoing studies analysing the macro, meso and micro changes taking place in professional groups, and their potential outcomes. However, in general, these studies do not take into account the interconnection of different dimensions in the production of these changes. Some of these dimensions are, as seen earlier in this Introduction: the state-reforming role, the relationship between the knowledge society and professional specialised knowledge and expert skills, and the reconfiguring of bureaucracies towards soft bureaucracies (Diefenbach & Todnem 2012) and post-bureaucratic regimes of professional work. Furthermore, the focus of most of the literature is on one profession and does not allow us to identify and to analyse, in a more comparative perspective, changes and/or transformations in wider-ranging professional fields.

This is the case, for instance, of the academic profession. The academic profession, for a long time regarded as a key profession (Perkin 1969), is expected to fulfil a central role in the knowledge society and knowledge economy (Olsen & Peters 2005). Nevertheless, empirical studies into the way academy responds to such transformations suggest that there is no single model in the way the profession is both affected by, and responds to, it (Carvalho & Santiago 2010a, 2010b; Santiago & Carvalho 2012; Neave 2013). Research in HE tends to focus exclusively on academics as a singular case study, just as the majority of studies on professions tend also to focus on one specific professional group.

The focus on one single profession does not allow the construction of either a comparative perspective or a holistic one. Cross-professional group comparison can be useful in finding out more about changes in the professions and in professionalism, with respect to differences in national, institutional and professional contexts, as well as in a single profession. Thus, cross-group comparisons allow the possibility of addressing the range of changes and variations that may operate, at the same time, across different professions, but, additionally, in different national and institutional contexts in response to externally driven pressures.

Based on these assumptions, the main purpose of this book is to trace a panoramic view of changes in professions and professionalism from a comparative perspective. The comparative level includes different national contexts – Portugal, England and Finland – two institutional sets – health institutions (hospitals) and higher education institutions (HEIs) – and three professional groups – academics, doctors and nurses. Such an approach may well open up a more nuanced understanding of the way in which contemporary challenges faced by these professions are perceived. This may also help to expand knowledge on what, why and how professional groups respond differently to state and organisational pressures, considering their different professional cultures and history, and thus their professional identities. In short, the aim of this book is to enlarge the conceptual possibilities with regard to the analysis of changes in professions and professionalism, enabling contacts between different theoretical and empirical constructions.

Changes in the professions of academics, medical doctors and nurses in three welfare state systems

In European societies, health and HE have been key welfare sectors in which, under the state direction, structural reforms had, and still have, a strong – perhaps the strongest – impact. Hospitals (and primary healthcare units), universities and polytechnics (in the Portuguese and Finish case) were submitted to market and new public management (NPM)-driven pressures, which were not only directed towards re-engineering their organisational structures and modus operandi, but also towards producing a different role model for their professional groups' *habitus* (Bourdieu 1997) and practices.

Each of these groups has been shaped by a specific national history and moulded by distinct social processes. They also have important similarities in the way their professional project was developed and consolidated under welfare state political and social logic. Firstly, in different degrees, the three groups have maintained a paradoxically but interconnected contingent and a co-evolution relationship with their organisations. In most organisational situations, professionals acted, and may still act, as the co-producers of bureaucratic and managerial rules, or, at least, as having a significant influence over their definition and implementation. Secondly, the three professional groups shared a similar position, since the core of their members work in services central to the welfare state apparatus. Thirdly, as suggested previously, they have also historically followed a similar successful route with regard to the consolidation of their professional projects – based on the definition of a body of formal knowledge and expert skills, legitimated by credentialism, state legitimacy, social recognition, and the development of economic and political strategies for social closure. Fourthly, all three professional groups have been submitted to similar wide reform principles. The way these principles are perceived and interpreted inside each nation, sector, institution and professional group will condition the processes of formation and implementation of health and HE public policies, which will differ according to distinct national and institutional contexts.

The three professional groups are examined from the standpoint of different national models of the welfare state. These models are the Southern or Mediterranean model represented by Portugal; the Scandinavian or social democratic variant, drawing on the experience of Finland; and the liberal – or Anglo-Saxon – model (primarily England). This focus provides a cross-national setting, allowing a closer examination of the political and social, as well as the economic, contexts that are being brought to bear on these three models; contexts which can be considered significant components of the European welfare state diversity.

Outline of the volume

This Introduction is completed by a brief outline of the contents of the other chapters. However, it is important to recall briefly the main original contribution this book expects to make to the study of HE. This expectation is principally based on the theoretical and empirical conviction that using a comparative perspective may generate a more robust purchase over the impact of deep external transformations on key professions and professionals. This comparative perspective comprises three distinct dimensions: comparison between different professional groups, distinct national environments and institutional settings. Taken as a whole, the different chapters included in the book, even if some of them resort to an analytical basis anchored in a single profession and national context, try to overcome the literature's more conventional approach, which tends to examine the way a single profession accommodates and adjusts to radical change.

The eight chapters of the book are embedded in the set of concepts and issues discussed in this introduction; that is, the macro, meso and micro elements that are inducing significant changes in the institutional environment of the three professional groups, and in their structural, organisational and professional practices. The book is organised in two parts: the first part – professionals in HE – which comprises three chapters, concentrates predominantly on a global analysis of the contemporary structural position of the academic profession in the European HE systems, as well as on changes occurring in respect to professional autonomy; the second part – professionals in health – includes five chapters related mainly to health professions – nurses and medical doctors. These chapters focus mainly on changes in the professional markets, and in the new control and regulation mechanisms under which these professionals are placed.

Guy Neave's chapter critically analyses the concept of the academic profession, looking at three historical scenarios of the relationship between state and HE – the British, the American and the Western European or Continental one. Referring mainly to Western Europe, Neave proposes two evolutionary paradigms to approach changes in academia's assigned social and institutional roles – a first paradigm shift from the academic guild to the academic estate (from guild to state service); and a second paradigm shift from the academic estate to the academic constituency (from state service to the academics as agents of production in the knowledge economy). With regard to these changes, the authors question if the term 'profession' is the most suitable to use when analysing contemporary changes in academia.

Teresa Carvalho and Rui Santiago provide an extended analysis of recent NPM-driven changes of professional autonomy. This concept is key to the sociology of professions, even if it has different meanings, and even if, in a great number of studies, it is used without an adequate clarification. In theoretical terms, Carvalho and Santiago propose a model to approach the autonomy concept based on three interconnected levels: the structural autonomy, related to the social and political contingencies framing the jurisdictional fields and professional groups' collective behaviour and power; the organisational autonomy, associated with the space in which professionals have to participate in the institutions' decision-making processes (particularly in respect to the general rules and conditions under which their professional work is done); and the autonomy of practice, connected to the protection of the sphere of working processes from the interference of management and hierarchy. Within the framework of the Portuguese national scenery, the authors empirically tested their conceptual framework in two sectors – HE (universities and polytechnics) and health (hospitals) – and in three professional groups – academics, doctors and nurses. Based on the analysis of the three professional groups' discourses, the chapter allows concluding that there are distinct perceptions of changes in the three levels of autonomy, not only between different professional groups, but also inside them.

In the last chapter of the first part of the book, Timo Aarrevaara traces a panorama of the challenges that academics are facing in Finland as a consequence of HE reforms, particularly regarding the decrease in public funding; the expanded access; the merger policies; and the emphasis on quality assessment and interdisciplinarity. To clarify what these challenges signify for the present and future of the academic profession, Timo proceeds to analyse the Finish academics' perceptions of their new social and institutional roles, using, as an example, academics who are affiliated to the disciplinary areas of medical sciences, health-related sciences and social services. The data supporting this analysis was obtained from the Changing Academic Profession (CAP) and the Academic Profession in Europe (EUROAC) international studies, undertaken from 2008 to 2012.

The second part of the book – professionals in health – has five chapters. The first two chapters are devoted to an analysis of the changes in the nursing profession in Finland and Portugal that have occurred as a result of the knowledge society, NPM and austerity policies that have affected the public health services in the two countries.

Helena Hirvonen argues that nurses, compared with doctors, face more challenging contingencies enacted by the transformations of the structural and institutional conditions of the public health sector in Finland, namely in respect to their professional autonomy. Supported by feminist theories and by a critical analysis of NPM assumptions and managerial technologies, Helena's argument contends that the use of information and communication technologies in health and social care audits, within the context of the transition of the Finish society to a knowledge society, is gendered marked. Contemporary welfare state forms of professional work control and regulation tend to favour a disembodied professionalism and, in this sense, culturally feminine aspects of nursing and care work become categorised as non-professional activities. Helena uses empirical data, based on qualitative interviews, concluding by the existence of hybridism between forms of disembodied care professionalism, which are explicitly gender neutral, and forms that implicitly reproduce the traditional gender expectations and skills in the care work.

Joana Sousa Ribeiro's chapter addresses the relation between the development of the nursing profession and the labour market in the Portuguese context. Issues such as the Portuguese nursing process of de-professionalisation, (de)-nationalisation of professional projects and professionalism are discussed within the scope of neo-liberal, managerialist and, more recently, austerity policies, in the reorganisation of health-care services. After tracing the profile of the nurses' professional group, which is the most numerous of various health groups in Portugal, Joana Ribeiro analyses the Portuguese nurse's emigration movement to other European countries (such as Germany, the Netherlands and Switzerland) and the opening of the Portuguese nursing market to foreign nurses, namely of Spanish and East European extraction. Along with these new dynamics of professional mobility, linked to international recruitment by agencies, she discusses other issues which alter the configuration of the nursing profession in Portugal: the overproduction of graduates; the increase of the nurses' precarious labour conditions and proletarisation; and external interference in nurses' control over the monopoly of their work.

The remaining three chapters of the book are dedicated to the doctors within the British and the Portuguese national contexts. Mike Dent, starting from the analysis of the various waves of NPM and governance in Britain (primarily in England), concentrates his reflection on the influence of those waves in the respecification of hospital doctors as hybrid doctors. He appeals to the new institutionalist perspective, based on the script notion, to examine how changes at the hospital organisational level have induced a shift from the dominant autonomous doctor to a hybrid doctor who is also engaged in management. According to Mike, this does not mean that there is a process of de-professionalisation or proletarianisation, but simply that doctors are adapting to the new regimes of control and regulation – accountability systems, transparency and efficiency – dominant in the NHS and in the British (primarily English) hospitals' organisational landscape.

Starting from a different conceptual framework, affiliated to the neo-Weberian approach – namely by endorsing the Weber proposal on social closure – Mike Saks examines the changing position of doctors as a profession in England. Mike argues that the achievement of formal exclusionary social closure, which emerged in the mid-19th century, has been subjected to increasingly critical scrutiny since the second half of the 20th century. State policy reforms, new bureaucratic regimes of control, regulation and surveillance, market pressures and the increasing power of users, are all aspects that have, in some sense, changed the doctor's position and role at the macro, meso and micro levels. However, almost following Mike Dent's arguments, Mike Saks contends that these changes do not configure a de-professionalisation process. In fact, strategies were developed by doctors to counteract threats to social closure and professional autonomy, even if the English doctors' profession has been re-stratified. Saks also argues in his chapter that social closure exclusionary mechanisms in HE have less amplitude when compared with the medical doctors' mechanisms.

Tiago Correia, Graça Carapinheiro and Helena Serra have reached, in their chapter, similar conclusions to Mike Dent and Mike Saks, but this time when analysing the impact of Portuguese neo-liberal and NPM health reforms on doctors. According to the authors, doctors have succeeded in developing strategies to protect their professional position in the workplace, by reconfiguring their jurisdictions and influencing organisational structures and decision-making processes. Correia and colleagues support their conclusions by using the empirical results of three sociological studies developed on the interplay between the state and medical self-regulation. The studies aimed to analyse the way doctors interpret and respond to the externally imposed pressures coming from state policies, and from its translation by professional managers to the organisational landscape of public hospital. The authors' general purpose is to suggest a set of theoretical and empirical insights with regard to knowledge improvement, allowing a more advanced interpretation of doctors' resistance (and adaptability) to pressures from the state, other professional groups and users.

The concluding chapter, written by Teresa Carvalho and Rui Santiago, based on reflections over the content of the different book chapters, propose a comparative analysis of the major elements associated with the way the professional groups face changes of state policies and organisational landscapes. Additionally, these comparative analyses are focused on how these changes can potentially affect the three professional groups' positions and practices. Special attention is given to the common themes that emerge from the comparison of academics with doctors and nurses, as well as to the identification of some important differences. Finally, some important issues for further research are also presented in this concluding chapter.

References

Abbott, A. 1988. *The System of Professions: An Essay on the Division of Expert Labour*, University of Chicago Press, London.
Bleiklie, I. & Michelsen, S. 2008. 'The university as enterprise and academic co-determination', in A. Amaral, I. Bleiklie & C. Musselin (eds.), *From Governance to Identity: A Festschrift for Mary Henkel*, Springer, Dordrecht.
Bourdieu, P. 1997. *Les usages sociaux de la science: pour une sociologie clinique du champ scientific*, INRA editions, Paris.
Brint, S. 1994. *In an Age of Experts: The Changing Role of Professionals in Politics and Public Life*, Princeton University Press, Princeton, NJ.
Carvalho, T. 2012. 'Shaping the "new" academic profession: Tensions and contradictions in the professionalisation of academics', in G. Neave & A. Amaral (eds.), *Higher Education in Portugal 1974–2009: A Nation, a Generation*, Springer, Dordrecht.
Carvalho, T. & Santiago, R. 2010a. 'NMP and "middle management": How do deans influence institutional policies?', in L. Meek, L. Gooedgbuure, R. Santiago & T. Carvalho (eds.), *The Changing Dynamics of Higher Education Middle Management*, Springer, London.
Carvalho, T. & Santiago, R. 2010b. 'Still academics after all ...', *Higher Education Policy*, Vol. 23, pp. 397–411.
Champy, F. 2009. *La sociologie des Professions*, PUF editions, Paris.
Champy, F. 2011. *Nouvelle théorie sociologique des professions*, Presses Universitaires de France, PUF, Paris.
Diefenbach, T. & Todnem, R. 2012. 'Bureaucracy and hierarchy: What else?', in T. Diefenbach & R. Todnem (eds.), *Reinventing Hierarchy and Bureaucracy: From the Bureau to Network Organizations*, Emerald Group Publishing Limited, Bingley.
Evetts, J. 2002. 'New directions in state and international professional occupations: Discretionary decision-making and acquired regulation', *Work, Employment and Society*, Vol. 16, No. 2, pp. 341–353.

Evetts, J. 2006. 'Short note: The sociology of professional groups: New directions', *Current Sociology*, Vol. 54, No. 1, pp. 133–143.
Foucault, M. 2004. *Naissance de la biopolitique. Cours au collége de France (1978–1979)*, Seuil/Gallimard, Paris.
Fournier, V. 1999. 'The appeal to "professionalism" as a disciplinary mechanism', *Social Review*, Vol. 47, No. 2, pp. 280–307.
Freidson, E. 2001. *Professionalism, the Third Logic*, Polity Press, Cambridge.
Greenwood, R. & Lachman R. 1996. 'Change as an underlying theme in professional service organizations: An introduction', *Organization Studies*, Vol. 17, No. 4, pp. 563–572.
Johnson, T. 1972. *Professions and Power*, Macmillan, London.
Kirkpatrick, I., Ackroyd, S. & Walker, R. 2005. *New Managerialism and Public Sector Professionalism*, Palgrave Macmillan, London.
Kuhlmann, E. & Mike, S. (eds.) 2008. *Rethinking Professional Governance: International Directions in Healthcare*, Policy Press, Bristol.
Larson, M. 2013. *The Rise of Professionalism: Monopolies of Competence and Sheltered Markets*, Transaction Publishers, New Brunswick and London.
Mintzberg, H. 1979. *The Structuring of Organizations: A Synthetics of Research*, Prentice Hall, Englewood Cliffs, NJ.
Neave, G. 2013. *The Evaluative State, Institutional Autonomy and Re-Engineering Higher Education in Western Europe*, Palgrave Macmillan, Basingstoke.
Olsen, M. & Peters, M. 2005. 'Neoliberalism, higher education and the knowledge economy: From the free market to knowledge capitalism', *Journal of Education Policy*, Vol. 20, No. 3, pp. 313–345.
Perkin, H. 1969. *Key Profession: The History of the Association of University Teachers*, Kelley, London.
Reed, M. 2002. 'New managerialism, professional power and organisational governance in UK universities: A review and assessment', in A. Amaral, A. G. Jones & B. Karseth (eds.), *Governing Higher Education: National Perspectives on Institutional Governance*, Kluwer Academic Publishers, Dordrecht.
Reed, M. 2007. 'Engineers of human souls, faceless technocrats or merchants of morality? Changing professional forms and identities in the face of neo-liberal challenge', in A. Pinnington, R. Macklin & T. Champbell (eds.), *Human Resource Management; Ethics and Employment*, Oxford University Press, Oxford.
Rose, N. 1996. 'Governing "advanced" liberal democracies', in A. Barry, T. Osborne & N. Rose (eds.), *Foucault and Political Reason: Liberalism, Neo-Liberalism, and Rationalities of Government*, University of Chicago Press, Chicago.
Santiago, R. & Carvalho, T. 2012. 'Excellence rhetoric in Portuguese higher education', *Minerva*, Vol. 50, No. 4, pp. 511–532.
Weber, M. 1995. *Économie et société/1. Les catégories de la sociologie*, Librairie Plon, Paris.

Part I
Professionals in Higher Education

1
The State of the Academic Estate

Guy Neave

Introduction

Regardless of whether as individuals, we count ourselves as members of the Academic Estate or hope to become so, one thing is blindingly clear: few periods in the history of the universities in Europe, have witnessed so many changes and that across so many dimensions as has been the lot of higher education over the course of the past two decades. And, given the current situation, it is very unlikely indeed that the adaptability the Academic Estate has shown over the past half century is fated to diminish in the foreseeable future. On the contrary, if Portugal, France and Spain are still digesting the changes that legislation in 2007 introduced in both governance and evaluation of higher education (Neave & Amaral 2011, pp. 40–62; Neave 2012a, pp. 46–60) further legislation is currently being debated in France, while the introduction of new tools of varying degrees of vexatiousness – risk management being one – is under active contemplation in the United Kingdom (McClaran 2014, pp. 106–116; Rosa & Amaral 2014, pp. 13–31).

Teeming disciplines

Those who study higher education take for granted that HE is a multidisciplinary domain, if not always an interdisciplinary one. Indeed, much heat and not always great light have been generated – rarely accompanied by success – to define what ought to be the core disciplines in the study of higher education. For the American sociologist of organisations, the late Burton R. Clark, four disciplines formed the core of higher education as a field: Sociology, Politics, Economics and History (Clark 2000, pp. 1–38). To this, in the mid-1990s, Frans van Vught, shortly before his Elevation as Rector Magnificus of Twente University pressed to add Public Administration. The cries of dissent his modest proposal invoked were very far from modest. They were testy, outraged and exceedingly intolerant. In short, scholars in higher education, like the late Chairman Mao, agreed – as, indeed, they tend to do in other areas of intellectual endeavour – 'to let a thousand flowers bloom'. To the pragmatist, who, even if she or he is not always aware of it, owes much to the late Tony Becher, the early 1990s saw some two dozen different perspectives feeding into the study of higher education. They ranged alphabetically from Anthropology to Women Studies (Becher 1992, pp. 1763–1776). Since then, other perspectives have joined the throng. One thinks, for instance, of International Relations – effectively inter-system flows of staff and students – and the rise of the twin perspectives of Quality and Evaluation, which came into their own during the 1990's.

Given the range of higher education's contributing perspectives – and the myriad facets they display – it is not surprising that higher education is a domain, both fertile and dynamic. Yet such variety is not without ambiguity. It may indeed be a blessing. It can just as easily be a curse. When different perspectives act in a complementary fashion, the study of higher education may yield insights both fruitful and original. Multidisciplinarity coalesces into interdisciplinarity. But such a happy state is not always guaranteed. Nor can we always count upon it as an inevitable feature of our domain.

Still, precisely because the study of higher education brings together researchers from widely differing disciplinary backgrounds, by the same token such meetings maximise the opportunity to learn something of benefit and advantage from colleagues.

Our task

Our task is twofold. Principally, we are focused on the Academic Estate and its changing lot in our respective systems – Finland, Portugal and the United Kingdom. But we are also engaged in dissecting the anatomy of one historic Guild within the Academic Estate – the medical profession – and the rise to fortune and recent access to enhanced status of the nursing profession. Over the years, I have spent a little time trying to weigh up the significance and the consequences of changes in the condition, tasks, responsibility and accountability that the Academic Estate today is asked to take on board. But, I have equally to admit that the worlds of medicine and nursing remain, to use a Scottish vernacular, 'beyond my ken'. My task, as I interpret it, is to provide a broad conceptual framework within which they may be located.

Apologia

Given the many perspectives that gather around the study of higher education, it is only right that I make mine explicit. I trained as a political historian, specialising in the history of the French labour movement and then, in the rousing days that followed the French student upheaval in May 1968, found myself strangely and suddenly seduced by the sociology of education. Today, what I call my stamping ground is Comparative Higher Education Policy. This focuses primarily on the macro and system levels; more particularly on the relationship between government and higher education.

We all have our personal ideas, which we take for granted. Mine is this: it is excessively difficult to weigh up the enduring – as opposed to the passing – significance of higher education policy in its contemporary shape, priorities and demands without placing such aspects against a medium – or a long-term – backdrop. The short-term vision is not always the same thing as its long-term consequences, intended, perverse or otherwise.

Such a view does not hold that what happened in the past of necessity determines what happens today. Rather, it simply suggests that we are better placed to grasp what precisely is at stake if we are aware of what present initiatives set out to replace and what the origins of these initiatives were. Furthermore, one advantage an historical analysis brings to issues of the moment is precisely to winnow out the substantial and enduring significance of the issue from the chaff, rhetorical justification and rodomontade that so often accompany the unveiling of that issue, in contrast to the objective condition which it is supposed to remedy. The way change is perceived by its proponents at the outset is not always how it is subsequently viewed:

> when the tumult and the shouting dies,
> The captains and the kings depart.
>
> (Kipling, 1919)

The Bologna process provides an excellent illustration of this unwitting phenomenon: judgement maturing 'as time goes by' (Neave & Amaral 2008, pp. 40–62).

A few dilemmas

When we embark on the comparative analysis of academia, we are, from the very start, faced with one fundamental dilemma. Despite today's siren calls for convergence, for accountability, for performance demonstrated and for the 'good practice' of some systems to be rapidly taken up by the rest, the status, identity, standing and structure of the 'Academic Estate' was – and, for that matter, still is – largely defined and moulded by national circumstance. From this, it follows that neither the Anglo-Saxon notion of an 'academic profession', nor, for that matter, the various historical models found in Continental Europe which integrated academia into the nation's civil service, are adequate in grasping the subtleties of the other. Furthermore, the willingness of both British and American scholars to accept the concept of academia as a profession in a magnificent belief that one term fits all, plays down marked differences in the formal legal relationship between academia and authority, both political and institutional, that characterises the Academic Estate in those two nations.

Clarity, clarity

So, a very good case can be made for drawing a clearer line between the British, on the one hand, and the Americans, on the other; very particularly so in respect of the particular balance of power and thus the relationship between the Academic and the Administrative Estates as two of the three constituent orders in the world of higher learning.

Arguably, British academia preserved, far longer than its Continental counterparts, many of those characteristics that hark directly back to the medieval Guild. As a parenthesis, it was precisely the notion of the university as a medieval Guild – or corporation – that the revolutionaries in France of 1792 abolished as an intolerable example of one of the many ancient privileges of that *ancien régime* (Neave 2012b, pp. 129–162). British universities, like the medieval guilds, were each a separate self-governing entity. Each university was created by individual Parliamentary Act that brought the individual university into being. Likewise, the conditions of governance, work, institutional control over career and expenditure were set down in each specific Act (McKlintock 1974, pp. 21–27). Members of the guild were selected by their peers. Their advancement was determined by the same. And, no less important, academia determined who should enter university. In short, the British Academic Estate determined the size of the Student Estate.

In its classic form, which largely survived intact until the early 1970s, British universities were less a system subject to the principle of 'legal homogeneity' (Neave 2012a, pp. 48–62), than a loose confederation, which came together around the University Grants Committee to negotiate the overall university budget with the Treasury (Ministry of Finance). Furthermore, British academia exercised operational expression over two values, key for higher education in any democracy: namely, identifying and rewarding merit and worth. British academia determined, and that on an individual basis, who merited a place at university (Rothblatt 2006). For the social historian Harold Perkin, British academia was the 'key profession' (Perkin 1969). In effect, academia decided who would be admitted to the training that ultimately fed into the liberal professions – law, medicine, engineering – and into what, following the model developed by the American political scientist Robert Dahl, are sometimes presented as 'the value allocating bodies in society' – education, the church, law, medicine and the national civil service.

Whilst many of these practices are also present in American higher education, the central feature that sets off the American model of the academic profession from its British counterpart is the issue of ownership. Since 1819, the year when the so-called Dartmouth Judgement was passed, ownership, unlike in the British Guild model, was formally and legally vested in trustees (Trow 2003, pp. 9–26). Trustees, sometimes called Regents, essentially represent the interests of the local community or region. They appoint the university president. He both acts in their name as the chief administrative officer and is directly answerable to them. In turn, after due consultation with academia, the president appoints deans who are responsible for the development of their respective Faculties, for individual appointments to post, for career review and for personal advancement. In essence, the dean is an administrative emanation of presidential will, authority and strategy.

Such an interpretation of ownership marked off the American academic 'profession' from its British guild counterpart. The American construct placed responsibility for coordinating institutional development firmly within the purlieu of the Administrative Estate, as well as ensuring the means to do so. Indeed, as Clark Kerr, one of the most influential figures in American higher education, once wryly pointed out, much of presidential toil lies in ensuring funding for the university, football for the alumni and parking for faculty. Effectively, institutional administration sets both targets and criteria for academia to achieve.

But, whilst the descriptor 'academic profession' applies to the United States, there is a further refinement. For Gary Rhoades, a sociologist of higher education, American academia is best viewed today as 'managed professionals' (Rhoades 1998, pp. 10–15). Whether being 'managed' contradicts the established criteria of a 'profession' – that is, a body which determines who may enter it, assigns standing and status within it, decides what behaviour on the part of peccant individuals is worthy of expulsion and, finally, which has a 'professional ethic' (*déontologie*) – is a very nice point indeed. Still, as managed professionals, American academia is responsible and answerable to, institutional administration. This relationship presumes a significant degree of hierarchical subordination. Academia is driven by, and accountable to, central institutional administration. It reflects a power relationship grounded in, and developed out of, the university, defined in terms of internal governance underpinned by the key concept of ownership.

Pitfalls as contrast

In latching on to the general concept of academia as a profession, it is as well to be alert to the considerable variations that lurk beneath the terminological common denominator. True, I have dwelt a trifle long on British and American differences. But this is not unjustified. With the 20/20 vision that hindsight unfailingly provides, both systems are important for two reasons. If British academia up to the early 1970s, seen from a mischievous and Dickensian perspective, represents the Ghost of Christmas Past, by the same metaphor, many features current in the American system may, from a European perspective, be seen as the Ghost of Christmas Yet to Come.

There is, however, a second justification for so Anglo-Saxon an attitude. It is this. Using the most prominent Anglo-Saxon systems as referents allows us to draw an even starker contrast with the classic European construct of academia's place in the polity, and to set it against a backdrop that brings out to the full the radical nature of the current changes in contemporary Europe.

So, how does academia in Europe fit into this scheme of things?

From guild to estate: An earlier shift in paradigm

The outstanding feature of academia in Western Europe, by contrast with either its British or American counterparts, has been its formal status as a state service; that is, a service provided by the State funded overwhelmingly from that same source, and with its members and their conditions of service aligned on parallel ranks and conditions similar to those in the national or regional administration (Neave 1986, 1987). It is precisely these characteristics which today are roundly upbraided as deeply dysfunctional to the imperative demands of quality, efficiency and enterprise, those non-negotiable credos that uphold *la pensée unique* and sustain national competitiveness in a global economy. What is less remembered are the equally radical changes to the polity that assimilation of the Academic Guild and its conversion into the Academic

Estate were intended to achieve. This too may be seen in terms of a shift in *political* paradigm, though obviously this term is as gross an anachronism as ever one might wish for.

Harnessing learning to the technical, administrative and ethical demands of state service and the upholding of a particular political order is not the work of a moment. And whilst this saga may, in certain instances, be clearly identified with marked political events – for example, Wilhelm von Humboldt's Memorandum on the establishment of the University of Berlin in 1806 and the setting up of the French Université Impériale five years later (Durand-Prinborgne 1992, p. 217) – in other nations, the process of incorporation was more protracted. In Portugal, it lasted for the best part of the 19th century, if not beyond (Sobral 2011, pp. 58–62; Torgal 2011, pp. 67–88).

Bringing the State into higher education had two primordial purposes. First, political reconstruction (Nybom 2003, pp. 141–149) and setting in place the rule of law as opposed to the rule of might. Second, the putting in place of national instruments for identifying talent and merit – and thus, in turn, to meet that basic principle that opened state service to meritocracy – the revolutionary message of *la carrière ouverte aux talents*. For those interested in the chronology of setting 'national standards', the French Baccalauréat was first established in 1832. Two years later, in Prussia, the Abitur became the sole qualification granting university entry.

With higher education defined, governed and explicitly protected by the central state – a situation some have identified as a species of 'guardian relationship' and others have qualified as 'state control', the Academic Estate in mainland Europe stood clearly apart and distinct from its Anglo-Saxon fellows. Such differences emerged in several respects. First, Academia's mission – or outreach – was national, rather than local. The prime responsibilities of teaching and research did not include what American parlance calls 'community service', a notion that only recently emerged in Europe under the guise of 'the Third Mission' (Laredo 2007, pp. 441–456).

Rather, higher education, and the Academic Estate by extension, served in the self-modernising nation state as a national, not a local, community. Again, if we indulge in creative anachronisms, the Academic Estate acted as a force for national integration rather than sustaining local particularism.

Merit and worth

However, the Academic Estate in Europe did not, as was the case in the United Kingdom, or, for that matter, in the United States, determine either merit or worth at the point of entry to higher learning. This function, again a powerful device in operationalising national identity and cohesion amongst the nation's future elites, lay either with the national Ministry or delegated agencies responsible for assessing the achievements of those graduating from academic secondary schools. Hence, unlike the situation in the United Kingdom, the Academic Estate in Europe did not, in first instance, determine the size or profile of the Student Estate. Unlike the British Guild or its American offshoot, however, the Academic Estate in Western Europe did indeed serve to identify merit, worth and the qualities necessary for public service. But it did so through a system of dual qualifications at the end of first-degree programmes. This duality was to be seen in qualifications that conferred eligibility on their holder to apply for a place in public service, a condition that went under various guises – the *effectis civilis* in the Netherlands, *grades scientifiques* in Belgium, *diplômes nationaux* in France or the *Staatsexamen* in Germany. Alongside these qualifications ran others. They certified scholarly attainment alone: the *grades légaux* in Belgium, *diplômes universitaires* in France, doctorates in Germany. Other countries, notably Spain and Italy, combined both functions in the first degrees awarded.

Neither in Britain nor in the United States, did this direct – and, it should be noted, highly prized – curricular pathway to state employ exist inside the university; a separation fully in keeping with the tenets of Lockean or Jeffersonian democracy. Certainly, the American federal agencies and the British civil service were no less demanding in the qualities they expected of their candidates. But competitive entry was set by public service itself. It did not penetrate back into academia. In short, if the Academic Estate in Western Europe did not possess the power to shape the Student Estate at the *input* stage, it fulfilled an explicit and preliminary screening function for future candidates to the middle and upper ranges of national bureaucracy. Academia exercised a very explicit filtration of merit, identified ability, at the *output* stage, prior to entering the world of work. It did so as much on behalf of the State as it did on behalf of learning and scholarship.

The Academic Estate shaped by legal homogeneity and political theory

Yet the Academic Estate in Western Europe was itself both the subject and the object of what has been termed 'the principle of legal homogeneity' that is, legal enactment, definition, oversight and verification applied in the same manner to the same type of higher education establishments across the national territory (Neave 2012a, p. 49). This highlights a fundamental difference, both conceptually and operationally, between the place the State occupied in higher education in Continental Europe and those systems based on Anglo-Saxon theories of the proper relationship between state and citizens, whether Jeffersonian or Lockean (Neave 2012b, pp. 129–162).

Succinctly put, both these interpretations of democracy, American or English, drew a line around culture and education. Neither was held to come under the responsibilities of the State. Both were deemed a direct responsibility of the local community. The State was the guarantor of liberty only so long as the State could be confined to defence, foreign policy and taxation.

Without going into the finer points, theories of 19th-century Anglo-American political liberalism had no purchase over shaping the transition of academia from a Guild to a state service in Europe. Rather, a strong State was, at one and the same time, the means of translating the general interest into operational reality, a guarantor of equality before the law and the law as an expression of that equality (Neave & Amaral 2011, pp. 15–47; Neave 2012b, pp. 129–162). Bringing academia within the purlieu of the State transformed higher education into a system, as opposed to a loose confederal *entente à l'anglo-saxonne*, precisely because higher education was subject to uniform legal enactment of national scope. Thus, the Academic Estate served two vital functions. It upheld national integration. It also provided and transmitted a statement of national identity and achievement.

Second paradigm shift

So much for the Ghost of Christmas Past. Today, much has changed. It is changing still, which is why this book has been written. Not least amongst these changes are new priorities, together with instrumentalities that require compliance by academia, and redistribution of responsibilities between Academic and the Administrative Estates (Whitchurch 2008a; 2008b, pp. 337–398; Machado & Cerdeira 2012, pp. 353–383). Nor does the litany of reform end there. It also sees the take-over into the public domain by external agencies of public purpose and oversight (Trow 1980, pp. 5–10) taking over instruments of assessment and performance, achievement and efficiency – previously the private means by which Academia distributed what Clark elegantly called 'the gold coin of academic excellence' (Clark 1983, p. 135) – into the public domain. These are now the principle 'drivers' of higher education. Some are pleased to see this in terms of a new 'professionalism', a higher degree of organisational rationality to higher education's timeless mission – teaching, learning and research – and to its burgeoning support services. Others see the enforced flight away from state service and the rapid embrace of entrepreneurial utilitarianism (Neave 2013, pp. 170–198) as a transnational set of priorities represented in 'new public management' (Pollitt & Bouchaert 1999).

Not surprisingly, there are other analytic frameworks to trace what may be seen as the second great transformation of academia – from Estate to Constituency. And they are legion. They hail variously from political science or public administration: the gradual substitution of a government/university relationship grounded in a long-standing state control over the legal framework, over finance and the rise of what some claimed to view in terms of 'a facilitatory state' (Neave & van Vught 1991, p. xi). Or others, more optimistically still, cast as the 'Offloading State'. Last, there is that most pervasive of all perspectives – reinterpreting the university's purpose as no longer an extension of the Welfare State, still less as a vehicle for redistributing wealth or enhancing social opportunity. Rather, in a world defined in terms of trade and competition, its purpose is directly and explicitly to engage in 'creating wealth'. The Academic Constituency is now cast as a major generator of knowledge in an economy where knowledge is legitimately regarded as a saleable commodity. Knowledge creation thus becomes a non-negotiable yardstick for comparing the competitiveness of any one system against others, almost inevitably held up as its rivals and competitors.

Academia: From estate to constituency

So radical a redefinition of the task universities are now called upon to fulfil is a paradigm shift of the first magnitude. It is also, if you accept the interpretation I have placed on the transition in Western Europe of academia from a Guild to an Estate, a second paradigm shift. This second paradigm shift reconstructs the Academic Estate not as serving the State but rather the market. This shift in purpose alters the Academic Estate profoundly. If its mutation into 'managed professionals' – to revert to Rhoades' vocabulary – is not accelerated, then, at very least, academia becomes an interest group, a 'stakeholder', or a Constituency. From the standpoint of government/higher education relationships the shift in paradigm clearly reflected a shift in academia's purpose (Neave 2013, pp. 170–198).

Let me suggest that the focus of the literature on the Academic Estate, the medical and the nursing professions lend themselves nicely to a grounded exploration of what follows from this shift in purposiveness. All three – Estate, Guild or profession, call them what you will – serve as a singularly sensitive litmus paper to higher education's shift, from being impelled by the imperatives of the Welfare State, to being subsequently reshaped around 'the market', urged on, to use a most unfortunate Anglo-Saxon expression, by 'corporate practice' grounded in 'entrepreneurial utilitarianism' (Neave 2013, pp. 170–198). Corporatism in Spain, Italy and Portugal carries very different historical connotations with it, not the least of which is outright dictatorship, a far cry indeed from the benevolent association it has with large enterprises in the vocabulary of the English-speaking business world.

Internal or external perspectives

We are, in effect, tracking change. And this may be done from two main approaches. These are: the internal and the external perspectives.

The internal perspective may be seen as an example of what Roger Dale terms 'higher educationism' (Robertson & Dale 2009). That is, analysing developments within higher education as self-standing phenomena, without seeking to relate to them to anything beyond the university. The 'internalist' approach focuses on changes within the Academic Constituency. What such changes are, their weight or significance, and thus their impact as perceived by Academia, their consequences for the self-perceived identity of Academia, and the consequences that arise from whatever the Academic Constituency perceives to be shifts in the balance of power and responsibility between the Constituent Orders in higher education: namely, the academic, administrative and student interests. A variation on this approach sets out to ascertain the impact of a particular issue – governance, accountability or performance assessment, for example – on the Academic Constituency. Such issues, in turn, may draw upon techniques from public administration, organisational sociology, the impact of managerialism or the testing of implementation theory *entre autres*. And, since what is being examined is a dynamic process, there is, though more often tacit than explicit, a dimension across time. What *is* changing, by contrast with what went before.

Two interpretations

The internalist perspective, however, builds around two very different *interpretations* of change (Neave 2012c, pp. 19–40). The first involves a retrospective view of change. It asks where we have come from and what is currently mutating over a particular period. It assumes change as a departure from a previously stable state. It asks the question 'How far have we come from the previously "even tenor of our ways"?' What are considered to be the most telling elements, the most 'challenging' for the Academic Estate in the distance travelled so far? Clearly, such an approach – and I have used it here – tends to stress the degree of change so far accomplished. However, it may well overestimate the capacity of the Academic Estate to accommodate change.

But there is a second string to this particular bow. The second string sees change not as *retrospective* so much as *prospective*. The prospective interpretation of change seeks to assess how far new and publicly assigned objectives, responsibilities or tasks that policy, government or institutional leadership lay upon the Academic Constituency are taken up and embedded in its behaviour and response. In other words, what is examined is the distance – or degree of accommodation – the Academic Estate displays in reaching or, as an alternative metaphor, assimilating or moving towards fulfilling the publicly stated objective. The main issue posed by the *prospective* interpretation of change makes policy – or the particular dimensions contained in that policy – the independent variable. By the same token, the Academic Constituency provides the dependent variable. Change, seen in this light, is the distance covered by the Academic Constituency towards attaining the objectives of a given policy. And, just as the retrospective approach tends to maximise progress made, so, on balance, the prospective approach tends to minimise it. Or, to take a more charitable viewpoint, it tends to dwell on the difficulties faced by the Academic Constituency in adapting.

Of these two approaches to change, the retrospect or the prospective, clearly the latter is more weighty by far, for one very simple reason. In effect, it sets the success of policy – or, for that matter, its failure – in terms of the reception such a policy receives from the Academic Constituency, as the ultimate test not merely of the relevance and sensitivity of the operational details that policy introduces, but also – though this tends to receive rather less attention – the basic assumptions, political or national circumstances, theories and political rhetoric that brought about the launching of the policy: by what I have termed '*le pays politique*' (Veiga & Neave 2013, pp. 59–77).

Sizing up policy impact: A tale of gastronomy

In short, the *prospective* approach sees policy as 'moving towards' as opposed to 'moving away'. Or, to give this a slightly different emphasis, it sees policy as attainment, rather than policy as departure. As with the homely British proverb 'The proof of the pudding is in the eating', so with the Academic Constituency. Digestion, indigestion – or outright gagging – are seen as proof of policy fulfilled, rejected or suspended. One way or the other, the stance taken by the Academic Constituency is a pragmatic pointer to the timeliness, frivolous or vexatious nature of a given policy as judged by those called upon to carry it out.

The external perspective

Finally, there is 'the external perspective'. The external perspective, when applied to the Academic Constituency, differs subtly, I would argue, from change interpreted as prospective. It does so inasmuch as today's Academic Constituency is placed in the role of providing evidence for, and thus reflecting, broader and long-term changes in society at large, as opposed to change that is the direct product of specific legislation, ministerial decree and enforcement. Key amongst these 'organic developments', as opposed to 'ordered developments', is the composition of the Academic Constituency, from the standpoint of the social class origins of its members, their breakdown by gender, their career trajectory, and the particular disciplines that serve as spearhead for this process of social equity. To this litany, one can add which sector of higher education – university, non-university, public or private – has been the most responsive to these trends in social advance and collective mobility. Clearly, the disciplines at the centre of the external perspective draw on sociology, the sociology of education, Women's Studies and the sociology of the professions.

Conclusions

In this chapter, I have sought to set out a long-term backdrop to our discussion. I have unpicked – comparatively – the evolving lot of academia through two paradigm shifts. These shifts have taken it from Guild to state service, and from state service to its present condition as an agent of production in the knowledge economy. In doing so, I have deliberately, though without malice aforethought, played down the usual definition of our corps as a profession. Some may see such a demurral as a latter-day heresy. This implies, of course, that there is an orthodox view of academia *en tant que telle*.

The question I leave the reader with is this: In the light of the changes the analyses reveal, is the concept of 'profession' still relevant, accurate? Does the term 'profession' give us a full purchase over the evolving status, standing, identity, tasks and the conditions under which academia works today and has its being? In persisting in the convention of seeing academia as a 'profession' are we not, to use a culinary metaphor, simply trying to put a quart in a pint pot? *Hélas, trois fois hélas.* I was forgetting. We are all global consumers. So what we might well be doing is scrabbling to put a litre into a 50 centilitre tetrabrick!

References

Becher, T. 1992. 'Disciplinary perspectives on higher education', in B. Clark & G. Neave (eds.), *The Encyclopedia of Higher Education*, Pergamon Press, Oxford.

Clark, B. 1983. *The Higher Education System: Academic Organization in Cross-National Perspective*, University of California Press, Berkeley/Los Angeles/London.

Clark, R. 2000. 'Developing a career in the study of higher education', in J. Smart (ed.), *Higher Education: Handbook of Theory and Research*, Vol. 15, Agathon Press, New York.

Durand-Prinborgne, C. 1992. 'France', in B. R. Clark & G. Neave (eds.), *The Encyclopedia of Higher Education*, Vol. 1, *National Systems of Higher Education*, Pergamon Press, Oxford.

Kipling, R. 1919. 'Recessional', in A. T. Quiller-Couch (ed.), *Oxford Book of English Verse 1250–1900*, Clarendon Press, Oxford.

Laredo, P. 2007. 'Revisiting the third mission of universities: Toward a renewed categorization of university activities?', *Higher Education Policy*, Vol. 20, No. 4, pp. 441–456.

Machado, M. L. & Cerdeira, L. 2012. 'The rise of the administrative estate in Portugal', in G. Neave & A. Amaral (eds.), *Higher Education in Portugal 1974–2009: A Nation, a Generation*, Springer Books, Dordrecht/Heidelberg/London.

McClaran, A. 2014. 'Risk management: Implementation', in M. J. Rosa & A. Amaral (eds.), *Quality Assurance in Higher Education: Contemporary Debates*, Palgrave Macmillan, Basingstoke/New York.

McKlintock, M. 1974. *Quest for Innovation: History of the First Ten Years of Lancaster University*, University of Lancaster Press, Lancaster.

Neave, G. 1986. 'European University Systems Part I.', *CRE Bulletin*, No. 75, 3rd Quarter [Standing Conference of Presidents, Rectors and Vice-Chancellors of the European Universities], Conférence des Recteurs Européens, Geneva.

Neave, G. 1987. 'European University Systems Part II.', *CRE Bulletin*, No. 77, 1st Quarter, Conférence des Recteurs Européens, Geneva.

Neave, G. 2012a. *The Evaluative State, Institutional Autonomy and Re-Engineering Higher Education in Western Europe: The Prince and his Pleasure*, Palgrave Macmillan, Basingstoke/New York.

Neave, G. 2012b. 'Contrary imaginations: France, reform and the California master plan', in S. Rothblatt (ed.), *Clark Kerr's World of Higher Education Reaches the 21st Century. Chapters in a Special History*, Springer, Dordrecht/Heidelberg/London.

Neave, G. 2012c. 'Change, leverage, suasion and intent: An historical excursion across three decades of change in higher education in Western Europe', in B. Stensaker, J. Valimaa & C. Sarrico (eds.), *Managing Reform in Universities*, Palgrave Macmillan, Basingstoke/New York.

Neave, G. 2013. 'On meeting the mass in higher education', in M. Feingold (ed.), *History of Universities*, Oxford University Press, Oxford.

Neave, G. & Amaral, A. 2008. 'On process, progress, success and methodology or, the unfolding of the Bologna process as it appears to two reasonably benign observers', *Higher Education Quarterly*, Vol. 62, No. 1–2, pp. 40–62.

Neave, G. & Amaral, A. 2011. *Higher Education in Portugal 1974–2009: A Nation, a Generation*, Springer Books, Dordrecht.

Neave, G. & van Vught, F. 1991. *Prometheus Bound: The Changing Relationship between Government and Higher Education in Western Europe*, Pergamon Press, Oxford.

Nybom, T. 2003. 'The Humboldt legacy: Reflections on the past, present, and future of the European University', *Higher Education Policy*, Vol. 16, No. 2, pp. 141–159.

Perkin, H. 1969. *Key Profession: The History of the Association of University Teachers*, Kelley, London.

Pollitt, C. & Bouchaert, G. 1999. *Public Management Reform: A Comparative Analysis*, Oxford University Press, Oxford.

Rhoades, G. 1998. *Managed Professionals: Unionized Faculty and Restructuring Academic Labor*, State University of New York Press, Albany.

Robertson, S. & Dale, R. 2009. *The World Bank, the IMF and the Possibilities of Critical Education*, Routledge, London.

Rosa, M. & Amaral, A. 2014. *Quality Assurance in Higher Education: Contemporary Debates*, Palgrave Macmillan, Basingstoke/New York.

Rothblatt, S. 2006. *Education's Abiding Moral Dilemma: Merit and Worth in the Cross-Atlantic Democracies, 1800–2006*, Symposium Books, Oxford.

Sobral, J. 2011. 'National identity and higher education: From the origins till 1974', in G. Neave & A. Amaral (eds.), *Higher Education in Portugal 1974–2009: A Nation, A Generation*, Springer, Dordrecht.

Torgal, L. 2011. 'University, society and politics', in G. Neave & A. Amaral (eds.), *Higher Education in Portugal 1974–2009: A Nation, A Generation*, Springer, Dordrecht.

Trow, M. 1980., 'Dilemmas of higher education in the 1980s and 1990s', *Presentation to the Conference of Learned Societies*, Montréal, June.

Trow, M. 2003. 'In praise of weakness: Chartering, the University of the United States and Dartmouth College', *Research & Occasional Paper Series: CSHE.2.03*, University of California, Berkeley, CA.

Veiga, A. & Neave, G. 2013. 'The Bologna process: Inception, "take up" and familiarity', *Higher Education*, Vol. 66, No. 1, pp. 59–77.

Whitchurch, C. 2008a. 'Shifting identities, blurring boundaries: The changing roles of professional managers in higher education', *Occasional Papers Series 10–2008*, Centre for Studies in Higher Education, Berkeley, CA.

Whitchurch, C. 2008b. 'Shifting identities and blurring boundaries: The emergence of third space professionals', *Higher Education Quarterly*, Vol. 62, No. 4, pp. 377–396.

2
Professional Autonomy in a Comparative Perspective

Teresa Carvalho and Rui Santiago

Introduction

Two contradictory tendencies can be found in advanced capitalist societies regarding professionals and professional work. On the one hand, transformations in these societies are said to impose logics that result in the weakening of the traditional *power and status* of professions and professionalism in society; but, on the other hand, the number and the importance of professional groups, as well as those aspiring to see their occupational groups socially, politically and culturally acknowledged and rewarded with the profession 'label', have been increasing.

In the context of neo-liberal assumptions regarding the global economy, public organisations are increasingly conceptualised as efficient mechanisms, and top management is conceived as having the main role in leading them to a more competitive and entrepreneurial culture. At the same time, the welfare state, which has sustained the emergence of new professional groups and has consolidated the presence of others within public organisations (Larson 2013), is increasingly being questioned. Political impositions aimed at shifting the public sector towards a more market-oriented and managerially led direction through its engagement in private-like management policies and practices, usually described as new public management (NPM), have been deployed, using different modes in accordance with different national historical and cultural contexts (Blank & Burau 2010; Kuhlmann et al. 2011; Pollitt & Bouckaert 2011). Additionally, the widespread dissemination and popularisation of the so-called knowledge society and knowledge economy narratives (Olssen & Peters 2005) are said to promote knowledge commodification, privatisation and commercialisation (Ward 2012). Important areas of knowledge have become conceptualised through the lens of knowledge usefulness to the market, which has turned it into a potential source of change directed at the 'epistemic ground' of professions. These tendencies are expected to induce de-professionalisation processes, or, at least, relevant changes in professionalism (Freidson 2001).

The joint effects of these phenomena have usually been assumed to promote decreases in the social position of professional groups in society, and decrease their autonomy within institutions. However, it is still unknown whether professional autonomy is destined to erode or is more likely to spread across a growing number of expert occupations.

Autonomy is a key notion in the analysis of professions and professional groups, and has been assumed to be a central condition for professionals since sociologists first started reflecting on this social phenomenon. However, the concept is still used today, albeit with different meanings, and researchers sometimes assume that the concept is well known in the field and do not clarify how they are conceptualising it. As Julia Evetts (2002) claims:

> The issue of autonomy of professions and its decline has, then, been inadequately conceptualised in sociology of professions literature, despite being an important interpretation of professions' current condition. (p. 342)

In this sense, the notion can be classified, according to Bourdieu (2000), as a meaning that is based on misrecognition, which is used without a conscious idea of the context in which it is structured. In fact, Bourdieu (2001, 1997) referred only to the notion of 'relative autonomy' when conceptualising 'metiers' and intellectuals' work and social roles, and connected it to the also 'relatively autonomous' field of social and professional practices, such as the domains of science, arts, literature, and academic and research institutions.

In Portugal, the number of professionals has been growing due to the country's successful evolution from an agrarian economy to an economy dominated by the industrial and service sector (Pereira & Lains 2012), and, since 1974, the development of the welfare state. More recently, policy and managerial devices framed within the NPM context have been deployed with the political aims of 'modernising' the public sector and containing public expenses. Attempts to introduce market coordination mechanisms have resulted in a transformation in the way institutions are reorganised and professionals are regulated and controlled. As has been the case for reforms developed in other Western countries, public organisations have been empowered, at least rhetorically, and attempts have been made to shift them in a direction that is more vertically integrated, as well as to influence the (re)conceptualisation by professionals of the institutionalised aims of public services and public entities.

Different authors have tried to analyse the potential effects of these changes on professionals (Carvalho 2009, 2012; Carvalho & Santiago 2010; Correia 2012). Their main conclusions highlight the fact that transformations in the public sector have had a complex and multidimensional impact on professionals. Based on a structure–agency perspective, these studies reveal the way that professionals develop different strategies to maintain their positions and power in public organisations. Nevertheless, all of these studies have focused on only one professional group.

This chapter is developed based on the assumption that professional groups have different positions in the system of professions, and, consequently, they also have distinct levels of autonomy. In this sense, political initiatives and their transposal into institutional policies and practices may have different impacts on professional groups inside the same institution and within different institutions.

The aim of this chapter is to reflect, in a comparative way, upon professionals' perceptions of professional autonomy with respect to changes in the public sector. The main questions, which are at the core of the discussions in this chapter, are: How do professionals perceive autonomy? And, is it possible to find the same dimensions of autonomy in professional groups that are developing their work within the same sector and in different sectors? In order to answer these questions, three professional groups were selected: academics, doctors and nurses.

The chapter is outlined as follows. First, it proposes a reflection on the concept of autonomy, which follows a critical description of health and higher education (HE) policies, and of the professions of doctors, nurses and academics in Portugal. Second, following the definition of the methodological guidelines, the main results are presented and discussed. Finally, a conclusion is offered which emphasises additional potential directions for analysis in this field.

Autonomy – What's in a concept?

Autonomy is one of the most fundamental concepts in the sociology of professions. It has been identified as an important trait of professional groups ever since they were initially studied in the 1930s. The functionalism approach, which has been closely influenced by the specificities of the concept of a profession in the Anglo-Saxon context (Brint 1994; Freidson 2001; Sciulli 2005; Larson 2013), determined that autonomy was indispensable for a group to be considered a profession, as opposed to an occupation. The notion of a profession, based on a liberal conception, led functionalism to interpret professionals idealistically, as those whose professionalism is supported on social trust (Brint 1994), and who are able to develop their work without being employed by an organisation, and are thus relatively independent from hierarchical and market pressures (Carr-Saunders & Wilson 1933).

In the 1970s, reflections regarding professionals highlighted the important role of the state in legitimating and protecting the jurisdictional fields of professional groups. Johnson (1972), Larson (2013) and Freidson (1977) revealed how the state has allowed professionals to have control over both those who belong to their groups and their clients.

For Johnson (1972), power relations should be analysed as focusing the control and domination of the producer over the customer of services. The relations of social distance between professionals and clients, and the dependence of the latter, are based on professionals' expertise, which is not dominated by the client.

Larson (2013) identified social closure as the main endeavour and goal of professionals. In analysing professionalisation processes, primarily of doctors, lawyers and engineers, she stresses that professional projects are also organisational projects, which organise 'the production of producers and the transaction of services for a market', and which provide privileges to 'organisational units in the system of stratification' and culminate in 'distinctive organisations', such as professional schools and professional organisations (Larson 2013, p. 74). In doing this, professional projects have incorporated a historical process in which the professions have attained a legal knowledge-based monopoly over certain services or activities, and, in this way, have created markets for specific professionals. However, this has only been possible as a result of the state's legal recognition and protection of their activities, as well as the credentials of higher education institutions (HEIs). As a result, professionals have also increased their material and symbolic privileges in democratic societies. It is this monopoly over the market for professional services and cultural specificities that defines the processes of social closure (Parkin 1979; Murphy 1988; Weber 1995).

For Freidson (1977), a profession results from an organisation of the labour market, which is based on three key elements that underpin its power: technical autonomy (as a professional expert); monopoly over an area of specialised and institutionalised knowledge; and credentialism, which restricts access only to those who hold the credentials. Freidson (1994) maintains that professional autonomy includes three different types of monopolies: economic (control of recruitment, training and credentialism, number of practitioners and income); political (control of area of expertise, expert guidance for legislation and administrative rules); and administrative or supervisorial (control of work standards, direction and evaluation). Further, Freidson (2001) came to recognise that professional power and autonomy is better preserved in the context of an ideal type, which is a 'third logic' – professionalism – as opposed to the other two logics – market and bureaucratic/managerialism. However, Freidson recognised that this 'third logic' needed to be guaranteed structurally, that is, by the state, through credentialing.

What is common to these different authors is their tendency to emphasise professional autonomy based more on a macro perspective. The macro social, cultural and political conditions which allow professional groups to have more power and control over their work are the main concern for these authors. So, this perspective, which emphasises the importance of macro elements in defining a profession, can be classified as structural autonomy.

Structural autonomy highlights collective professional power, which is translated as control over authority mechanisms (namely, macro control over expert knowledge and the labour market), as the main requisite for creating a profession. The main question for structural autonomy is how professional groups are able to define the macro conditions which ensure their privileges and high status in society.

Another perspective that has been developed concerning professional autonomy can be conceptualised as organisational autonomy. Within this context, autonomy is also identified as one of the main elements that distinguish professionals from other workers.

Since the development of Taylor's scientific management theory (Taylor 1914), the organisation of work in modern societies has rested on a clear division between two groups of workers in all organisations: those who conceive the 'best way' for work to be done (managers), and the others, who do the work as previously defined by the first group (workers). For Weber (1995), the division of work does not entirely conform to a Tayloristic 'epistemic' logic, which is based on the division between conception and execution; rather, it conforms more to a different functional logic. The primacy of the impersonal rules which frame the configuration of authority over the personal action and conduct of office holders, ensures that the bureaucracy functions as a network of social groups, each occupying different hierarchical positions and based on disciplinary systems of knowledge, which are 'either professionally [or] organisationally formulated' (Clegg 2012, p. 61). This has enabled co-determination and alliances (Bleikie & Michelssen 2008) between the groups that hold this knowledge and, subsequently, the permanent negotiation of each group's autonomy. Nevertheless, when Mintzberg (1996), who is anchored by a Weberian and neo-functionalist vision of organisations, developed a typology of organisational models, he specifically identified the professional bureaucracy as the group in which professionals have central power, with the coexistence of two structures – the bureaucratic-professional and the techno-administrative (the 'mechanistic' component of professional bureaucracies). Professionals within professional bureaucracies work without technical supervision and have a high degree of freedom in making decisions, based on their expertise.

However, in general, the coexistence of professionals and bureaucracies tend to be seen in a dichotomous way, and organisations are usually seen as an obstacle to the process of professionalisation (Noordegraaf 2007). Nevertheless, other authors maintain that the bureaucracy, as seen, is an important ally of the professional strategy of social closure (Larson 2013). In reflecting on workers' conditions, Gouldner (1954) states that, even in less favourable working contexts, actors can obtain some level of autonomy and have a role in establishing the organisational order. Crozier and Friedberg (1977) highlighted the existence of 'areas of uncertainty' that actors seek to control and through which they win more power within organisations, with the aim of enlarging their margins of autonomy. Anselm Strauss and his colleagues (1964) refer to the notion of 'negotiated order' to account for the contributions of all those involved in professional work towards building rules for indispensable cooperation within their working environments. Nevertheless, some of these last-mentioned authors have been criticised for not taking into account the influence of pre-determinate meso (and macro) structures and rules as an organiser of actors' social interactions, at least in formal terms.

In sum, the main concern of authors mentioned in previous paragraph is how professionals win autonomy within their organisational fields. One can say that the main question in organisational autonomy is how the interplay between professionals and bureaucracies allows professionals the space to make decisions concerning their own groups.

It is likely that organisational autonomy has principally been cited and studied in recent years for two main reasons. First, professionals increasingly work in organisations and not in liberal solo practices (Freidson 2001; Evetts 2002; Larson 2013). Second, the majority of organisations are still organised in a hierarchical way and have been subjected to increasing market and state pressures (Clegg 2012; Diefenbach & Todnem 2012). These trends have called attention to changes in the relation between organisations and professions, particularly under the influence of NPM. NPM, which is defined as the adoption by public organisations of management policies and practices that have traditionally prevailed in the private sector, has fuelled the discussion regarding the relation between professionals and organisations.

Much of the literature on the effects of NPM on professionals has been very pessimistic, based on the idea that more managerialism in public organisations would result in diminishing professional autonomy (Oakley 2000; Pollitt 2003; Hunter 2006). To Kirkpatrick, Ackroyd and Walker (2005), the intention of NPM, to increase managers' power within public organisations, could be defined as a strategy to intensify the control of organisations over professionals. Nevertheless, other empirical studies have revealed that the effects of NPM on professionals are difficult to analyse and point in different directions. For instance, in analysing doctors, nurses, academics and social workers, different authors claim the existence of complex relations that do not allow a confident assertion of the existence of a process of de-professionalisation (Kitchener & Whipp 1995; Ferlie et al. 1996; Kitchener 2000; Kirkpatrick & Ackroyd 2003; Carvalho & Santiago 2010; Kuhlmann et al. 2011; Carvalho 2012). The way that professionals respond to NPM is not only adaptive, but also creative introducing new nuances in the equation between increasing organisational control and diminishing professional autonomy (Muzio et al. 2007; Carvalho 2012, 2014).

Finally, there is also a perspective on autonomy that rests mainly on the way that professionals develop their working practices. This perspective can be classified as the autonomy of practice.

Professionals primarily work within organisations as salaried employees, and submit to the formal and legal rules of employment of those organisations (Freidson 1994, 2001). Under the influence of NPM, even public institutions are increasingly relinquishing collegial norms of governance and are moving towards more hierarchical ones, with power highly centralised at the top (Santiago et al. 2014). Traditionally, even in hierarchical organisations, it can be said that professionals have benefited from a high level of freedom in developing their working practices, based on two legitimating elements: the possession and use of scientific knowledge and the existence of a professional ethos. It is still scientific knowledge that legitimates discretionary practices (Evetts 2002) or allows prudential practices (Champy 2011).

Evetts (2002) maintains that discretion is better than autonomy in describing professional judgement and decision-making in professional work. In her words: '[P]rofessional discretion enables workers to assess and evaluate cases and conditions, to assert their professional judgment regarding advice, performance and treatment' (p. 345). Nevertheless, professional judgements do not solely take clients' needs into consideration; rather, they also consider needs in a wider corporate, organisational and economic context.

According to Champy (2011), prudential practices are what distinguish the professions from other occupations. Prudential practices mean work expertise, solving unusual and complex situations, a professional culture or identity based on expert knowledge and specialised skills, and autonomy of reflection – professionals as reflective practitioners (Schon 1994) – over complex professional practices.

However, there are more doubts about the way that a professional ethos still legitimates autonomy in working practices. There is currently a discussion regarding the possibility that the ethics of service will be replaced by a commercial spirit or by a managerialist ideology (Brint 1994; Evetts 2002; Carvalho & Santiago 2010). At the same time, there is an increasing tendency for professional practices to be more standardised and less discretionary as a consequence of the introduction of more technology and the emergence of accountability and audit systems, as well as a movement towards 'quality and performance cultures', which proclaim the need for evidence-based practices and international comparisons.

The three different levels of autonomy are presented here as ideal types. They are, in fact, only conceptual abstractions, because, in practice, they are closely related and mutually influenced. As Abbott (1988) indicated, in identifying the system of professions, the way that professional groups are positioned in organisations depends on their *locus* in the system of professions. At the same time, their structural and organisational positions also constrain professionals' autonomy in their working practices.

Changes in the professional landscape

Health and HE systems have been among the welfare state's more emblematic and symbolic sectors; in this sense, they also have been one of the major targets of the foremost recent neo-liberal and NPM-inspired reforms. In Portugal, health and social welfare programmes were only established after the April 1974 democratic revolution (Carvalho & Bruckmann 2014). At that time, a National Health Service (NHS) was created and HE was assumed to be one of the mainstays of the country's democratisation. To promote a more equitable and extensible provision of health services, a national public network of local primary care units and central or local public hospitals was implemented. In the same way, to allow HE democratisation, a binary system (with polytechnics and universities) was consolidated with the emergence of new public HEIs.

Within this context, new legal careers were defined for academics, with distinct careers for those at universities (Decree-Law 448/79) and those at polytechnics (Decree-Law 185/81), as well as for health professionals. Medical and nursing careers were legally defined in the 1980s (Decree-Law 310/82 and Decree-Law 305/81), and had a highly hierarchical structure.

At the end of the 1980s, an extraordinary increase in the number of private HEIs began to be promoted by the state (Teixeira 2012). In 1990s, the basic law of health was approved in Parliament, with a major new element: the inclusion of private providers in the NHS framework. At the same time, the first experience of private management in a public hospital was developed.

This period was particularly important for the nursing profession, because nursing schools were integrated into the polytechnic subsystem, and their training programmes were accredited as an academic degree (bachelor). A professional association was created (1998) with legal status ('Ordem'), which spelled out a professionalisation process based on credentialism, similar to other European countries (Dingwall et al. 1983; Dent 2002) and mirroring that in the medical profession.[1]

Nevertheless, NPM was only politically effective in the beginning of the new millennium. In 2002, a health reform agenda was implemented with the aim of increasing the role of the private sector in the NHS (Carvalho 2009). Major changes were noted in the governance and management of hospitals, with 31 traditional public hospitals being transformed into state enterprise-like corporate organisations. Attempts to institutionalise accountability and audit cultures resulted in annual budgets based on performance contracts that were negotiated with the Ministry of Health. It was also the time for a split between purchasers and providers, with the creation of Public–Private Partnerships (PPP), and the possibility of adapting private human resource strategic management policies and practices.

Traditionally, the top management structure of public hospitals constituted a team consisting of a general manager (administrator), a doctor (clinical director) and a nurse (supervisor nurse), all of whom made the same contribution to hospital management decisions. At the clinical level, a partnership consisting of a doctor (unit director) and a nurse (chief nurse) was in charge of management, although doctors always had the more authoritative and powerful position. The new legal framework for hospitals led to the centralisation of management policies and power. The new governance and management structures of hospitals now included four bodies: the administration council (composed of one president, two executives and technical direction, which included a clinical director and a nurse director, who only had a consultant role) and a consultant council (composed of representatives of the central and local governments and all professional groups). At the mid-level of organisation, clinical departments were transformed into 'operationally decentralised' centres with a specific budget allocation for staff, small equipment and pharmaceuticals. Heads of departments (directors of units), from a clinical management perspective, were made responsible for issues of quality, practice protocols and budgets. In many hospitals, the top management structure began to be replicated at the middle level, which promoted the recruitment of many middle managers.

The governance and management of HEIs later changed, pursuant to Law 62/2007. The most noticeable changes introduced by the law were both the opportunity given to HEIs to choose between two different institutional models (foundational or public institute), and the implementation of a new government and management structure; the General Council replaced the General Assembly and the Academic Senate, which had been in place previously. With this new board, there was a clear reduction in the number of members who constituted it, as well as increased participation by external members in its composition (30 per cent), although academics still made up the majority (50 per cent), along with students and administrative staff (20 per cent). There was also a reinforcement of the executive power of rectors and presidents.

However, as Carvalho and Bruckmann (2014) maintain, there are important differences in the legal changes in governance and management in the two sectors. The changes were imposed in a more coercive way in hospitals, and the legal discourses were embedded, to a greater extent, in economic rationality. By contrast, in HE, the changes were more evidenced in the *locus* of decision-making, which questioned, in a more direct way, the culture and traditional participation in decision-making of those professionals.

Careers for health professionals were also changed legally. Decree-Laws 176/2009 and 177/2009 changed the medical careers and Decree-Law 248/2009 changed the nursing careers. Hospital careers have three ranks: assistant, graduate assistant and senior graduate assistant (previously chief director). In the first two, doctors have, as their main task, the treatment of patients, while in the last (senior graduate assistants) they can also be appointed as service, departmental or clinical directors. The new careers for nurses were now based on only two ranks: nursing and principal nursing. The main role for nurses in those two ranks was patient care. Nurses could also hold positions of leadership and direction, but only when appointed by the management of the health institution.

In HE, Decree-Law 205/2009 (for universities) and Decree-Law 207/2009 (for polytechnics) changed the academic career structure. The new academic careers in universities imposed the PhD degree as a minimum requirement and a tenure position was created. Simultaneously, the number of academic ranks was reduced to only three: full, associate and auxiliary professors. The new legal polytechnic career also reduced the number of ranks to three: adjunct professor, coordinator professor and principal coordinator professor. A PhD or a specialist title also became the minimum career requirement.

At present, the main impact of the financial cuts on the organisation of the health system was the merger of several primary health centres and hospitals, with a huge concentration of clinical units and the subsequent closure of others. These changes have been followed by the increasing mobility of health professionals. In the HE sector, there has been a political discussion regarding the need to reorganise the system and to decrease the number of HEIs.

Qualitative data collection

The empirical approach of this chapter emphasises professionals' perceptions (in order to avoid a classical analysis structured from a top-down perspective) and embraces three professions: academics, doctors and nurses.

In line with the research objectives, the study is based on a qualitative approach, which is mainly grounded in document analysis and semi-structured interviews. Semi-structured interviews were carried out with 17 academics, 18 physicians and 20 nurses. Keeping in mind the internal heterogeneity of each of these professional groups, we selected the actors to interview according to the organisational positions in which they have developed their professional activities: the middle organisational level. The reasons underlying this option are connected to the fact that these professionals assume a mediation role between the organisational policies and the professional groups at the 'shop-floor' level. The guideline that served as a reference to conduct the semi-structured interviews was structured around seven thematic groups: the perceptions of changes in the profession, the main dimensions of the professional role, perceptions about reforms and the process of decision-making, the relation to specialised knowledge, perceptions about management relations, personal questions about the future of the profession and further management posts, and socio-demographic characteristics.

The empirical qualitative data supporting the analysis in this chapter was mainly selected from three thematic groups: perceptions of changes in the profession, perceptions about reforms and the process of decision-making, and perceptions about management relations. Although the aim of this chapter is to analyse professionals' discourses regarding organisational autonomy, there were no explicit questions about this. The references in the discourses were selected from questions such as: How do you look at recent changes in the legal framework of your career? What are the effects of the recent reforms on your organisation? Did you notice any kind of changes in the decision-making process? Can you talk a little bit about the relations you have developed with the organisation's general manager?

All interviews were conducted in the first six months of 2013. The participants were contacted by phone, although the majority of the interviews were conducted face to face, in locales chosen by the interviewees (the workplace was chosen by almost all of the interviewees); there were two exceptions, which were conducted by phone. The interviews took, on average, 45 minutes, and they were recorded with the permission of the interviewees and a guarantee of anonymity. All of the interviewees were informed of the aim of the study and of the purpose of the interviews. The interviews were transcribed and subjected to classical thematic content analysis procedures (Bardin 1993).

Findings: Autonomy in professional discourses

The empirical component of this chapter is related to an analysis of the professionals' discourse regarding organisational autonomy, as intersected by the structural autonomy and the autonomy of practice at the organisational micro level. These different levels of professional autonomy were transformed into content analysis categories aimed at describing and interpreting the discourse of the three professional groups. The structural autonomy category is intended to analyse the impact of exogenous 'forces' on professionals' organisational autonomy, and is linked to the way that state policies interfere in the professional status that each group is granted or not in society (see Freidson 2001): the *locus* of their work in the division of labour, the way their jurisdictions are defined, the type of relations they establish with 'consumers', and the support for and legitimation of their knowledge and training programmes, credentials and professional associations.

The other two categories can be interpreted as being endogenous. In different terms, the endogenous side of organisational autonomy is related to the greater or lesser opportunity that professionals have to be locally involved in the definition of the organisational conditions, rules and norms (formal or informal) under which their professional practices are developed. With respect to the autonomy of practice, this endogenous side is connected to the greater or lesser amplitude of the sphere of activity that is under the professionals' self-direction in the face of the organisation's hierarchical and managerial control.

In sum, structural autonomy is mainly related to changes that are external to the organisation. This means that this category included all of the elements to which professionals refer that are related to their organisations' external environment, and, in this sense, can be common to all of the institutions within a specific sector. These elements are mainly related to the regulatory framework of the specific sector. Within this category, professionals referred mainly to the professional bureaucracy and their own careers. Organisational autonomy stresses those elements identified by professionals which are related to the specific internal and singular context of each institution. Within this scope, professionals, from an agency perspective, can actually have a relevant role in their professional autonomy, although, obviously, this is constrained by the structural autonomy of the group. Finally, the autonomy of practice is related to the capacity that professionals have to make decisions related to their day-to-day activities at the organisational micro level.

Structural dimension of organisational autonomy

In accordance with Max Weber's ideal type, a bureaucracy implies the existence of legal and formal rules that, in the specific case of public institutions, emanate from government (Weber 1995). However, within this context, following Weber (1989) and Mintzberg (1996), in professional knowledge-intensive organisations, such as universities and hospitals, some singularities are present which are connected to their relation to the state and to its internal governing forms. Admittedly, the bureaucratic regime of control and structural organisation has been the dominant state-governing mode of hospitals and universities. However, the state allowed, enabled and legitimated a special structural configuration that Weber (1995), for instance, considered to be 'archaic' – collegiality – and Mintzberg (1996) renamed as the professional bureaucracy. Weber (1995) acknowledged that elected collegial bodies limit the more rational governing mode through 'monocracy' (Weber 1995).

NPM turned its attention towards neutralising these two articulated logics: bureaucratic and collegial/professional. The aim was to make public organisations more efficient and externally accountable through the application of a set of principles inspired by a market-oriented and managerially led 'philosophy' of self-governance, and sustained by the decentralisation of decision-making. Political expectations arose regarding the possibility of shifting the system, that is, steering it from hierarchy to contractual-coordination devices and an at-a-distance 'output-driven' mode of control. This could potentially have an impact on professionals' structural autonomy. The new logic behind the recomposition of the system brought new power and governing technologies which were not necessarily mainly founded on the beliefs, values and ideology of professionalism. Therefore, it is possible that the professions (and professional associations) have lost some of their power to impose their standards and norms as the main principles that back the structure and modus operandi of public services and public organisations, particularly in the fields of health and HE.

As highlighted in the section entitled 'Changes in the Professional Landscape', NPM has made its way through Portuguese public institutions from the mid-1990s onwards, and some legal arrangements have been introduced in the governance and management of both health and HE, to promote more 'self-governed' and decentralised organisations. Nevertheless, in spite of some coercive changes, because there was a similar power 'architecture' at the central level, in each sector, institutions were delegated the jurisdiction to design their own local policies and strategies, as well as to define their management operational devices and basic organisational structures.

In mentioning changes in their professional autonomy, the interviewees referred to the importance of the alterations they have perceived in their own institutions. However, these changes are not viewed by professionals as defining a path through decentralisation, but, rather, as configuring a process of centralisation. In fact, various authors (Hoggett 1991; Henkel 1997; Reed 2002; Carvalho & Santiago 2010) have already called attention to this phenomenon. Governments maintain control over a few 'variables', such as financing and the rules regarding access to services, which are key structural variables to oversee the systems and to control and regulate the organisational dimensions of institutions. Moreover, in intending to increase efficiency, the value of money and accountability, governments are also increasingly placing more demands and guidelines on public institutions, which, in this way, restrict their autonomy.

This process can be defined as a 'centralised decentralisation' (Hoggett 1991; Henkel 1997; Reed 2002), in which there is a considerable degree of autonomy, but it is, nonetheless, within centrally defined parameters that are designed to ensure careful 'steering at a distance'. In this context, Neave and van Vught (1991) classified the new role of the state as configuring a supervisory or evaluative state. Subsequently, Neave (2012) reviewed this concept and referred to a 'new regulative state', which is now permeated much more by neo-liberal ideology. This 'new state' retreats from some organisational inputs, but, at the same time, increases its control at a distance over its institutions, based on their output, with an emphasis on efficiency, economy and accountability.

There is a dimension in the discourse of the three professional groups (especially academics) that highlights the ways that the new state role impact institutional autonomy and, in this way, also interfere with the groups' organisational autonomy.

> I think that the most painful is the loss of the autonomy of the university. Each time, it is more regulated by the directives and by outside pressures: many are indirect, are by budgetary and regulatory constraints, and other things. Each time, there is less space for the institutions, their departments, their groups, to seek their space, their own partnerships.
> (Int.14A; Academic, University, Man)

So, the sense of the loss of autonomy that seems to be present in this discourse is mainly related to the more general context of the loss of institutional autonomy, and is interpreted as affecting all of the groups within academia.

The autonomy of HEIs, and especially the autonomy of universities, is historically assumed to be one of its foundational elements, along with academic freedom. Academics, as a professional group, have always been very sensitive to the question of autonomy. It is interesting to note that expressions related to a decrease in structural autonomy are also present in the discourse of health professionals:

> At present, I think the loss of autonomy has much to do, as I mentioned, with the shortage of human resources and with the new guidelines that are sent by the Ministries of Health and Finances. But, this is not just in nursing; it is in all other professions in the civil service or in public functions. Budget constraints and these new guidelines for cost containment, the resource contention, all this leads to a loss of autonomy.
>
> (Int. 20E; Nurse, Woman)

So, there is a first element in professionals' perception of autonomy which is related to the external environment that surrounds public institutions. Professionals assume that because public institutions have lost autonomy, the same tendency is present in their own professional groups. However, even if one assumes that this will actually occur, it is also important not to forget that the discourse of professionals may only be reproducing dominant ideas, and, also, that organisational autonomy is a complex phenomenon which incorporates many other dimensions.

Changes in the legal framework of careers, a typical element of the structural autonomy of professional groups, also seem to have had an impact on professionals' perceptions of autonomy. In fact, the legal framework of professional careers depends on state regulatory practices and on limits in the capacity of professional groups to bargain with the state regarding their structural autonomy. The positioning and roles of professionals within institutions are directly linked to the results of this negotiation, which determines, through formal secured rules, the internal jurisdictional boundaries for the division of work, the roles prescribed to each position, and professional and management authority lines. Although professional groups are segmented and fragmented, the existence of a formal career statute, which is protected and legitimated by the state, ensures stability against internal forms of market instability, and contributes towards making their work's jurisdictional boundaries less permeable by local 'management authority' and control at different organisational levels. Comparing the three groups, health professionals were those who mentioned the most changes in the legal framework of their careers. In fact, academics scarcely mentioned it. This may be the result of the distinct capacity that professional groups have to negotiate their working conditions with the state. In sum, within the three groups under analysis, nurses are the ones who referred most to threats to their autonomy which have resulted from changes in the legal framework of their careers, followed by doctors; this topic is almost absent in the discourse of academics. Eventually, this may also mean that the organisational autonomy of academics is stronger, because, when compared with doctors and nurses, academics are less dependent on state legitimacy for their professional autonomy. This has occurred due to the distinct organisation of academics' work (which is much more individual and independent than other professional groups), but it may also be a result of different negotiation strategies at the macro level. In fact, while the structural autonomy of doctors and nurses is mediated by their professional associations, in the case of academics this does not happen. In general, all of the actors involved in the negotiation processes are peers (since the 1974 democratic revolution, the majority of Ministers of Education and HE have come from the academic world).

Nurses perceived changes in the legal framework of their careers as an element leading to a decrease in their professional autonomy. They compared the improvements that changes in professional regulations have promoted in past decades to what they perceive as a retreat that has occurred recently, which constitutes, from their standpoint, a process of de-professionalisation:

> Over the past 10 years, we had some improvements. It was when the professional association emerged ('Ordem') and the academic reorganisation allowed the autonomy of the discipline, as a science, because we already have masters and doctorates in nursing. (...) Now there is a clear deregulation of careers; there is a clear devaluation of career and work, and this has been very much expressed in the context of the work (...)
>
> (Int.5E; Nurse, Man)

Doctors referred mainly to changes in recruitment policies, due to the possibility that professionals may be hired by health enterprises and not directly by hospitals:

> Because now, there is an attempt for doctors to be hired by intermediates, which are the companies, and then companies 'have a doctor on hand'. It's a bit like the fishermen... those who win the money are the entrepreneurs. Like farmers... and it will be the same with us..., those who win are those who are not working... you know?
>
> (Int.5M; Doctor, Woman)

In fact, nurses identified changes in the legal framework of their careers as a threat to their autonomy. They perceived these changes as a regression in the successful process which had developed since the end of the 1990s to improve their status and prestige in society. Doctors also seemed to identify changes in their careers as a threat to their autonomy, but they saw it as mainly due to changes in their contractual relations with the state. Finally, academics are moving in the opposite direction, with no references to changes in the legal framework of their careers.

Dimension of organisational autonomy

Organisational structures are highly constrained by legal frameworks, and, as mentioned in the section entitled 'Changes in the Professional Landscape' there has been a tendency to dismantle professional bureaucracies, both in health and HE. Nevertheless, organisations still have some room to reinterpret the legally imposed changes and to reorganise their units and services, namely at the intermediate level, which may incorporate logics that are different from the ones which are politically expected.

The literature on the governance and management of organisations highlights the way that (re)configured bureaucracies intend to limit collegial bodies and to concentrate policy and strategic decisions at the top (Magalhães & Santiago 2012). This encompasses the deployment of line management mechanisms towards the vertical integration of organisations, and their reconfiguration as more unitary (Carvalho & Santiago 2010) or complete organisations (Enders et al. 2008). In a more specific way, this tendency means that collective decision-making is giving way to the empowerment of top governance and management bodies, particularly at the executive level. In fact, this tendency was acknowledged by our interviewees, who referred to it as a threat to their autonomy. This seemed to be especially relevant for academics. When referring to professional autonomy, academics emphasised the relevance of the decrease in their presence in collegial bodies:

> I would say we have lost our voice. Lost our voice (...). We do not always have this ability as directors, because we do not always carry weight in the right bodies. (...) To get directions to the school, therefore, the director is like an 'adviser' of the school principal and no more, isn't he?
>
> (Int. 11A; Academic, University, Man)

Claims of decreased participation in collegiate bodies are also accompanied by more specific references to a loss of control over organisational processes that involve decisions directly linked to professional groups. Decisions regarding recruitment and performance evaluation occur at this level. This area seems to have initiated a loss of control over professional self-regulation, something which was also stressed by nurses when they referred to the external control of the profession through evaluation systems:

> Now, it is clear that the evaluation systems that currently exist, and those that are being implemented, are systems that regulate, control... We had an evaluation system that was very independent, very autonomous... This new one, from my point of view, will be more restrictive and impose some values. We know that the norms which are presented for the evaluation can't be modified in any way by us. I know... I know that even if 50% of my team are very good professionals, I can't make that assessment. It is something that is imposed on me; this is an external control of the profession. (...) The legislation imposes on me, and this is a way to control the profession.
> (Int. 5E; Nurse, Man)

These quotations accurately express the impact of the formalisation of the accountability systems on professional autonomy, as it is perceived by professionals. Inspired by NPM assumptions, these systems have been transferring, often in a tacit way, the prerogative of professionals to define the general rules of the 'game' to externally imposed explicit norms that work as new templates for professional actions and professional values. In other national contexts, different authors have also maintained that there has been a loss in the autonomy of professionals which has resulted from these new templates. For academics, Rhoades and Slaughter (1997) and Slaughter and Leslie (1997) found this tendency in the USA and Australia, and Trowler (1998), Henkel (2007), and Deem, Hillyard and Reed (2007) found it in the United Kingdom.

The decrease in the participation in collegial bodies has been recognised as proportional to the increase in power at the top, and this has mainly been mentioned by nurses and doctors. This increasing power has been perceived as more individual than collegial:

> When we speak of a public corporation, in any area, one thing everyone should know is the organisation's strategy. It must be shared with employees, and this is not happening... We live in obscurity; no one has the faintest idea... The information is simply not shared. What do I mean by this? Nobody has the faintest idea of what you're doing.
> (Int. 7E; Nurse, Man)

The absence of participation by professionals in decisions at the central administration level has been manifested by the perception of an unclear definition of management objectives and strategies for the organisation, which has presented professionals and managers as being on opposite sides. In this sense, professionalism and managerialism have been identified as opposite and conflicting (Oakley 2000; Hunter 2006).

> To me, what is more painful and takes more time is the huge number of documents we need to have to respond to management and administration. Sometimes, things are a bit repetitive, because it gives me the idea that managers who are in health still do not know much about health. Often, when a document is requested, it is the duplicate of another, and they end up not realising where the problem of the patient is in the middle of those squares, where there are only numbers and braces. Therefore, the relationship with directors and top management is sometimes a bit tricky.
> (Int. 4M; Doctor, Woman)

However, there was not a single discourse or tendency concerning professionals' participation in decision-making. Although these examples of discourse focused on the negative impact of organisational changes in professionals' autonomy, others referred to professionals' autonomy being maintained or even increased in the present institutional context.

There was clear evidence in the discourse that academics have been called to make decisions that affect them or their professional group. At the same time, a collegial way of working is still in place and is highly appreciated by health professionals (especially doctors):

> We are called too, and I am also called to participate in decisions related to management, with the reallocation and reorganisation of resources, especially economic and financial resources, which then has implications in terms of hiring people, the reorganisation of the distribution of teaching services, and all this at the moment, this is the problem that is affecting us more.
> (Int. 1A; Academic, Polytechnic, Man)

> We have two meetings a week in which we discuss clinical cases and issues regarding the organisation of the service. There are always those first ten minutes or quarter of an hour to address how the service is going, what is going well and wrong, and therefore, I

have something that encourages people to give their opinions, what they think is right and what is wrong, and I think I have tried to act according to these opinions, whether they are in the majority and I do not think they're silly. I'm trying to focus on these aspects.

(Int. 8M; Doctor, Man)

These quotations reinforce some conclusions from other studies in the field that maintain that NPM and professionalism are interrelated in a complex manner and that autonomy cannot be defined by simply using a lost or gain perspective (Carvalho & Santiago 2010; Champy 2011; Kuhlmann et al. 2011; Correia 2012, 2014). In fact, it seems that there are differences in the discourse about organisational autonomy, which are not only distinct from an inter-professional perspective (academics referred more to the loss in organisation autonomy, while nurses referred to the loss in professionals' self-regulation), but also from an intra-professional one, with different actors from the same professional groups maintaining different positions.

The relevance of inter-professional relations in autonomy was mainly identified by health professionals. This was expected, because the organisation of work in health care is mainly based on teamwork and on an inter- and multidisciplinary basis, in contrast to academic work, which (with the exception of research projects) is mainly developed from an individual perspective. Nurses referred to the loss of autonomy over their work due to the increasing power that the new legal frameworks concede to doctors with managerial duties:

It is not a recent thing. For some time now, from the moment that the head of service became the director and became the medical director... This may not be exceptional. We lost some autonomy.

(Int. 20 E; Nurse, Woman)

This tendency confirms previous studies that have revealed that NPM has induced nurses to redefine their professional boundaries (Carvalho 2012). Actually, the same nurse confirmed, in her discourse, that she and her colleagues were continuously negotiating the boundaries of their work with doctors:

If we have a good relationship with the service director (a doctor), everything goes well. If we are in conflict, in some situations, it is very complicated. Therefore, we have to circumvent this issue. If we have a good relationship and it recognises an important role for us... If he does not recognise it, you are not in a good role. What happens? It happens... they often delegate their service to us, because many roles that we have are for them, but they rely on us. And that's important. But we need delegation. Because when they do not delegate, I simply cannot do. What happens, for example, in the evaluation of auxiliary nurses, they depend on me, but my director has that responsibility. Okay, we lost some space, but that space is gained because of the delegation of powers, which is not equal.

(Int. 20E; Nurse, Woman)

With the emergence of NPM, there has been a tendency to value management and managers within public institutions. Giving institutions more autonomy and freedom to manage implies having more 'general managers' who are trying to legitimate this knowledge as a 'superior form' of organising and controlling the professional work, instead of professionalism. However, they also have the important role of making professionals more accountable. In this way, the emergence of this group may introduce some imbalance in the already complex interprofessional relations that exist within public institutions (Carvalho 2012).

In fact, the emergence of managers is a phenomenon that has been frequently noted in the health sector. Both doctors and nurses referred to a decrease in autonomy due to the work of managers:

I think the perspective they have is not the same as mine. Managers say... 'you need to lower 10%', we need to decrease... but how can they give me such orders if they often have no idea of the complexity of the techniques and stuff I try to use. For example... look, even today, I spent a half an hour explaining to my manager what a bone marrow transplant is, the steps through which it needs to pass, because I think that only by understanding can they realise what is involved... so that's why I think the ultimate responsibility has to belong to a doctor.

(Int. 5M; Doctor, Woman)

The dominant perspective of these professionals seemed to be that they are continuously negotiating their relationship with managers and their field of action within health organisations, and, often, doctors have actually been able to impose 'their rules', even when they are against the law:

> Because when the new law appeared, when recording the presence became mandatory for everyone, I went to management and said: 'You will spoil my service.' This service has the highest productivity in the hospital; its written statement is not bloated, but it is written by the administration. Therefore, we have productivity that is above the benchmark, even internationally, ok. So, my team does not mark its presence (...); you can't record their presence. (...) And the administration intelligently accepted this. Since I came to Portugal and I have held positions, I have never signed a point, never signed a paper for a holiday. (...) In fact, we have some special conditions, but we fought, so we have had, until now, we have a great understanding with the management.
>
> (Int. 1M; Doctor, Man)

However, this discourse of successful negotiations with managers was not exclusively from doctors, who are usually considered to be a very powerful professional group within health organisations. Nurses also referred to episodes when they were able to maintain their position against managers' decisions:

> It is not so easy, with a manager who is an administrator, to notice these things. For example, a very basic thing that they say is: 'No, you can't have two people working at night, you can only have one' and I say 'I can't work with one person, because I put people at risk here', 'But I do say that you have to', 'But I can't. You'll have to write it on paper for me, and when I receive it, then I will do it', and this paper never comes, and I do not do it. You see?
>
> (Int. 5E; Nurse, Man)

The relationship with general managers was almost absent in the discourse of academics. Once again, this means that, even if NPM policies and practices refer to market-oriented and managerially led principles that are widespread and 'popular', and similar in different public sectors, they do not affect different professional groups in the same way; they also do not affect all the professionals inside a group in the same manner. A professional group's prestige and position in society – the social, cultural, intellectual and symbolic capital that supports its structural autonomy – may explain some of the differences; in addition, the way each group mobilises this acts to preserve and/or develop their 'organisational autonomy' and 'autonomy of practice' in the 'heartland' of each of their institutions. However, there is also an individual dimension to the sense of the loss of autonomy, which results from the agency capacity of professionals.

Dimension of autonomy in practice

Autonomy in practice is directly connected to professionals' relationship with their 'technical autonomy', or, in other words, with the way they conceptualise and act in their working sphere. Their autonomy, at this level, is related simultaneously to the application of professional knowledge and expert skills in the narrow context of working practice: the 'technical' decisions made on a daily basis. This implies some subjective and personal choices that are related to the indeterminacy and uncertainty of their specialised knowledge, which is confronted with specific situations/problems (Freidson 2001; Brint 1994, 2006). It is this indeterminacy and uncertainty that partially legitimates what Evetts (2002) described as discretionary practice (Evettts 2002), or what Champy (2011) described as prudential practice in work. Autonomy in practice allows the existence of spheres of activity that are subjected only to professional judgement and are protected from organisational hierarchical control (Brint 1994).

More recently, however, the need to increase professional accountability within a NPM framework, has resulted in the emergence of formal systems, such as quality assessment and performance evaluation, which are more oriented towards organisational output (Santiago & Carvalho 2012; Bruckmann & Carvalho 2014; Carvalho & Bruckmann 2014). As these accountability processes allow information to be gathered and transformed into standardised organisational knowledge that can be used to control professionals' spheres of activity, these processes have been interpreted, by some authors, as technologies of control (Fournier 2000; Reed 2002). Moreover, attempts to ensure efficiency and cost control at the unit level has induced a top-down style of decision-making, which also has been assumed to potentially interfere with professionals' autonomy, because it may constrain the dominant values that underlie professional decision-making processes.

In the three professional groups, it was possible to identify two main positions. Some assumed that the introduction of new models of organisation and governance in institutions, as well as the top-down style of management, has produced undesirable effects in professionals' practice. Within this context, nurses placed special emphasis on the way that the changes in the organisation of work, which have involved increasing bureaucratisation, have translated into an extraordinary work overload, which has an effect at the level of practice:

> Every year, we have to develop standards, criteria, talk to people, set up meetings. I mean, we have a brutal workload in preparing paperwork for management, which almost prevents us from having contact with patients.
>
> (Int. 17E; Nurse, Man)

A decrease in autonomy in practice seems to be felt more by nurses. They actually assume that the changes in hospitals' organisation, management and governance are a way to increase control over their work, which results in undesirable consequences for their daily activities:

> I feel that this can serve as a way to control our work. I mean, we are often limited, it serves to control... and, more important, it may divert nurses from what is essential. It shifts the energy to other aspects, which are less essential than our main activity, which has to do with the patient.
>
> (Int. 2E; Nurse, Woman)

In fact, it seems that, as nurses have fought for their autonomy more recently, and as the new law has given more power to doctors in the administration and management of wards, nurses have also felt that they are not entirely autonomous in their professional judgements and decisions, because they do not believe that their expertise is given enough recognition:

> It is undeniable that, we, in our day-to-day lives, feel disappointed due to a lack of recognition of our knowledge. People do not recognise that we are professionals, with higher education degrees, and we also have our own autonomy. We are not anyone's employees or anyone's helpers. We work on a team; we develop a role that is as important as any other element on the team. And we also have our areas of autonomy.
>
> (Int. 2E; Nurse, Woman)

In addition to a lack of recognition of their knowledge, their employment is perceived as insecure, which nurses mentioned as a threat to their autonomy in practice:

> The work is increasingly precarious; there is substantial insecurity in our employment, and this is reflected in the quality of practice. If people had more security, it is evident that the quality of their practice would improve. You cannot ask professionals who are always at risk of losing their contracts and may end up being unemployed, to focus on their work as much they would if they had some security in their jobs. A person who has a stable contract is more likely to invest in her education. If you are here today, tomorrow is another service, and in 3 months, you may be unemployed, you cannot do the same thing.
>
> (Int. 9E; Nurse, Woman)

In contrast, other professionals within each group, but especially among doctors and academics, asserted that they are doing exactly the same things, and they are doing them in the same way that they have always done them. For these professionals, one cannot argue that they feel that their autonomy in the domain of their daily practice has been placed in question. In fact, some doctors argued that there has been no interference in their technical or clinical autonomy:

> So far, the board is hearing us... and they never interfere in the clinical area. (...) Apart from financial interference, I have never felt any attempt to interfere with our techniques, saying 'do this', 'make that' or 'your resources have to be directed in this direction or in another'. Technical decisions have been, as yet, always delivered with clinical direction. There are bureaucratic problems and funding cuts, but I have not noticed any significant interference in practice. I have not found any direct interference by the board in the clinical issues of service (...).
>
> (Int. 2M; Doctor, Man)

Academics also maintained the existence of this autonomy, especially in references to their teaching role:

> Basically, when we talk about academic autonomy... this is restricted to teaching activities, to the classroom space. (...). Even in research priorities, we are limited to what is demanded by the provision of

research by the external market...we have to conform with the possibilities which are offered to us.

(Int. 4A; Academic, University, Man)

Although it was less dominant in the discourse of nurses, there were also some statements that referred to the existence of autonomy in this domain:

I think we have lost autonomy in the administrative part, but not in the domain of the area of caregiving; I do not think so.

(Int. 9E; Nurse, Woman)

To sum up, one can say that there is no consensus in professionals' perceptions of the ways that new management and governance models in hospitals and HEIs are interfering with autonomy in practice. The professionals' perceptions of these topics present some divergence: either between groups or within each group. Academics were the group that referred less to this type of autonomy; they were followed by doctors, and finally, by nurses. Although there were some references to constraints on autonomy in practice, they were mainly indirect, which means that they were related to an increasing workload, and changes in both the organisation and management of institutions – with increasing bureaucratisation – and in working conditions. Nurses' assertions of a decrease in their autonomy in practice may also be related to a lack of recognition of their legitimate decision-making expertise at the level of clinical practice. Nevertheless, a considerable number of professionals in all three groups also assumed that their technical autonomy remains intact, and that they are still able to make decisions concerning their professional practices.

Conclusions

This study demonstrates that the relation between NPM and professionalism has a different tonality according to the global context of the national and social sectors, as well as the institutional, organisational and practical fields of professional action. As previous international studies have highlighted, there are important differences between the distinct public sectors (Ferlie et al. 1996; Kirkpatrick et al. 2005), which is a phenomenon that also has been observed in the Portuguese landscape (Santiago & Carvalho 2012; Carvalho & Bruckmann 2014). Here, important differences between professionals in academia and health have been revealed. Academics tend to focus more on the exogenous side of organisational autonomy, which implements 'forces' that attempt to lead them to heteronomy, rather than on the endogenous side. At the same time, the references to inter-professional relations are almost non-existent, which is not the case, for instance, for nurses. Much more than doctors, nurses, on a daily basis, must negotiate their margins of professional autonomy with both doctors and managers.

Although HEIs have also been opened to 'non-academics', namely, to management and techno-bureaucratic roles at the central and middle organisational levels, and professionals have lost representative 'power' in collegial bodies, manager–professional relations are not equally present in the discourse. This may be because managers have not entered HEIs in such high numbers and with such a high degree of power as in health institutions (hospitals), or it may express their inability to interfere with work which is essentially individual and somewhat diversified with respect to disciplinary fields, and is multidimensional in its specific objectives. Otherwise, it may also simply mean that professionals in health are using the professional–manager discourse more as a strategy or tool to allow the prevalence of their professionalisation process. This implies self- and peer-control over their work (autonomy in practice) and over the organisational conditions under which it is developed (organisational autonomy).

As another exogenous contingency, academics did not mention changes in the legal framework of their careers as a threat to their autonomy. Doctors and nurses placed more emphasis on this subject, with nurses, once again, feeling that the changes in the structure of nursing careers represent a threat to their professional autonomy.

These sets of differences in the three professional groups may be related to the specificities of the two sectors. Knowledge production and dissemination and the role of HEIs as the 'production of producers' (Larson 2013) has always implied professional autonomy; also, academia is based on more individual work, but this may be the result of the introduction of different modes of NPM in the two sectors. The state has delegated more institutional autonomy to HEIs, which may also correspond with the transference of career issues and conflicts to each single institution. Academics have become more dependent on each institution's policies regarding career management than doctors and nurses. In this sense, the structural autonomy of academics is loosely coupled with their organisational autonomy, while the structural autonomy of doctors and nurses is tightly coupled with their organisational autonomy, and they are much more dependent on the mediation of their professional association in the negotiation of their career pathways with the state.

These analyses of two distinct professions in the same sector are also relevant to more fully expose the differences between the sectors. Nurses referred more often to the degradation in their working conditions. This may mean that professional groups with a high level of social prestige and symbolic capital, as well as a more consolidated 'structural autonomy', as is the case for doctors, may have more favourable ground for resistance, to adapt or shift the intrusion of NPM at the organisational level to their advantage. However, the majority of members in the three professional groups emphasised that their participation in organisational decision-making has been restrained by top-down impositions. The centralisation of more policy, and strategic and executive power, in the top levels of governance and management bodies seems to have limited collegial decision-making. Academics are more sensitive to this, because collegiality, at least in symbolic terms, has been a historical and strongly institutionalised 'archetype' in the university landscape.

Claims of decreased participation in collegiate bodies are also accompanied by more specific references to the loss of control over organisational processes, which involves decisions that are directly linked to professional groups. Decisions about the definition of the general rules regarding work management and conditions, and regarding recruitment and performance evaluation, occur at this level. This area seems to show a loss of control over professional self-regulation, which was also stressed by nurses, when they referred to the external control of the profession through the evaluation systems. Moreover, policies and management practices aimed at efficiency and cost control, which have a strong impact at the unit level, seem to interfere differently with the autonomy in practice of the three professional groups. While academics and doctors mentioned that the sphere of their working process was still more or less preserved – although academics differentiated between their different roles – nurses, in contrast, felt that their autonomy in practice had largely been exposed to external control.

The professionals' perceptions regarding these topics reveal some divergence, both between groups and within each group. Doctors, as a group, referred less to this type of autonomy; they were followed by academics, and finally, by nurses. Although there were some references to constraints in their autonomy in practice, they were mainly indirect, that is, they were related to an increasing workload and changes in both the organisation and management of institutions – with increasing bureaucratisation – and in working conditions. The nurses' assertions of a decrease in their autonomy in practice may also be related to a lack of recognition of their expertise in legitimate decision-making at the level of clinical practice.

However, there were also important differences in the professionals' discourse within the same group. Some talked about losses in autonomy, while others mentioned gains. This may be the result of bilingualism, surface compliance or non-consent, but it may also be interpreted as the result of distinct power relations based on intra-group professional elites and hierarchies, and/or the competence and recognition of individuals.

Professionals (especially in health) use the dichotomy between the discourse of professionals and managers as a strategy for professionalisation and for the 'insulation' of professionalism, perhaps as a counter-movement against the threats of the market and NPM. However, further studies are needed to understand whether managers' attempts to be socially and culturally acknowledged and legitimated as a professional group will introduce new elements in this relational context within public institutions, namely, in health and HE. Are managers really different from other professional groups within public institutions? How do they view the current changes? Does their professional *ethos* also include a public service ethos? How, in a comparative perspective, do they perceive the *locus* of management knowledge in the social, cultural, symbolic 'worlds' of professional knowledge?

Note

1. The medical professional association 'Ordem' was created in 1938.

References

Abbott, A. 1988. *The System of Professions: An Essay on the Division of Expert Labour*, The University of Chicago Press, Chicago & London.
Bardin, L. 1993. *L'analyse de contenu*, Presses Universitaire de France, Paris.
Blank, R. & Burau, V. 2010. *Comparative Health Policy* (3rd edn), Palgrave, Houndmills.
Bleikie, I. & Michelssen, S. 2008. 'The university as enterprise and academic co-determination', in A. Amaral, I. Bleikie & C. Musselin (eds.), *From Governance to Identity: A Festschrift for Mary Henkel*, Springer, Dordrecht.
Bourdieu, P. 1997. *Pour une sociologie clinique du champ scientific*, Institut National de la Recherche Agronomique (INRA), Paris.
Bourdieu, P. 2000. *Pascalian Meditations*, Polity Press, Cambridge.
Bourdieu, P. 2001. *Science de la science et reflexivité, cours au collège de France*, Éditions Raisons d'Agir, Paris.

Brint, S. 1994. *In an Age of Experts: The Changing Role of Professionals in Politics and Public Life*, Princeton University Press, Princeton, NJ.

Brint, S. 2006. 'Saving the soul of professionalism: Freidson institutional ethics and the defense of professional autonomy', *Knowledge, Work & Society*, Vol. 4, No. 2, pp. 101–129.

Bruckmann, S. & Carvalho, T. 2014. 'The reform process of Portuguese higher education institutions: From collegial to managerial governance?', *Tertiary Education and Management*, Vol. 20, No. 3, pp. 193–206.

Carr-Saunders, E. & Wilson, P. 1933. *The Professions*, Clarendon Press, Oxford.

Carvalho, T. 2009. *Nova gestão pública e reformas da saúde. O profissionalismo numa encruzilhada*, Edições Sílabo, Lisbon.

Carvalho, T. 2012. 'Shaping the "new" academic profession: Tensions and contradictions in the professionalisation of academics', in G. Neave & A. Amaral (eds.), *Higher Education in Portugal 1974–2009: A Nation, a Generation*, Springer Publishers, Dordrecht.

Carvalho, T. 2014. 'Changing connections between professionalism and managerialism: A case study of nursing in Portugal', *Professions and Organization*, Vol. 1, No. 2, pp. 1–15.

Carvalho, T. & Bruckmann, S. 2014. 'Reforming Portuguese public sector: A route from health to higher education', in C. Musselin & P. Teixeira (eds.), *Reforming Higher Education: Public Policy Design and Implementation*, Springer, Dordrecht.

Carvalho, T. & Santiago, R. 2010. 'Still academics after all', *Higher Education Policy*, Vol. 23, pp. 397–411.

Champy, F. 2011. *Nouvelle théorie sociologique des professions*, Presses Universitaires de France – PUF, Paris.

Clegg, S. 2012. 'The end of bureaucracy?', in T. Diefenbach & R. Todnem (eds.), *Reinventing Hierarchy and Bureaucracy: From the Bureau to Network Organisations*, Emerald, Bingley.

Correia, T. 2012. *Medicina. O agir numa saúde em mudança*, Lisboa, Editora Mundos Sociais/CIES-IUL.

Crozier, M. & Friedberg, E. 1977. *L'acteur et le système*, Editions du Seuil, Paris.

Deem, R., Hillyard, S. & Reed, M. 2007. *Knowledge, Higher Education, and the New Managerialism: The Changing Management of UK Universities*, Oxford University Press, Oxford.

Dent, M. 2002. 'Professional predicaments: Comparing the professionalization projects of German and Italian nurses', *International Journal of Public Sector Management*, Vol. 15, No. 2, pp. 151–162.

Diefenbach, T. & Todnem, R. 2012. 'Bureaucracy and hierarchy: What else!?', *Research in the Sociology of Organizations*, Vol. 35, pp. 1–27.

Dingwall, R., Simon, P. & Lewis, C. 1983. *The Sociology of the Professions: Lawyers, Doctors, and Others*, Palgrave Macmillan, Basingstoke.

Enders, J., de Boer, H. & Leisyte, L. 2008. 'On striking the right notes: Shifts in governance and the organisational transformation of universities', in A. Amaral, I. Bleiklie & C. Musselin (eds.), *From Governance to Identity: A Festschrift for Mary Henkel*, Springer, Dordrecht.

Evetts, J. 2002. 'New directions in state and international professional occupations: Discretionary decision-making and acquired regulation', *Work, Employment and Society*, Vol. 16, No. 2, pp. 341–353.

Ferlie, E., Ashburner, L., Fitzgerald, L. & Pettigrew, A. 1996. *The New Public Management in Action*, Oxford University Press, Oxford.

Fournier, R. 2000. 'Boundary work and (un)making of the professions', in N. Malin (ed.), *Professionalism, Boundaries and the Workplace*, Routledge, London.
Freidson, E. 1977. 'The futures of professionalisation', in M. Stacey, M. Reid, C. Heath & R. Dingwall (eds.), *Health and the Division of Labour*, Croom Helm, London.
Freidson, E. 1994. *Professionalism Reborn*, Polity Press, Cambridge.
Freidson, E. 2001. *Professionalism, the Third Logic: On the Practice of Knowledge*, The University of Chicago Press, Chicago.
Gouldner, A. 1954. *Patterns of Industrial Bureaucracy*, Free Press, Glencoe, IL.
Henkel, M. 1997. 'Academic values and the university as corporate enterprise', *Higher Education Quarterly*, Vol. 51, No. 2, pp. 134–143.
Henkel, M. 2007. 'Can academic autonomy survive in the knowledge society? A perspective from Britain', *Higher Education Research & Development*, Vol. 26, No. 1, pp. 87–99.
Hoggett, P. 1991. 'New modes of control in the public service', *Public Administration*, Vol. 74, No. 1, pp. 9–32.
Hunter, D. 2006. 'From tribalism to corporatism: The continuing managerial challenge to medical dominance', in D. Kelleher, J. Gabe & G. Williams (eds.), *Challenging Medicine* (2nd edn), Routledge, London.
Johnson, T. 1972. *Professions and Power*, Macmillan, London.
Kirkpatrick, I. & Ackroyd, S. 2003. 'Archetype theory and the changing professional organization: A critique and alternative', *Organization*, Vol. 10, No. 4, pp. 731–750.
Kirkpatrick, I., Ackroyd, S. & Walker, R. 2005. *New Managerialism and Public Sector Professionalism*, Palgrave, London.
Kitchener, M. 2000. 'The "bureaucratization" of professional roles: The case of clinical directors in UK hospitals', *Organization*, Vol. 7, No. 1, pp. 129–154.
Kitchener, M. & Whipp, R. 1995. 'Quality in the marketing change process', in M. Martinez & I. Kirkpatrick (eds.), *The Politics of Quality*, Routledge, London.
Kuhlmann, E., Burau, V., Larsen, C., Lewandowski, R., Lionis, C. & Repullo, J. 2011. 'Medicine and management in European healthcare systems: How do they matter in the control of clinical practice?', *International Journal of Clinical Practice*, Vol. 65, No. 7, pp. 722–724.
Larson, M. 2013. *The Rise of Professionalism: Monopolies of Competence and Sheltered Markets*, Transaction Publishers, New Brunswick & London.
Magalhães, A. & Santiago, R. 2012. 'Governance, public management and administration of higher education in Portugal', in G. Neave & A. Amaral (eds.), *Higher Education in Portugal 1974–2009, A Nation, a Generation*, Springer, Dordrecht.
Mintzberg, H. 1996. *Estrutura e dinâmica das organizações*, Circulo de Leitores, Lisbon.
Murphy, R. 1988. *Social Closure: The Theory of Monopolization and Exclusion*, Clarendon Press, Oxford.
Muzio, D., Ackroyd, S. & Chanlat, J-F. (eds.) 2007. *Redirections in the Study of Expert Labour: Established Professions and New Expert Occupations*, Palgrave Macmillan, Basingstoke.
Neave, G. 2012. *The Evaluative State, Institutional Autonomy and Re-Engineering Higher Education in Western Europe: The Prince and His Pleasure*, Palgrave

Macmillan, Basingstoke.
Neave, G. & van Vught, F. 1991. *Prometheus Bound: The Changing Relationships between Government and Higher Education in Western Europe*, Pergamon Press, Oxford.
Noordegraaf, M. 2007. 'From "pure" to "hybrid" professionalism: Present-day professionalism in ambiguous public domains', *Administration Society*, Vol. 39, No. 6, pp. 761–785.
Oakley, A. 2000. *Experiments in Knowing*, The New Press, New York.
Olssen, M. & Peters, M. 2005. 'Neoliberalism, higher education and the knowledge economy: From the free market to knowledge capitalism', *Journal of Education Policy*, Vol. 20, No. 3, pp. 313–345.
Parkin, F. 1979. *Marxism and Class Theory: A Bourgeois Critique*, Tavistock, London.
Pereira, Á. & Lains, P. 2012. 'From an agrarian society to a knowledge economy? The rising importance of education to the Portuguese economy, 1950–2009', in G. Neave & A. Amaral (eds.), *Higher Education in Portugal 1974–2009: A Nation, a Generation*, Springer, Dordrecht.
Pollitt, C. 2003. 'Public management reform: Reliable knowledge and international experience', *OECD Journal on Budgeting*, Vol. 3, No. 3, pp. 121–136.
Pollitt, C. & Bouckaert, G. 2011. *Public Management Reform: A Comparative Analysis – New Public Management, Governance, and the Neo-Weberian State*, Oxford University Press, Oxford.
Reed, M. 2002. 'New managerialism, professional power and organizational governance in UK universities: A review and assessment', in A. Amaral, G. Jones & B. Karseth (eds.), *Governing Higher Education: National Perspectives on Institutional Governance*, Kluwer University Publishers, Dordrecht.
Rhoades, G. & Slaughter, S. 1997. 'Academic capitalism, managed professionals, and supply-side higher education', *Social Text*, Vol. 15, No. 2, pp. 9–38.
Santiago, R. & Carvalho, T. 2012. 'Managerialism rhetoric's in Portuguese higher education', *Minerva*, Vol. 50, No. 4, pp. 511–532.
Santiago, R. Carvalho, T. & Ferreira, A. 2014. 'Knowledge society/economy and managerial changes: New challenges for Portuguese academics', in J. Brankovic et al. (eds.), *Global Challenges, Local Responses in Higher Education. The Contemporary Issues in National and Comparative Perspective*, Sense Publishers, London.
Santiago, R., Carvalho, T. & Ferreira, A. 2015. 'Changing knowledge and academic profession in Portugal', *Higher Education Quarterly*, Vol. 69, No. 1, pp. 79–100.
Schon, D. 1994. *Le praticien reflexive: À la recherche du savoir caché dans l'agir professionnel*, Les Éditions Logiques, Montréal/Québec.
Sciulli, D. 2005. 'Continental sociology of professions today: Conceptual contributions', *Current Sociology*, Vol. 53, No. 6, pp. 915–942.
Slaughter, S. & Leslie, L. 1997. *Academic Capitalism: Politics, Policies, and the Entrepreneurial University*, The Johns Hopkins University Press, Baltimore.
Strauss, A., Schatzman, L., Bucher, R., Ehlirch, D. & Sabshin, M. 1964. *Psychiatric Ideologies and Institutions*, Free Press of Glencoe, New York.
Taylor, F. 1914. *The Principles of Scientific Management*, Harper, New York.
Teixeira, P. 2012. 'The changing public-private mix in higher education: Analysing Portugal's apparent exceptionalism', in G. Neave & A. Amaral (eds.), *Higher Education in Portugal 1974–2009: A Nation, a Generation*, Springer Publishers, Dordrecht.

Trowler, P. 1998. *Academics Responding to Change: New Higher Education Frameworks and Academic Cultures*, SRHE, Open University, London.
Ward, S. 2012. *Neoliberalism and the Global Restructuring of Knowledge and Education*, Routledge, New York & London.
Weber, M. 1989. *Sobre a universidade*, Cortez Editora, São Paulo.
Weber, M. 1995. *Economie et société. 1, Les catégories de la sociologie*, Plon/Pocket, Paris.

Legislation

Decree-Law 176/2009.
Decree-Law 177/2009.
Decree-Law 185/81.
Decree-Law 248/2009.
Decree-Law 305/81.
Decree-Law 310/82.
Decree-Law 448/79.
Law 62/2007.

3
The Finnish Academic Profession in Health-Related Sciences and Social Services

Timo Aarrevaara

Introduction

The societal interest in higher education (HE) in the welfare context is strong in the Nordic countries. In Finland, HE is predominantly publicly funded, which imposes high expectations on policies and practices of modernisation. HE is expected to facilitate the building of a stronger economy, efficiency in education and research processes, and change in society through research and education. It is expected to improve the well-being of citizens. Universities are also expected to bring changes to employment in a way that will improve the culture, innovation and growth of society. However, research is also required to meet society's high expectations.

Higher education institutions (HEIs) and the academic profession have traditionally been relatively autonomous and had high social status. The autonomy of universities has been a key line of development in Finland throughout the 2000s. Their autonomy has been primarily in financial and administrative areas, but it has also led to society paying attention to changes in the academic profession. Reforms since 2000 in Finnish HE have been influenced by the demand for universities to improve their strategic areas of focus, the defining of their responsibility to society, attempts to increase the diversity of the funding base and the growing role of external stakeholders, improved global competitiveness, and the clash of contradicting bureaucratic and entrepreneurial attitudes. Finding a balance between expectations and reality is, however, problematic (Maassen & Olsen 2007). Under these demands, HEIs compete for research funding, students and staff in the sustainable European labour market for researchers (Fumasoli et al. 2015).

The purpose of this chapter is to discuss how the academic profession can meet society's challenges, as described. The chapter examines the characteristics of Finnish HE, the available data on the academic profession and the development of the profession, and the internal and external demands for dynamic changes. In this context, Finland is an example of this change of role, as shown in this chapter by the views of those within 'medical sciences, health-related sciences and social services', as reported in the Changing Academic Profession (CAP) survey and in 'The Academic Profession in Europe: Responses to Societal Challenges' (EUROAC) research.

Finnish HE

Large-scale changes have occurred over recent decades in Finnish HE. These reflect newer generations' expanded access to HE, and the fact that the level of public funding has remained high – 80 per cent of Finnish HE recurrent funding is publicly sourced. The situation in Finland is in line with the other Nordic university systems, which have also had a traditional dependence on state funding and been under tight government control. The expansion of HE has typically been based on regional development, a dimension reflected in the expansion of the university sector in the 1960s and the establishment of the polytechnic sector in the last 20 years. The Nordic model combines economic growth with high levels of social protection, inclusion and equality. Gornitzka and Maassen (2012) find government policies concerning university autonomy and the development of public funding to be at the core of governance reforms in Nordic HE.

The national characteristics in the Finnish case are strongly connected with the nation-building of the Finnish state. The first Finnish university was established in 1640, long before Finland became a sovereign state, and it is closely linked to the country's national tradition (Kogan 2002; Aarrevaara et al. 2011). In common with the rest of the world, Finnish universities were elitist institutions, a model that was prevalent up until the 1960s, and massification did not occur until the 1990s. In the case of Finnish HE, there have been broad and substantial changes since the early 1990s, when massification of HE enrolment was boosted by the establishment of a second HE sector, comprising polytechnics. The aim of government policy was to channel HE growth into polytechnics, these having been developed through the amalgamation and consolidation of former post-secondary institutions and upper vocational institutions within each region (MinEdu

2001). This is an ongoing process in Finnish HE, and changes to academic practices are taking place in relation to the curriculum, degree structure and research (Laiho 2010). Reforms are also taking place in several other European countries with a non-university sector. For example, in Portugal new legislation on the framework of public academic careers was established, and there have been significance changes in the polytechnics (Dias et al. 2013).

The functional dimension is also well documented in the Finnish university sector, since performance management reform was undertaken from the early 1990s – reform that strengthened universities' administrative and financial autonomy, but not necessarily their academic autonomy. Important characteristics in Finnish HE are its strong regional emphasis; the existence of a binary system with different goals; and two official national languages – Finnish and Swedish. Finnish citizens have the right to demand that public services, including all levels of education, be provided in either language.

Following several university mergers in the early 21st century, by 2015 the number of universities in Finland had been reduced to 14 universities, 12 of which are institutions subject to public law, and the other 2 are foundations subject to private law (Aarrevaara et al. 2009; Universities Act 558/2009, amended 12 August 2011). In addition, the National Defence College is a university that comes under the Ministry of Defence. In 2015, the 24 polytechnics under Ministry of Education and Culture ceased being responsible to local government councils or the state, and became independent legal entities. However, the bulk of their funding still comes indirectly from the national government, as before 2014. There is also one polytechnic under licence to the semi-independent Province of Åland (a collection of islands that lie between the Finnish mainland and Sweden) and a police academy that is the responsibility of the Ministry of the Interior. The Universities Act (2009) can be seen as a part of the development of the HE system: the government's main goals were to reduce the number of universities as a whole; to aggregate academic units into larger and more effective entities; and to facilitate the creation of strategic alliances.

The polytechnics under the Ministry of Education and Culture have also undergone changes in governance, which has seen them move from under the local government umbrella to become independent legal entities in 2015 with the status of a limited company. Their administrative and financial autonomy have increased in a way similar to that experienced by universities following the new Universities Act effective from 2010.

Data on the academic profession

This chapter is based on data from the CAP survey, an international questionnaire-based survey of 25,282 staff in 18 countries (Teichler et al. 2013). The participants of the CAP survey in Finland consisted of salaried full-time employees with teaching and research responsibilities. The questionnaire was addressed to a 20 per cent sample of full-time teaching and research personnel. The Finnish sample comprised useable responses from 1,374 full-time academic staff from the 18 universities and 24 polytechnics in existence at the time, divided into 12 main discipline-based groups (1,125 identified as being in the Humanities, Natural Sciences or Health). CAP also provided information on gender and seniority. Although the Finnish sample corresponded well with the general academic population in terms of their various occupations and gender, senior academics were overrepresented relative to their junior colleagues (Table 3.1).

A follow-up study to the CAP survey, entitled EUROAC, was conducted during 2011. It was a qualitative study of the impressions of academic staff conducted among academics from eight European countries (Teichler & Höhle 2013). Several countries participating in EUROAC that had not participated in CAP in 2007/2008, provided CAP survey information in 2011. The EUROAC research was based on a broader scope than the CAP project. The European survey comprised 16,467 respondents in 12 countries. The EUROAC interviews were carried out in 2011 in Finland and Germany, which had participated in the CAP survey, plus Austria, Croatia, Ireland, Poland, Romania and Switzerland, with interviews covering three fields:

(1) Humanities (languages and cultural studies (history, philosophy, theology), sports, arts, law, economics/business administration, social sciences, education, social work).
(2) Natural Sciences, including life science (mathematics, natural sciences, agriculture, forestry, nutrition sciences, engineering sciences, architecture).
(3) Non-clinical staff in Medical Sciences (medicine, veterinary medicine, dentistry, pharmacy, health sciences, nursing, health care).

This chapter reviews the CAP survey and EUROAC results in general, while adding comments made by EUROAC respondents in the health disciplines. Among the respondents of the Finnish CAP survey, 13.4 per cent of university respondents and 19.4 per cent of

Table 3.1 Respondents according to disciplines, in the CAP survey and EUROAC interviews in Finland

	CAP 2008		EUROAC 2011	
	Respondents N	Respondents %	Respondents N	Respondents %
Humanities	497	44	36	41
Natural Sciences	451	40	41	47
Health	177	16	10	12
	1,125	100	87	100

polytechnic respondents identified themselves as being from the medical sciences, health-related sciences and social services (hereafter, *Health*). It was the second largest category in both sectors, behind engineering, manufacturing and construction, and architecture. Ten of the 87 interviewees from the Finnish EUROAC survey were from *Health* disciplines.

The CAP survey obtained an overall picture of the academic profession, including how work conditions are changing. The study examined many key issues, including documenting the interconnections between the academic community, universities and relationships with society at large. The CAP survey is a database from which can be produced detailed comparative research-based information on the national HE systems, research and HEIs of the participating nations.

The Finnish Universities Act (2009) has emphasised the quality of education and the quality and impact of research. Universities' separation from the state administration was effected from the beginning of 2010, and the changes in polytechnics' financial and administrative autonomy occurred in 2011–2014. For the scholarly community, the impact of these changes can be seen in some practices. For example, within universities, an important change has been in the bureaucratic context of employment (Aarrevaara et al. 2009). University staff were previously 'civil servants', in effect employed by the national government. Since the Universities Act of 2009 came into force, members of university staff have become the direct employees of the universities themselves. From the academic profession's perspective, this has meant a more diversified labour market and variable working conditions. In the early 2000s, the government's interest was focused on the processes and procedures in universities, with a view to making HE more effective in society. University management's role has changed from traditional public administration to focusing on achieving results and taking responsibility for doing so (Hughes 2012). Senior academics recognise such changes in HE, as described in the following quotation from a EUROAC interview:

> The changes at the national level affect me especially by applying more pressure on us to make students graduate faster. It is a question of balancing between high quality in the studies and better and faster flow-through. Also, the structural reforms even at the European level and the recognition of international degrees, studies, qualifications and experience take a lot of my time. In my subject areas (*Health*) these things are really difficult but also important. I don't think that the power of managers and leaders has increased, at least not in our unit. We have been very stable in that sense, probably because of the low turnover among the managers and leaders.
>
> (Female, Senior, Polytechnics)

The traditional expectations of government control of HE based on regulation, budgetary control and control by information management, have been partly replaced by increased expectations with regard to institutional autonomy and self-governance. For traditional HEIs, balancing teaching, research and service according to the new Finnish system is now more complex than it was (Enders & Teichler 1997; Aarrevaara et al. 2011). Both halves of Finnish binary education are now more dependent on interaction with society, and global trends linked with national characteristics and scattered interests in HE.

The 'modernisation' project is still in progress in Finnish HE. This can be seen, for example, by respondents expressing dissatisfaction with the top-down management model. A minority of respondents in the European countries in the CAP survey identified that there was *competent leadership* in their institutions (Teichler & Höhle 2013). This statistical view is confirmed by these comments from EUROAC interviewees, indicating that managers' posts are not considered to be an attractive option:

> There is an opportunity to apply for a position with responsibility for administrative tasks, but there are not many of those. Managers have emphasised that additional training is taken into account and it affects the content of the work.
>
> (Male, Junior, Polytechnic)

I have had university work experience and now I have experience in this polytechnic, too. At first I was surprised when I saw the extent of managers' power here, but I've realised that universities have followed a similar trend, with new managers at the faculty level now wielding increased power.

(Female, Junior, Polytechnic)

A minority of respondents in all the European countries in the CAP survey rated leadership competence in their institutions as being high (Teichler & Höhle 2013).

Many of the respondents have worked outside HE, and have had experience in management. Nevertheless, many have no interest in managerial posts in academe. In *Health*, the stakeholders' role is strong and there is preparedness for engagement or public service motivation (van Eijk & Steen 2014). However, the difference between academic responsibilities and the lack of resources is evident, as impressed in the next few quotations:

In a way we cannot yet tell if collegial power has been diminished in these new structures. The external influence is really big in medicine. We have jobs that are partly funded by the university and partly by the regional and municipal hospitals. Sometimes the hospital stresses the clinical qualities rather than the academic qualities too much.

(Female, Senior, University)

There is a lot of professionalisation beyond traditional academic tasks, for instance in leadership and administration. This holds especially for professors I think. The structural reforms together with a lack of funding led to frustration among many of my colleagues. Many say it is ridiculous that half of the working hours go on preparing funding applications.

(Male, Senior, University)

Demand for dynamic HE

The Finnish HE system is an interesting combination of institutions with regional strengths, disciplines and research, with the major funding role continuing to be played by the Ministry of Education and Culture. The Finnish HE system is characterised by multi-level governance, complex national decision-making and dispersed HE policy interests. The most important players are the National Technology

Agency (TEKES), the Academy of Finland, the Finnish National Fund for Research and Development, and other groups connected with the university system (FinnSight Georghiou et al. 2003; FinnSight 2006, 2015). The success in winning the competitive funding provided by these agencies, as well as that made available via international programmes, has become a part of the Ministry of Education and Culture's funding model, amounting to 9 per cent of all government funding for universities in 2014. Under the current funding model, universities can accumulate resources by improving students' completion rates and quickening their transfer to the workforce, improving their administration, and improving the quality of education and research.

The regional interests of all HEIs are important, but it could be argued that Finland has too many HEIs for such a small country. However, the government has drawn attention to the fact it has reduced the number of university departments by combining them, aiming to improve efficiency. Government policy to increase the overall size of academic units could mean that all HEIs become financially, academically and administratively stronger.

The new context of global HE requires improved competitiveness for all HEIs, and it is assumed they will have to compete globally for students and staff. Major changes would require professional management and leadership, but Finnish HEIs are not traditionally very strong actors in this regard, and the system has thus not been dynamic in character. This can be seen in the EUROAC interview data. In recent decades, universities have seen reduced state control and an increase in the use of market mechanisms in the academy. This means that universities compete for research funding, students and staff. In practice, the shift in this 'market' direction can be seen in following interview quotations from the EUROAC survey 2011:

> For one's career, it is not important to keep in contact with stakeholders such as the pharmaceutical industry. In the clinic there is a very precise way of working. All treatment decisions must be justified. In research, there are meetings to figure out what is a sensible and ethical way to go forward.
> (Female, Senior, University)

> One thing that has definitely changed since the 1980s is the increased (doubled) number of staff members. Previously there was a two stage, very vague academic career model with assistants and professors.

Now there is a four stage model with doctoral students, university researchers, university lecturers and professors. The amount of external and competitive funding is also much greater nowadays than it was a couple of decades ago.

(Male, Senior, University)

The interrelations between HE policy actors presuppose relative stability (Kauko 2013). Promoting the dynamics of the HEIs in both sectors would require extensive freedom of operation for the different actors applying the entrepreneurial and accountable operating culture. It will probably take a generation before the requisite structural reforms can move ahead.

Developments in the 21st century have seen both HE sectors increasing their involvement in the wider innovation system. A recent evaluation on the Government Research and Innovation Council (Pelkonen et al. 2014), identified problems in its operating model, position and effectiveness. The remarks can be generalised more largely to apply to the European research and innovation systems, the driving forces behind the model which are identified as internationalisation, globalisation of the economy and increasing complexity in society. The evaluation report stresses that there are more general problems relating to the innovation system, namely segregation between the areas of education, research and innovation. The ongoing structural reforms since 2010 have established the universities' separation from the state administration and polytechnics' separation from local governments. Closer partnerships and cooperation have developed between the sectors, but the dynamics of the HE sector have been such that there is little interaction between the two, and the sectors have remained distinct and separate. In this landscape, there have been several mergers within each HE sector, but none between the two sectors. This chapter sheds light on the reasons behind the policy of maintaining two separate HE sectors.

The academic profession has developed in response to the new system of HE

HE reforms can be characterised according to their focus on structural reforms. In the 2010s, it seems that there is a stronger focus on universities' mode of operation. There are no consumers in the research and HE system in the sense that there are consumers in the economic system. Trends in research and academic organisations do not necessarily follow directly trends in society.

In the administrative reorganisation of the 2010s, the academic core and administrative support services were mainly separated in universities. As a result, there is specialisation, which is a positive outcome. Still, the desired division of work between academics and administrators and managers is not taking place as planned. As a result, there are more administrative duties than before, especially for senior academics:

> I accept that some of the [administrative] work has to be done by me, but I feel that administrative tasks take up a terribly large amount of time. So part of my work is not based on my formal education. Everybody here is tired and exhausted with the organisational reforms, which have not supported us to work more in research. I find it surprising and scary that people get tired and overwhelmed. Everyone gets tired in organisational development, a result that leads to a reduction in research.
>
> (Male, Senior, University)

In the EUROAC interviews, these problems are focused on two themes. First, the academic profession is closely working within the structures of HE connected specifically to either universities or polytechnics, which prevents mobility between sectors. The social costs of mobility in the Finnish case seem to be high. In many fields there are few units to choose between, as described in next quotation:

> Of course, in radiography education for nurses in Finland there are only five units right now, and it means that there are only five cities in which x-ray education is provided, plus one in the Swedish language.
>
> (Male, Junior, Polytechnic)

Second, the narrow funding base and economic recession have brought hard times to recruitment and working conditions. There is a great risk that potential newcomers will move to sectors other than HE.

As the procedural autonomy of HE has increased in the Finnish case, this has meant a reduction of direct government control and a growing role for other stakeholders. There is an increased demand for relevance, accountability and performance. All this development is partly dependent on actors outside the HE sector. Finnish HE is still under reform, based on influential actors rather than equal and institutionally fair opportunities. Under these conditions, all HEIs are expected to reach a high level of international success and emphasise performance in strategic development areas. Both HE sectors in Finland are struggling with the simultaneous demands to increase quality levels in core activities and to extend the role of HE itself.

In recent years, the government has emphasised structural reform and mergers as a tool for the implementation of this reform. The academic profession, in turn, is reacting to reform. The initiative for the relevance of research, improved quality of teaching and the pruning of operating information are the areas in which the scholarly community, taking into account disciplinary traditions, has the potential to influence the content of reforms. Structural reforms are seen as both good and bad as they provide a range of options – often outside the traditional academic heartland – for their implementation.

Finnish universities are now looking ahead to a time of even greater autonomy. How long this will take to achieve will depend not only on developments in HE's core fields, but also on economic trends and the universities' ability to maintain effective operations. Puusa and Kekäle (2013) have noted that members of staff commit themselves to their work. However, members of the academic staff are suspicious about institutional and system changes, and their commitment to scholarly work and familiar and more manageable units is stronger. Organisational support correlates with respect and organisational commitment (Boezeman & Ellemers 2014). The rigid bureaucracy identified in the CAP data of 2008 has restricted universities' abilities to compete in labour markets for new workers. This can also be seen in the following interviews from EUROAC 2011:

> The changes in management have not yet affected basic work. Organisational changes are least visible to the junior staff and affect their jobs the least. The role of collegial decision-making has decreased and this might make universities less attractive employees as hierarchy increases.
> (Male, Senior, University)

> I have been a member of different faculty and department boards for many years and I have to say that my influence in those bodies has been and still is quite limited. The really important decisions are made somewhere else. We can only meet the new structures which are planned by somebody else.
> (Female, Senior, University)

More than half of the Finnish CAP respondents in *Health* felt that their teaching was practice oriented, and that it is the nature of research for it to take place in work groups. More than half of the respondents indicated that their research is also multi- or interdisciplinary in character. This is also illustrated by the fact that almost half of the academics in *Health* departments undertake paid work other than their normal academic work. This is despite the fact that the Finnish sample included only those staff working full-time. Compared with respondents from other disciplines, those in *Health* are involved more often in ICT-based learning, and less in face-to-face interaction with students outside of class (Table 3.2).

The academic profession's role differs between universities and polytechnics, but also between the various disciplines, universities, research institutions, and between the private and public sectors. Research is the main function of academics at universities, but the main function of polytechnic academics is teaching.

For example, it is clear that working hours differ between disciplines. On the basis of the CAP survey, the number of teaching hours per respondent is second highest in the health disciplines, right after the engineering discipline. This trend can also be seen in following interviews:

> Teaching takes around 50 per cent of time, administration 20 per cent and the rest is research.
>
> (Male, Senior, University)

Table 3.2 Teaching activities of the respondents according to the discipline (per cent of named activities). Question: During the current (or previous) academic year, have you been involved in any of the following teaching activities?

	Humanities %	Natural Sciences %	Health %
Classroom instruction	79.9	68.1	73.4
Individualised instruction	70.8	62.1	70.6
Learning in projects	44.3	33.9	40.1
Practice instruction	45.5	59.0	58.8
ICT-based learning	36.8	25.3	40.1
Distance education	31.8	19.7	26.6
Development of course material	64.6	60.3	66.7
Curriculum development	64.6	44.6	59.9
Face-to-face interaction outside the class	61.2	50.8	46.9
Electronic communications	79.3	66.1	71.2
	N = 497	N = 451	N = 177

I used to work as an adjunct teacher and researcher for some years and in 2009 this position was established. I applied for and I got this job. I feel that I have achieved what I wanted so far because I have a very meaningful package of teaching in a field I feel I am an expert in and I can supervise a couple of doctoral students. I think my university expects me to become a more independent researcher soon so I can lead research groups of my own.

(Male, Senior, University)

Conclusions

The academic profession is changing, not only in terms of the content of the work, but also according to the age structure and the career paths of those in the profession. Over the next few years, the retirement rate of researchers and teachers will increase dramatically as demand for HE is increasing (Statistics Finland, Findicator). Perhaps universities should take the opportunity to enlarge the academic profession inside the universities. Almost half of the staff working universities are in non-academic positions (Aarrevaara & Dobson 2014). However, some 'non-academic' staff also undertake traditional academic duties, mainly in teaching and research. Their tasks may also be related to student services, ICT, research or running laboratories. Universities seem to find it difficult to identify this academic capacity within staff occupying administrative positions.

This can result in structural reforms within universities, as they continue their quest for expansion and society demands more efficient HEIs. In Finland, state research institutes are being folded into universities, delegating the responsibility for basic research to the universities, in line with government policy. This objective requires universities to accept this opportunity; in practice, this means, for example, that they must substantially strengthen their support for scholars. This policy is also the basis for increasing the number of members in the Finnish academic profession.

Based on the CAP and EUROAC data on *Health* academics, it seems that the changes in HE have influenced our understanding of the academic profession. The academics in *Health* are more practically and multidisciplinary oriented than average scholar in Finnish HE. The views expressed in the EUROAC interviews indicate that the newer generation of academics do not share the values and attitudes of the previous generation. The traditional role of the academic profession is to educate for academic occupations, and traditional expectations have been important within *Health*. Research is growing in interdisciplinary fields, and the profession is becoming more fragmented. On top of this, many of the welfare state expectations are not being realised in the 2010s, as economic growth has been declining for the past few years. Based on the CAP and EUROAC data, the interpretations of changes at the institutional level will be studied in the coming years in the wider social and societal context. We know that younger cohorts prefer a different type of academy from that preferred by older cohorts. We also know that universities are striving for world-class status and research based on future needs, and that polytechnics are looking for stronger regional impact and international capacity.

Finland still has high levels of public funding with regard to HEIs, but the government's declining commitment is evident. Universities have seen the rise of education and research markets in the academy, as they compete for research funding, students and staff with the rest of society. The 'red tape' aspects of the bureaucracy in HE and its strong legislative basis have restricted the capacity to compete. The conditions for HE are changing, and the academic profession also has to change.

References

Aarrevaara, T. & Dobson, I. 2014. 'Job satisfaction among general staff in the Nordic countries: A preliminary examination', *NUAS Report*.
Aarrevaara, T., Dobson, I. & Elander, C. 2009. 'Brave new world: Higher education reform in Finland', *Higher Education Management and Policy*, Vol. 21, No. 2, pp. 87–104.
Aarrevaara, T., Dobson, I. & Pekkola, E. 2011. 'Finland – captive academics – an examination of the binary divide', in W. Locke, W. Cummings & D. Fisher (eds.), *Changing Governance and Management in Higher Education: The Perspectives of the Academy*, Springer, Dordrecht.
Boezeman, E. & Ellemers, N. 2014. 'Volunteer leadership: The role of pride and respect in organizational identification and leadership satisfaction', *Journal of Leadership*, Vol. 10, No. 2, pp. 160–173.
Dias, D., Machada-Taylor, M. L., Santiago, R., Carvalho, T. & Sousa, S. 2013. 'Portugal: Dimensions of academic job satisfaction', in P. Bentley, H. Coates, I. Dobson, L. Goedegebuure & L. Meek (eds.), *Job Satisfaction around the Academic World, Series the Changing Academy: The Changing Academic Profession in International Comparative Perspective*, n. 7, Springer, London.
Eijk, C. van & Steen, T. 2014. 'Why people co-produce: Analysing citizens' perceptions on co-planning engagement in health care services', *Public Management Review*, Vol. 16, No. 3, pp. 358–382.
Enders, J. & Teichler, U. 1997. 'A victim of their own success? Employment and working conditions of academic staff in comparative perspective', *Higher Education*, Vol. 34, No. 3, pp. 347–342.

FinnSight-2015, 2006. *The Outlook for Sciences, Technology and Society*, Academy of Finland and the Finnish Funding Agency for Technology, Helsinki.

Fumasoli, T., Goastellec, G. & Kehm, B. (eds.) 2015. 'Academic work and careers in Europe: Trends, challenges, perspectives', *Series: The Changing Academy, The Changing Academic Profession in International Perspective*, Vol. 12, Springer, London.

Georghiou, L., Smith, K., Toivanen, O. & Ylä-Anttila, P. 2003. *Evaluation of the Finnish Innovation Support System*, Ministry of Trade and Industry Finland Publications 5.

Gornitzka, Å. & Maassen, P. 2012, 'University reform and the Nordic model', in M. Kwiek & P. Maassen (eds.), *National Higher Education Reforms in a European Context, Higher Education Research and Policy (HERP) 2*, Peter Lang.

Hughes, O. 2012. *Public Management and Administration* (4th edn), Palgrave Macmillan, London.

Kauko, J. 2013. 'Dynamics in higher education politics, a theoretical model', *Journal of Higher Education*, Vol. 65, No. 2, pp. 193–206.

Kogan, M. 2002. 'National characteristics and policy idiosyncrasies', in *Higher Education in a Globalising World. Series: Higher Education Dynamics*, Vol. 1. Springer, Dordrecht.

Laiho, A. 2010. 'Academisation of nursing education in the Nordic countries', *Journal of Higher Education*, Vol. 60, pp. 641–656.

Maassen, P. & Olsen, J. (eds.) 2007. University Dynamics and European Integration. *Series: Higher Education Dynamics*, Vol. 19. Springer, Dordrecht.

MinEdu. 2001. 'Management by results in higher education', *The Ministry of Education, Publications of the Department for Education and Science*, No. 84.

Pelkonen, A., Nieminen, M. & Lehenkari, J. 2014. 'Tutkimus- ja innovaationeuvoston toiminnan ja vaikuttavuuden arviointi', *Publications of the Ministry of Education and Culture*, No. 14.

Puusa, A. & Kekäle, J. 2013. 'Commitment in the context of a merger', *Tertiary Education and Management*, Vol. 19, No. 1, pp. 205–218.

Statistics Finland 2014. *Findicator*. Retrieved 15 November 2014, http://www.findikaattori.fi/en.

Teichler, U. & Höhle, E. 2013. 'The work situation of the academic profession in Europe: Findings of a survey in twelve countries', *Series: The Changing Academy: The Changing Academic Profession in International Comparative Perspective*, Vol. 8, Springer, Dordrecht.

Teichler, U., Arimoto, A. & Cummings, W. 2013. 'The changing academic profession: Major findings of a comparative survey', *Series: The Changing Academy: The Changing Academic Profession in Comparative Perspective*, Vol. 1. Springer, Dordrecht.

Part II
Professionals in Health

4
Reconstructing Care Professionalism in Finland

Helena Hirvonen

Introduction

The public sector plays a special role in the Nordic welfare states through its commitment to the principle of universalism, and in relation to social security and publicly funded services in education, health and care (Rostgaard 2002). In the 21st century, the impact of economic austerity on public resources and a rapid aging of the population have forced welfare states to undergo an extreme reform. In Finland, the reform has meant streamlining the state, restraining public expenditure and recalibrating the universalistic ideals behind the Nordic welfare state model, as well as introducing new management models (Pollitt & Bouckaert 2011). The managerial reforms implemented in Finland have followed the ideology of new public management (NPM), altering the roles of the state and the clients, and influencing care work cultures, and health and social care workers' professional agency (Henriksson & Wrede 2008).

The welfare state reforms are intensified by an overlapping transition towards knowledge society. In the public service sector, this affects the professional power of public service workers. Clients and managers are now more empowered in relation to health and social care professionals, while professionals need to reassert their accountability through various audit techniques. Moreover, in 'technological societies' such as Finland, difficulties in improving the efficiency and quality of human service delivery are easily framed as technical problems that call for technological solutions (Barry 2001). Technologisation is validated by a strong optimism and hopes of more flexible service production, efficiency gains, better civic participation and improved transparency, documentation, quality and comparability of service outputs that would result in citizens' enhanced quality of life (Doupi et al. 2007; European Commission 2009; Heichlinger 2011). Technologisation of work is therefore a process that increases efficiency and reasserts trust in public services.

In the case of health and social care work, the parallel transformations towards knowledge society and a leaner welfare state has meant the introduction of complex and manifold audit techniques that are implemented through information and communication technologies (ICTs) as practices of record-keeping and checking (Saario 2014). These are used as a means for assessing health and social care workers' professional accountability, and for evaluating the results of their work as quantifiable and comparable outputs, representing a turn towards what Power (1997) calls an 'audit society'. As the end users of ICT solutions, workers are the key players in the success of technological investments, from the point of view of public economy and the quality of care.

Previous studies on the use of ICTs in health and social care work point to workers' resistive practices and improvised use of technology, which may compromise the expected outcomes of costly investments in technology (Koivunen et al. 2008). According to these studies, workers' dissatisfaction arises from the fact technologies are produced exclusively from the vision of their developers, and appear to end users as 'the design from nowhere' (Suchman 2002). Moreover, the gendered and corporeal nature of care work – which continues to be overwhelmingly female-dominated – has often been absent from policy discussions regarding the problematic aspects of the implementation and design of ICTs in care work (Balka et al. 2009).

The growing implementation of technology in health and social care work demonstrates the transition towards the knowledge society in the Finnish welfare state. From two points of view, the transition poses particular challenges to occupation groups in the lower ladders of professional hierarchies of health and social care work, such as nurses. First, as professional work, care work and nursing involves technical and medical expertise, but also a form of personal service, bodywork and emotional orientation to the needs of another human being. Due to the holistic nature of health and social care work, its outcomes are not easily transformed into quantifiable and comparable outputs to be audited and recorded. Nevertheless, ICTs have gained a growing role in monitoring and auditing workers' performance and care outputs (Saario 2014). Second, studies show that the occupational requirements of workers' interaction skills, emotion work and empathy are culturally essentialised as natural 'feminine skills', based on a normative cultural assumption of women's abilities in the fields of emotion work, empathy and corporeal care (Virkki 2008; Husso & Hirvonen 2012).

In this chapter, I use qualitative interview data (n = 25 – a sample size of 25 interviews) collected from Finnish health and social care workers to study the effects of the managerial transformation of the welfare state from two interrelated points of view: first, with regard to the overriding role that ICT-assisted practices of accountability work have gradually gained in health and social care work, and second, with regard to how this affects nurses' professional identities and agency as care professionals.

Restratification of care professions in a medico-managerial welfare state

In Finland, the education and professionalisation of health and social care occupations has taken place in accordance with the expansion of the welfare state, and in close relation to the public service sector. The period from 1960s to 1990s was especially characterised by a rapid expansion in the scope of the welfare state and its service provision. This encouraged women in particular to turn to careers in the welfare service (Wrede 2008). Today, however, rapid population aging and public sector austerity policies have forced the state to re-evaluate its means of sustaining the Nordic, universalistic welfare state model. In Finland, as in many Western welfare states, this has led to a reconstruction of the welfare state according to the principles of NPM, exerting pressure upon public finances, and the quality and efficiency of health and social care services (Pollit & Bouckaert 2011).

Despite cutbacks, and the consequential retrenchment of the universal coverage of the welfare state, the responsibility for the execution of health and social care services remains in the hands of Finnish municipalities, who rely primarily on the public service sector to produce statutory health and social care services (Anttonen & Häikiö 2011; Kröger 2011). Consequently, the development and organisation of care occupations continues to be strongly interlinked with the welfare state itself. Although welfare state reform has not led to a straightforward privatisation of welfare services, it signifies a great managerial and ideological transformation in the Nordic welfare states. According to critics, this has caused a conflict between the professional ethics of health care workers and the pressure to validate the managerial accountability and efficiency of care service work (Waerness 2005; Henriksson & Wrede 2008).

In feminist theory, care work is often analysed as a form of or in relation to biological and social reproduction (Bakker 2007). As an occupational practice, care represents a core task of health and social care work, that is cultivated through corporeal habits, emotion work and workers' occupational ethics. These require personal responsibility and commitment from individual workers to respond to the needs of another human being (Dahl & Rask Eriksen 2005; Twigg et al. 2011). The corporeal, situational and social nature of care can aid workers' imaginative ability to empathise with others. At the same time, it places care professionalism in contrast with the conventional idea of (health) professionalism that is impersonal, unemotional and science-based. Due to this, caring occupations have a complex and charged relationship with their aspirations towards professionalisation. Moreover, contemporary medico-managerial management culture prioritises medical care and emphasises workers' technical skills, further alienating workers' skills in corporeal and social care from the realm of professionalism.

Previous studies on the effects of public sector reforms estimate that established and autonomous professional groups, such as medical doctors, have fared rather well in terms of maintaining their autonomy (Kurunmäki 2000; Kuhlmann 2006). However, studies have also pointed to the emergence of both ethical and practical problems among less powerful and/or recently established occupations that are culturally more feminine and distant from the conventional idea of health professionalism (Dahl & Rask Eriksen 2005; Henriksson 2008; Tronto 2011). According to Wrede (2008), the new management culture points to both a deepening of the old and a creation of new divisions and inequalities, which build on mutually constituted, gendered and classed hierarchies in the field of health and social care work. The Finnish case, therefore, exemplifies a restratification of public professional work that Noordegraaf (2013) identifies as a key element in understanding its reconfiguration.

For one, in an effort to unite middle-grade care occupations in Finland, nine trans-sectoral study programmes in social and health care were united under the single umbrella curriculum of practical nursing in 1995. According to Henriksson (2008), the reconfiguration of occupational groups exemplifies the difficulties contemporary management culture has in associating professionalism with care service work. Moreover, practical nurses are the key occupational group involved in elderly home care services, which is an area of public care provision that is facing particularly strong pressure to streamline and rationalise.

Studies show that the scope of public responsibility of elderly home care has already shifted, from a holistic to a more narrow and medical account of care work (Henriksson & Wrede 2008; Anttonen & Häikiö 2011). This deepens the social–health care divide between various (semi-)professions, and compromises the professional status and power of recently established social care occupations in particular.

All in all, health and social care workers' formal competence requirements have increased over the past 30 years, while the value of the full range of their occupational skills and their chances to influence decision-making in the workplace have simultaneously decreased (Henriksson & Wrede 2008; Henriksson 2011). Regardless of the occupational and status differences between various groups of health and social care professions, the changing cultural, political and social environment in the welfare state has affected all grades of workers. In particular, the managerial, technological and cultural transition towards a knowledge society has aimed at a disembodied and gender-neutral conceptualisation of care professionalism.

Disembodied care professionalism in the knowledge society

Proximity between workers and service clients has traditionally been an essential requirement for the execution of corporeal and social practices of care. It transfers the 'feeling of being in good hands' and generates client trust. Consequently, the technical rationality and emergence of ICT-assisted practices of accountability affect client relations, and, in particular, the idea of client trust (Nicolini 2007). In human service work, such as nursing, trust is a mechanism through which the gap is bridged between the client's incomplete information and need for help on the one hand, and the impossibility of controlling professional work on the other (di Luzio 2006). Therefore client trust does not simply mean trust in a person but trust in an institution the person represents. In encounters between care professionals and clients, personal feelings, emotions and values are involved, together with the general, cultural value attributed to workers as knowledgeable specialists. In these encounters, trust is a social mechanism that helps clients to overcome uncertainties about the outcome of their treatment.

Recent studies on the reconfiguration of professional bureaucracies propose that the transition towards a knowledge society has altered the relations between professionals, service users and care managers. For example, Calnan and Rowe (2008) suggest that professional trust can no longer be assumed to be embodied in the professional. Instead, it has to be earned through careful, explicit documentation of daily work that Kuhlmann (2006) describes as 'checking-based trust'. Health and social care occupations are now faced with what Evetts (2009, p. 261) describes as a general decrease in the cultural value of professionalism. Evetts (2009, p. 261) claims that the association between trust, competence and professionalism has been questioned in recent years (see also Banks 2004; Hupe & Hill 2007; Brown & Calnan 2011). According to di Luzio (2006), the situation illustrates parallel changes in attitudes towards professionals, as well as a change in knowledge production and the organisation of professional work.

Moreover, Evetts (2009) suggests that public service managers and practitioners increasingly use professionalism as a discourse of occupational control, rationalisation and motivation. For example, total quality management (TQM) and International Organization for Standardization (ISO) 9000 approaches have been widely adopted by local governments to improve service quality and workers' professional accountability in Finland (Pollitt & Bouckaert 2011). This is despite the fact that service users continue to show strong trust towards the welfare state as the provider of services and social security (Kallio 2008).

Changes in the roles of professionals and service users influence the terminology that is used in health and social care settings. The term 'patient' remains in use only in hospitals, while the term 'client' defines the relation between workers and service users in outpatient clinics and health centres for ambulatory care. The Finnish legislation, however, continues to refer to health-care service users as 'patients' (Act on the Status and Rights of Patients 785/1992) and to social care service users as 'clients' (Act on the Status and Rights of Social Welfare Clients 812/2000). The workers interviewed for this study used both terms inconsistently when referring to service users. On the one hand, this inconsistency could be a result of the manifold expertise that many of them had in both health and social care work. On the other, it could be interpreted as a sign of their uncertainty and ambivalence towards the correct way to perceive and describe client/patient relations in the contemporary welfare state. The data extracts chosen for this chapter are faithful to the original terms used by the interviewees, while the rest of the chapter uses the term 'client' in reference to service users.

Besides a question of trust, feminist theorists have suggested that the ongoing technology-assisted transformation of care work cultures is a gendered process from the point of view of masculine and feminine characteristics culturally attached to work. They claim that the parallel changes towards a leaner welfare state and a knowledge society, promote managerial and technical rationality that renders the body invisible by overlooking the corporeal social and emotional nature of care, as well as the 'dirty work' that caring entails (Davies 1995; Twigg 2006, p. 150). Twigg and colleagues (2011, p. 7) refer to Grosz's (1994) pioneering work in *Volatile Bodies*, concerning the intertwinement of cultural and biological issues, and claims that the binary between mind and body is still a strongly gendered construction that identifies the body with women and the mind with men. The deep-rooted cultural idea(l)s then transfer to power dynamics in societal fields, such as the working life.

Recent studies show that the emotional burden and the 'dirty work' of care work continues to primarily fall on women, while men are encouraged to demonstrate leadership skills and physical strength, but also to have a restricted involvement in physical caregiving routines (Korvajärvi 2004; Evans 2006; Twigg et al. 2011). Kuhlmann (2006), on the contrary, presents a more optimistic interpretation of the technology-assisted transformation of social and health care work. She claims the transformation that highlights workers' skills in disembodied, medical and technical care, has the potential to roll back the gendered division and expectations regarding care occupations. As a compromise, rather than liberating people from gendered workplace binaries, Adkins (2001) calls for caution and an assessment of the ways in which contemporary flexibilities may instil new forms of power there. From the point of view of welfare service work this seems like sound advice, since the form of disembodied professionalism that the contemporary welfare state promotes, highlights first and foremost workers' medical and technical qualities, traditionally associated with masculinity and (health) professionalism.

Data and method

The data analysed in this chapter was originally collected for a PhD study (Hirvonen 2014a) concerning organisational change in welfare service work amidst the managerial, ideological and cultural transformation of the Finnish welfare state. The data includes qualitative interviews (n = 25) from welfare service workers. It was collected during the period 2007–2009, using snowball sampling and by recruiting interviewees through adverts posted in welfare service facilities. The interviewees were registered and practical nurses, social care workers and early education workers. They worked in public hospitals and clinics, municipal geriatric care units, home care service teams and kindergartens. Together, the aforementioned occupations represent the relatively highly educated welfare service workforce of the Finnish public service sector. The interviewees were between 25 and 61 years old and the sample consisted of interviews with 23 women and 2 men, representative of the gender distribution in social and health care occupations. The interviews, which had a semi-structured form, were recorded and manually transcribed, and lasted approximately one and half hours each (Corbin & Morse 2003, p. 340). Specific themes were introduced using key questions and prompts when necessary. Interview themes focused on the nature of the participants' jobs and their relationships with co-workers and clients, as well as the changing nature of care professionalism and public management. Overall, the aim was to map the respondents' accounts of organisational life and work practices in various locales within the contemporary public service sector.

The analysis used practice research as a conceptual and methodological vantage point to address professional and organisational transformation of care service work (Gherardi 2012). Health and social care work involves personal service, a form of bodywork, and emotional commitment to the needs of another human being. From this point of view, care is understood as a situational, social and embodied professional practice that is based on shared occupational ethics and values among various health and social care occupations. Practices are the 'organisational memory' of work that represent its persistent institutional knowledge and order (Schatzki 2001), and incorporate occupational values that are difficult to standardise, such as human dignity and compassion (van Wynsberghe 2011, p. 11).

Welfare state transformation affects these practices. Care work cultures are subject to various logics that predispose workers to cultural and structural change, such as the logic of patient choice, the logic of e-governance and managerialism, the logic of economy and the logic of care (Mol 2008, p. 84). These intersecting logics can generate innovative practices of care, but also moral dilemmas and contradictions concerning the appropriate use of scarce resources, such as time and money, in front-line care service work (Hirvonen & Husso 2012). In analysing the interview data, I have focused on the nature of the association between workers, the structural conditions of the labour market, and the ways in which the technical, socio-material artefacts, such as computers and mobile phones, are used in the interviewees' descriptions of their daily work practices. The excerpts were selected for this chapter to give an overview of the interviewees' responses regarding their professional accountability and practices of accountability work, and in relation to their reflections on care professionalism and gender. The results are presented in the following section.

Results: Towards a hybrid form of care professionalism

The results are presented in two parts. The first part deals with health and social care workers' perceptions of professional accountability in relation to the managerial reform of the welfare state and the parallel technologisation of health and social care work. The second part demonstrates workers' ambivalence towards the contemporary conceptualisation of care professionalism.

Practising accountability in care professions

To a growing extent, the everyday work of health and social care professionals, such as nurses, is framed by practices of 'accountability work'. This entails assessment, monitoring, budgeting and taking responsibility for administrative work (Banks 2004, p. 184; Hirvonen 2014a; Saario 2014). Health and social care work is subject to various audit techniques and systems that are defining professional practice to a growing extent. Many of the interviewees' accounts of the everyday practices of care work described an intensification of managerial control over care work and the novel practices it generated. A nurse with 20 years of work experience described her professional accountability as follows:

> There are demands from every direction, like we have these national requirements, EU regulations, instructions by STAKES,[1] and many from the Ministry of Social Affairs and Health. And then we have the municipal level guidance; how much money can be allocated to certain activities. So that, too, regulates to a great extent the work that we can do. So it has changed a lot, really. Like, now we have to report everything and compile statistics and (...) It takes an awful lot of our working time.
> (RN18, Acute Rehabilitation Unit, 53 yrs)

Assessment of workers' performativity according to impersonal and objective criteria relies on workers' willingness and ability to adopt practices of accountability work that subject them and the outputs of their work to various audit techniques. Accountability work produces quantifiable, comparable data, and extends the fiscal and managerial responsibility of the efficiency and transparency of care services to the level of the individual worker. Accountability work may improve the transparency of the daily work of care professionals and

90 *Professionals in Health*

bridge the information gap between workers and managers. However, it can also increase a sense of distance between the latter. A paediatric nurse explained how the alienation of her unit's chief nursing officer from the rest of the care staff weakened the information flows between staff and management, and how this had a deteriorating effect on the atmosphere in the unit:

> It feels as if there are more administrative personnel than ever, and fewer of us others, but it's not clear to us what their roles are. So, it almost feels like the chief nursing officer is afraid to visit us at the ward, since we don't see her much. So, our unit's head nurse is then there as the mediator who surfs between the chief nursing officer and us. But our head nurse can't always answer to all our questions. So it would be nice to somehow know the chief nursing officer ourselves, even if only by her face, or to have her visit us regularly to see how we're doing, and to see if we need help with something or if something is troubling us. And regarding the various projects we carry out, it would be nice to have meetings together with her instead of only receiving orders on a piece of paper.
>
> (RN13, Paediatric Intensive Care, 45 yrs)

Care managers' dissociation from front-line workers was a recurrent theme in the interviews. Medico-managerial management produce practices of accountability work to demonstrate workers' organisational accountability. However, practices of accountability work as such do not seem to meet workers' need for informal one-on-one communication and dialogue with the management. The extract just quoted illustrates the fact that asking the question of how to manage managerialism in the field of health care is as timely in Finland as it has been elsewhere (Dent et al. 2004; Carvalho 2012).

Another recurrent theme in the data concerned the use of technology as a social practice in care service work. As the end users of ICT-assisted audit techniques, care professionals are often excluded from decision-making concerning the development and introduction of technology into their workplaces. Previous studies suggest that this complicates the implementation of ICTs as a vehicle for accountability work, and may compromise the desired outcome (Koivunen et al. 2008). The interviewees' descriptions supported these findings, suggesting that one explanation for workers' resistance could be found in poor management of parallel tasks, that end up making care work more fragmentary. As a paediatric nurse explained:

Since this year, we've used electronic patient records, and it's taken a lot of time to learn to use the software. It's taking time away from patient work. Moreover, I now need to monitor a fragile child in a respirator that constantly sounds an alarm while at the same time reporting other tasks on a computer. So, I'm bouncing back and forth from the computer to the respirator, and both tasks suffer from it. At the time when we were filling reports on paper it wasn't that difficult, or at least it didn't disturb my work as much.
(RN13, Paediatric Intensive Care, 45 yrs)

Her explanation shows that it is not the technology-assisted practices per se that cause workers' resistance, but the poor management and planning of the use of technology as a social practice in care service work. Other interviewees described similar dilemmas regarding their need to prioritise one task over another, often meaning the prioritisation of accountability work over face-to-face client work.

The analysis shows that care professionals do recognise the benefits of using electronic records in terms of the good of the clients, the management and themselves, in particular when technologies are mobile and easily available. Nevertheless, workers are often at a loss with regard to the relevance of and the extent to which their work is being audited and recorded. A nurse from a municipal home care service team recalled the pros and cons of electronic records as follows:

We've recently begun to also report all the indirect tasks that are not part of our official job descriptions, such as phone calls and references. But I'm not convinced that this is good use of our time and skills (...) Then again, if I don't have the time to go to the electronic patient record to read the patient files, it seems crazy to go into the clients' homes because then I can only do the necessary basic tasks. I don't always have the time, but when I do, I try to read their files the day before, to check who I'm supposed to see the next day, to go through their medical history and their life history, to get an overall picture. It feels meaningful to be able to piece together their life situations. It allows me to help them the best way I can, so that it's not just separate tasks I do here and there.
(RN25, Home Care Services, 43 yrs)

The previous excerpt shows that the purposefulness of accountability work with regard to the core tasks of care work is a defining feature in the acceptance of technology-assisted management practices. On the one hand, when directly related to workers' job descriptions as care professionals, technology becomes a meaningful social practice. It can benefit workers' professional development and client relations in line with the normative value systems and ethics of care work, such as in the case of familiarising oneself with clients' histories through electronic patient records. On the other hand, more often than not technology as a social practice has little to do with direct client relations. It primarily serves managerial needs to audit and quantify care, instead of supporting workers' professional self-management in client work.

From embodied to disembodied professionalism

Further analysis revealed that technology-assisted accountability work has significant consequences for how trust and communication are built through everyday practices of care, especially in terms of how this affects client trust. Previous studies suggest that the rise of the knowledge society, together with the readjustment of power between bureaucratic authorities and citizens as informed consumers, have led to the diminishing of the professional power of front-line care workers in Western welfare states (Henriksson 2008; Van Loon & Zuiderent-Jerak 2011). The results here confirm that the growing choice and voice of clients as attentive consumers readjust the balance of power between care professionals and clients. A geriatric head nurse described this readjustment as follows:

> You need to be sensitive towards patients, sure, and to listen to them in as many ways as possible. But you also need to stay strong somehow. As I tell all our nurses, our work is truly under the microscope nowadays. Like, when you ride the bus or go to a hairdresser's, you don't begin to ask them if they're really sure they know how to ride a bus or how to give a haircut. But our skills and know-how constantly get questioned this way by patients and their families.
> (RN11, Head Nurse Geriatric Care, 38 yrs)

The extract highlights the growing consumer power in the Finnish welfare state. In a knowledge society, consumer power obliges public service organisations to tailor and market their services to citizens, and to rely on rational criteria and visible markers in creating transparency in the practice of care work so that they become assessable (Kirkpatrick et al. 2005; Kuhlmann 2006; Noordegraaf 2007). However, accountability work enacted from a distance and through disembodied professional practice does not necessarily contribute to the establishment of client trust, as a practical nurse from a geriatric care unit recalled:

> With some people it's like 'because we pay for this, we should get this and that', and no matter how much you try to explain that you don't always have the time, you are still expected to do more. And if you forget to write down or tick a box in some chart that states that you've given them the eye drops, it's like the end of the world to them – even when you actually carried out the procedure and only forgot to write it down. So, we joke about it, like 'Always remember to tick the box, even if you don't give them the eye drops!'
>
> (RN17, Geriatric Care Unit, 36 yrs)

Her account reveals the difficulty of generating client trust through disembodied and standardised practice of accountability work. Moreover, the analysis of the interview accounts showed that workers need to master a variety of skills in order to establish trustful relationships in face-to-face encounters with clients. Interviewees' descriptions of their everyday work showed how this embodied face-to-face accountability work takes place through the deceivingly mundane acts of touch, talk and closeness, which manage to convey the feeling of 'being in good hands'. The results suggest that for workers, establishing client trust often requires employing a variety of skills, some of which may seem insignificant for the judgement of workers' professional accountability from a managerial point of view, such as physical closeness. From a managerial point of view, workers' accountability, legitimacy and effectiveness are evaluated on the basis of standardised care outputs that detach care as a professional practice from closeness and corporeality. The transforming and somewhat conflicting image of care professionalism represents the shifts in management of care as paid labour, but also larger societal shifts in understanding professionalism. In the light of the results, it seems that 'digital relocation' – and sometimes dislocation – of public professional work (Noordegraaf 2013) is a key factor in evaluating the professional reconfiguration of health and social care work.

The results suggest that, despite the growing emphasis on disembodied professionalism, the work of front-line care personnel requires skills in corporeal and social care. Corporeal and social practices of care are crucial preconditions for good care. Together with good communication, they are care in and of itself, as anthropologist Annemarie Mol (2008, p. 76) has pointed out. Interviewees' accounts suggested that these practices are also important in terms of care workers' motivation and their professional identities. A majority of the interviewees described how the intimacy, empathy and responsibility involved in care work were crucial for workers' motivation and well-being. A nurse from an acute rehabilitation unit explained her motivation in the following way when asked what aspects of nursing brought her professional satisfaction:

> Well, it [satisfaction] comes from – I know it sounds naive and stupid – but it comes from seeing that someone clearly begins to feel better when you've performed a procedure. Or sometimes it's just your presence there, if they ask you to stay with them for a little while and just be there with them. That's where it comes from. And that's also when you know you've reached some kind of a trustful relationship with them, and the patient feels that you're worth their trust.
>
> (RN14, Acute Rehabilitation Unit, 29 yrs)

It is telling that the interviewee is belittling the importance of social, emotional and corporeal practices of care as a source of her professional satisfaction. Changes in the conceptualisation of care and care work also signify a transformation in professional values and ethics. As workers spend a growing proportion of their time reporting and managing care from afar, they are, paradoxically, increasingly dissociated from the face-to-face care that gives clients the chance to assess workers' trustworthiness, and, at the same time, reasserts workers' professional agency. Instead of managing the body, Twigg (2000) suggests, care work is now more concerned about managing the information concerning the body. As a consequence, workers' professional responsibility becomes defined on the basis of how they handle this information, rather than how they respond to clients' needs as they arise.

Furthermore, the analysis of front-line workers' accounts suggests that the transition from management of bodies to management of information should be understood in the light of the gendered and corporeal nature of care work. Professionalism is commonly associated with culturally masculine attributes such as scientific knowledge, emotional distance and reason, rather than the culturally feminine, less systematic and more abstract skills that nursing and care work entail (Davies 1995). Moreover, contemporary management styles are culturally associated with 'masculine' discourses of competitiveness, instrumentality and individuality (Thomas & Davies 2002, p. 390). Berg, Barry and Chandler (2012, p. 317) further suggest that pursuing these qualities in health and social care work could encourage female workers to behave in ways that challenge gender stereotypes in the field. Embracement of masculine managerial management styles may empower individual workers, but simply submitting to masculine styles of management does not resolve the question of the cultural misrecognition and disregard of the value of workers' corporeal and emotional skills as a part of their professional agency. Yet foregrounding the corporeality of care, Twigg (2006, p. 152) suggests, does not solve the problem either. On the one hand, it enables a recognition of the full range of nurses' professional skills in care work. On the other hand, it risks reproducing the idea that female workers' professional skills, especially, are natural (see also Calnan & Rowe 2008), making femininity a contested and ambivalent resource for identity work (Hirvonen 2014b).

Recognition is therefore a double-edged sword from the point of view of workers' empowerment. It exposes the nature of care work in ways that can erode rather than enhance the status of welfare service occupations, many of whom already have limited resources and professional power to defend their occupational status (Hirvonen 2014b). The interviewees' responses showed plenty of ambivalence towards the gendered cultural idea(l)s care work entails, particularly in relation to professionalism. A registered nurse recalled her thoughts about the societal value of care as follows:

> I feel that during nursing school I... it sort of just gave me some tips on how to do the job, but working has taught me these things, really. Maybe it's because this is the kind of job that's sort of like being a stay-at-home mom in the sense that it's not really valued. And the work, it only gets noticed when somebody hasn't done it. Sometimes even I myself find it hard to respect my work because of that! And it's only when I or one of my close ones gets sick that I realize that, yeah, somebody's running this show and taking care of them.
> (RN21, Geriatric Care Unit, 27)

The interviewee's reflection on the valuation of her work is telling with regard to the manifold ways in which the full range of welfare service workers' occupational skills are either misrecognised as 'natural' abilities, or otherwise neglected because they do not fit the predominant understanding of professionalism. Based on the results in this study, it seems that the conflict concerning contradictory values, goals and means of providing good quality care has been left to be resolved at the street level where front-line workers operate. As a consequence of the growing emphasis on ICT-assisted accountability work and related technical-skill requirements, the culturally feminine side of nursing and care work is further neglected as a domain of non-professional knowledge.

All in all, the results in this chapter suggest that care professionalism is increasingly assessed based on workers' medical and technical knowledge and skills in ICT-assisted accountability work. It is unlikely that a more holistic understanding of care professionalism will gain ground in the near future, despite its significance for workers' professional motivation and for the creation of client trust. Since the 1990s, welfare service reform and the parallel transition towards a knowledge society have had a significant impact on practices of care and on the societal understanding of care as a professional skill. On the one hand, the results suggest that medico-managerial management styles and application of technology as a social practice can support workers' professional growth and self-management. They enable a comprehensive utilisation of a variety of workers' professional skills and turn technology into a meaningful social practice in care work, as other studies have also suggested (Leppo & Perälä 2009; Van Loon & Zuiderent-Jerak 2011; Carvalho 2012). On the other hand, optimistic propositions tend to disregard the comprehensiveness of the consequences of technological transformation from the point of view of gendered cultural ideals and values related to care, and to the fundamentally corporeal nature of care work. The results suggest that disregard for these aspects may have negative consequences for workers' professional self-image and client trust.

Conclusions

In this chapter, I have discussed the consequences of the Finnish welfare state reform, and the technological and organisational transformation of the public service sector from the point of view of care work and care professionalism. The doctrine of NPM has brought economic rationality and 'management by numbers' to the public service sector. Through the quantification of the inputs and outputs of welfare service work, the goal of medico-managerial management is to increase transparency of and trust towards public service work. In contemporary welfare states, ICT-assisted accountability work has become the cornerstone that ensures the legitimacy of public service bureaucracies (Ferraris & Davies 2013). To a growing extent, acts of registration and documentation validate individuals' life histories and workers' organisational accountability in health and social care institutions.

The results of the analysis in this chapter suggest that, in the case of the Finnish public sector, medico-managerial management not only affects the institutional environment of service provision, but also remodels the practices of care and the cultural understanding of care professionalism. Care workers have become subject to the requirements of self-regulated professional development. To a growing extent, workers commit to the goals, ideals and efficiency targets of their workplaces, instead of the more universal, occupational values and principles that they acquire through education and training. In this sense, professionalism is defined by the needs of the organisation rather than the state.

According to Henriksson (2011, p. 120), the Finnish welfare state implicitly continues to rely on the gendered division in the society, according to which women in general, and welfare service workers in particular, are called upon to respond to care needs because they are considered to be 'natural carers' and flexible workers. Despite the hopes of generating a more gender-neutral idea of care professionalism, the contemporary promotion of disembodied and technical professionalism does not liberate care service workers from gendered cultural representations regarding care. Instead, it produces a hybrid form of disembodied care professionalism, as identified by other studies (see e.g. Carvalho 2014). In the case of Finnish health and social care staff it refers to professionalism that is explicitly gender neutral and technical, but implicitly gendered. It reproduces gendered expectations of workers' natural gendered skills in a way that leaves the question of gender and power unresolved in the labour market. In line with a conventional understanding of (health) professionalism, the ongoing transformations in the Finnish welfare state highlight workers' technical and medical competence as opposed to a more holistic understanding of care professionalism that is culturally gender sensitive. The narrow account of care professionalism may hamper workers' efforts to build positive professional self-images, and instead reaffirm the societal disregard of care as a professional skill.

In this chapter, I have also contemplated the welfare state reform and the turn towards a knowledge society from the point of view of client trust and workers' professional accountability. In the case of the Nordic welfare states, care professionals play a key role in reasserting the legitimacy of the welfare state. As front-line workers, they are the first to experience, and the ones to execute and arbitrate, the changes in the principles and values of service production to service users. Maintaining an empathetic attitude and conveying the experience of 'being in good hands' to the clients, while at the same time trying to adapt to these changes, can be a strain for workers. Improving client trust through manifold audit techniques and ICT-assisted accountability work do not, however, make up for the physical distance these methods tend to generate between managers, workers and clients. Making care more transparent consequently seems to increase the distance between actors. In care of the young, the old and the sick, ICT-assisted accountability work does not seem to make up for the benefits of physical proximity. Promotion of the corporeal and social aspects of care should, therefore, not be taken as a repetition of an outdated feminist agenda, but as a reminder of the challenges that the holistic nature of care poses in contemporary societies. This perspective is crucial in health and social care work for promoting care workers' well-being, and for the success of costly technological investments that are easily taken as a panacea in economic austerity policies concerning such work.

Note

1. National Research and Development Centre for Welfare and Health.

References

Adkins, L. 2001. 'Cultural feminization: "Money, Sex and Power" for women', *Signs*, Vol. 26, No. 3, pp. 669–695.

Anttonen, A. & Häikiö, L. 2011. 'Care "going market": Finnish elderly-care policies in transition', *Nordic Journal of Social Research*, Vol. 2, No. 2, pp. 1–21.

Bakker, I. 2007. 'Social reproduction and the constitution of a gendered political economy', *New Political Economy*, Vol. 12, No. 4, pp. 541–556.

Balka, E., Green, E. & Henwood, F. (eds.) 2009. *Gender, Health and Information Technology in Context*, Palgrave, Basingstoke.

Banks, S. 2004. *Ethics, Accountability, and the Social Professions*, Palgrave Macmillan, Basingstoke.

Barry, A. 2001. *Political Machines: Governing a Technological Society*, The Athlone Press, London.

Berg, E., Barry, J. & Chandler, J. 2012. 'Changing leadership and gender in public sector organizations', *British Journal of Management*, Vol. 23, No. 3, pp. 402–414.

Brown, P. R. & Calnan, M. 2011. 'The civilizing process of trust: Developing quality mechanisms which are local, professional-led and thus legitimate', *Social Policy & Administration*, Vol. 45, No. 1, pp. 19–34.

Calnan, M. & Rowe, R. 2008. 'Trust relations in a changing health service', *Journal of Health Service Research & Policy*, Vol. 13, No. 3, pp. 97–103.

Carvalho, T. 2012. 'Managerialism and professional strategies: A case from nurses in Portugal', *Journal of Health Organization and Management*, Vol. 26, No. 4, pp. 524–541.

Carvalho, T. 2014. 'Changing connections between professionalism and managerialism: A case study of nursing in Portugal', *Journal of Professions and Organization*, Vol. 1, No. 2, pp. 176–190.
Corbin, J. & Morse, J. 2003. 'The unstructured interactive interview: Issues of reciprocity and risks when dealing with sensitive topics', *Qualitative Inquiry*, Vol. 9, No. 3, pp. 335–354.
Dahl, H. & Rask, E. 2005. 'Introduction: Dilemmas of care in the Nordic welfare state', in H. Dahl & T. Rask (eds.), *Dilemmas of Care in the Nordic Welfare State: Continuity and Change*, Ashgate, Aldershot.
Davies, C. 1995. *Gender and the Professional Predicament in Nursing*, Open University Press, Buckingham.
Dent, M., Chandler, J. & Barry, J. 2004. 'Introduction: Questioning the new public management', in M. Dent, J. Chandler & J. Barry (eds.), *Questioning the New Public Management*, Ashgate, Aldershot.
Di Luzio, G. 2006. 'A sociological concept of client trust', *Current Sociology*, Vol. 54, No. 4, pp. 549–564.
Doupi, P., Hämäläinen, P. & Ruotsalainen, P. 2007. *eHealth strategy and implementation activities in Finland*, Report in the framework of the eHealth ERA project, STAKES, Helsinki.
Heichlinger, A. 2011. 'Introduction', in A. Heichlinger (ed.), *EPSA Trends in Practice: Driving Public Sector Excellence to Shape Europe for 2020*, EIPA, Maastricht.
Evans, J. 2006. 'Men nurses and women physicians: Exploring masculinities and gendered and sexed relations in nursing and medicine', in L. Andrist, P. Nicholas & K. Wolf (eds.), *A History of Nursing Ideas*, Jones and Bartlett, Sudbury, MA.
Evetts, J. 2009. 'New professionalism and new public management: Changes, continuities and consequences', *Comparative Sociology*, Vol. 8, No. 2, pp. 247–266.
European Commission. 2009. *Smarter, Faster, Better Egovernment: 8th Benchmark Measurement*, European Commission, Brussels.
Ferraris, M. & Davies, R. 2013. *Documentality: Why It Is Necessary to Leave Traces*, Fordham University Press, New York.
Gherardi, S. 2012. *How to Conduct a Practice-Based Study: Problems and Methods*, Edward Elgar, Cheltenham.
Grosz, E. A. 1994. *Volatile Bodies: Toward a Corporeal Feminism*, Indiana University Press, Bloomington, IN.
Henriksson, L. 2008. 'Reconfiguring Finnish welfare service workforce: Inequalities and identity', *Equal Opportunities International*, Vol. 27, No. 1, pp. 49–63.
Henriksson, L. 2011. 'Lähihoitaja – joustavaa työvoimaa sosiaali- ja terveysalalle', in A. Laiho & T. Ruoholinna (eds.), *Terveysalan ammatit ja koulutus*, Gaudeamus, Helsinki.
Henriksson, L. & Wrede, S. 2008. 'Care work in a context of a transforming welfare state', in S. Wrede, L. Henriksson, H. Host, S. Johansson & B. Dybbroe (eds.), *Care Work in Crisis: Reclaiming the Nordic Ethos of Care*, Studentlitteratur, Lund.
Hirvonen, H. 2014a. 'Habitus and care: Investigating welfare service workers' agency', PhD thesis, Jyväskylä Studies in Education, Psychology and Social Research, 497, University of Jyväskylä.

Hirvonen, H. 2014b. 'Doing gendered and (dis)embodied work: Care work in the context of medico-managerial welfare state', *Nordic Social Work Research*, Vol. 4, No. 2, pp. 113–128.
Hirvonen, H. & Husso, M. 2012. 'Living on a knife's edge: Temporal conflicts in welfare service work', *Time & Society*, Vol. 21, No. 3, pp. 351–370.
Hupe, P. & Hill, M. 2007. 'Street-level bureaucracy and public accountability', *Public Administration*, Vol. 85, No. 2, pp. 279–299.
Husso, M. & Hirvonen, H. 2012. 'Gendered agency and emotions in the field of care work', *Gender, Work & Organization*, Vol. 19, No. 1, pp. 29–51.
Kallio, J. 2008. 'Kansalaisten asennoituminen hyvinvointivaltion uudelleenmuotoiluun', *Sosiologia*, Vol. 45, No. 1, pp. 3–20.
Kirkpatrick, I., Ackroyd, S. & Walker, R. 2005. *The New Managerialism and Public Service Professions*, Palgrave Macmillan, Basingstoke.
Koivunen, M., Välimäki, M., Koskinen, A., Staggers, N. & Katajisto, J. 2008. 'The impact of individual factors on health care staff's computer use in psychiatric hospitals', *Journal of Clinical Nursing*, Vol. 18, No. 8, pp. 1141–1150.
Korvajärvi, P. 2004. 'Gender and work-related inequalities in Finland', in F. Devine & MC .Waters (eds.), *Social Inequalities in Comparative Perspective*, Blackwell, Malden, MA.
Kröger, T. 2011. 'Retuning the Nordic welfare municipality: Central regulation of social care under change in Finland', *International Journal of Sociology and Social Policy*, Vol. 31, No. 3, pp. 148–159.
Kuhlmann, E. 2006. 'Traces of doubt and sources of trust: Health professions in an uncertain society', *Current Sociology*, Vol. 54, No. 4, pp. 607–620.
Kurunmäki, L. 2000. 'Power relations in the health care field: Accounting, accountants and economic reasoning in the new public management reforms in Finland', PhD thesis, University of Jyväskylä.
Leppo, A. and Perälä, R. 2009. 'User involvement in Finland: The hybrid of control and emancipation', *Journal of Health, Organization & Management*, Vol. 23, No. 3, pp. 359–371.
Mol, A. 2008. *The Logic of Care: Health and the Problem of Patient Choice*, Routledge, London.
Nicolini, D. 2007. 'Stretching out and expanding work practices in time and space: The case of telemedicine', *Human Relations*, Vol. 60, No. 6, pp. 889–920.
Noordegraaf, M. 2007. 'From "pure" to "hybrid" professionalism present-day professionalism in ambiguous public domains', *Administration & Society*, Vol. 39, No. 6, pp. 761–785.
Noordegraaf, M. 2013. 'Reconfiguring professional work: Changing forms of professionalism in public services', *Administration & Society*, Vol. 20, No. 10, pp. 1–28.
Pollitt, C. & Bouckaert, G. 2011. *Public Management Reform* (3rd edn), Oxford University Press, Oxford.
Power, M. 1997. *The Audit Society: Rituals of Verification*, Oxford University Press, Oxford.
Rostgaard, T. 2002. 'Caring for children and older people in Europe: A comparison of European policies and practice', *Policy Studies*, Vol. 23, No. 1, pp. 51–68.
Saario, S. 2014. 'Audit techniques in mental health: Practitioners' responses to electronic health records and service purchasing agreements', PhD thesis, Acta Electronica Universitatis Tamperensis, 1391, University of Tampere.

Schatzki, T. 2001. 'Practice theory', in T. Schatzki, K. Knorr-Cetina & E. Savigny (eds.), *The Practice Turn in Contemporary Theory*, Routledge, London.
Suchman, L. 2002. 'Located accountabilities in technology production', *Scandinavian Journal of Information Systems*, Vol. 14, No. 2, pp. 91–105.
Thomas, R. & Davies, A. 2002. 'Gender and new public management: Reconstituting academic subjectivities', *Gender, Work & Organization*, Vol. 9, No. 4, pp. 372–397.
Tronto, J. 2011. 'Does managing professions affect professional ethics? Competence, autonomy and care', in P. DesAutels & J. Waugh (eds.), *Feminists Doing Ethics*, Rowman & Littlefield, Lanham.
Twigg, J. 2000. *Bathing, the Body and Community Care*, Routledge, London.
Twigg, J. 2006. *The Body in Health and Social Care*, Palgrave, Houndmills.
Twigg, J., Wolkowitz, C., Cohen, R. & Nettleton, S. 2011. 'Conceptualising body work in health and social care', in J. Twigg, C. Wolkowitz, R. Cohen & S. Nettleton (eds.), *Body Work in Health and Social Care: Critical Themes, New Agendas*, Wiley-Blackwell, Malden, MA.
Van Loon, E. & Zuiderent-Jerak, T. 2011, 'Framing reflexivity in quality improvement devices in the care for older people', *Health Care Analysis*, Vol. 20, No. 2, pp. 119–138.
Van Wynsberghe, A. 2011. 'Designing robots for care: Care centered value-sensitive design', *Science Engineering Ethics*, Vol. 19, No. 2, pp. 407–433.
Virkki, T. 2008. 'Habitual trust in encountering violence at work: Attitudes towards client violence among Finnish social workers and nurses', *Journal of Social Work*, Vol. 8, No. 3, pp. 247–267.
Waerness, K. 2005, 'Social research, political theory and the ethics of care in a global perspective', in H. M. Dahl & T. Rask Eriksen (eds.), *Dilemmas of Care in the Nordic Welfare State: Continuity and Change*, Ashgate, Aldershot.
Wrede, S. 2008. 'Unpacking gendered professional power in the welfare state', *Equal Opportunities International*, Vol. 27, No. 1, pp. 19–33.

5
Beyond the Portuguese Nursing Labour Market: Towards a Crisis of Professionalism?

Joana Sousa Ribeiro

Introduction

Nurses are the most representative professional group in several National Health Services (NHS). Being considered a welfare state profession, nursing is essential for meeting future challenges regarding health care (WHO 2000).

However, the nursing profession has been underresearched in social science analysis (Witz 1992; Carpenter 1993; Walby et al. 1994; Halford et al. 1997). This is in part due to the non-recognition of women's work in the public sphere (Carpenter 1993).

In the context of the neo-liberal reorganisation of health-care services, medical expertise and demand for evidence-based practices, curative provision tends to be seen as 'productive' labour, and caring as 'unproductive'. In contrast to technical competence – the jurisdiction of the medical professional (Abbott 1988) – caring work, recognised as a traditional core of nursing, is devalued.

In a similar vein, the health policy agenda rarely focuses on a comprehensive workforce policy at national and supranational levels,[1] and, when it does, it tends to concentrate on physician planning (Kuhlmann et al. 2013b).

The opening up of the health-care labour market to international professionals may create new work opportunities, but it also constitutes a challenge to professional governance, occupational integration and, therefore, to the transnationalisation of professional projects. Despite the importance of monitoring migration outflows and inflows in the health-care sector (Ribeiro et al. 2014), the European focus tends to be exclusively on physicians (Wismar et al. 2011).

This chapter aims to analyse the relationship between the development of the nursing profession and the labour market conditions in a Southern European country, which, in this case, is Portugal. The issues under consideration involve the nursing profile, the process of professionalisation and the professionalism debate. Additionally, the chapter analyses this 'unsettled' global health workforce through the report of a case study: foreign nurses working in the Portuguese NHS.

The Portuguese NHS and a nursing profile

In accordance with the Portuguese Constitution, the NHS is predominantly financed by general taxation. In 2012, the total expenditure on health represented 9.5 per cent of gross domestic product (GDP). Despite the guarantee of universal coverage, there are user fees for inpatient care. Out-of-pocket payments represent about 24 per cent of the total expenditure, one of the highest of the Organisation for Economic Co-operation and Development (OECD) countries (OECD 2013).

The NHS has been the largest owner and manager of most healthcare production means, and the most important purchaser of healthcare provision from the private sector.

In the last 20 years, important health policy reforms with a managerialist scope have been launched. These include, among others: a public contract model to fund health-care delivery; privatisation of public hospital management; creation of local health systems and hospital-integrated responsibility centres; new managerial models for health-care centres; development of quality assurance programmes; creation of family health units; restructuring of district hospitals; the shutting down of maternity and emergency services.

One of these reforms, which tends to promote 'the crucial role of primary care in the general system of care – 'primary health-care reform' – creates more attractive working conditions for health-care professionals, including for nurses. For instance, the increased responsibility of community care nurses and improvement in their work–life balance through flexible work schedules. Recently, the central importance of the nursing profession in health-care centres was de facto institutionally recognised by the Portuguese Health Ministry with the creation of the 'Family Nurse' staff category (Law-Decree 118/2004). This was an initiative promoted by the Portuguese Nursing Council, in line with the Munich Declaration (WHO 2000).

Conversely, another reform regarding terms of employment (the extension of individual contracts to some NHS institutions) increased turnover rates, job insecurity and professional socialisation deficits, which can be translated into higher social costs (Fronteira et al. 2008). The proletarianisation of nurses became socially visible when the Portuguese media began reporting the poor salaries paid in public health institutions (around 4 Euros per hour, which is below the Portuguese *minimum* wage) and the tough working conditions (heavy workload, added responsibilities with limited resources, few career paths). Pressure from the media had positive consequences, as it led to the Health Ministry requiring the health and labour inspection authorities to put in place supervisory measures to control what could only be termed a social dumping procedure.

Devaluing skilled workers, mainly with regard to dignity at work and the occupational identity of salaried employees, is a way to reinstate the proletarianisation argument that was conceived in the 1970s, when the negative impact of the development of the capitalist society was in its infancy (Braverman 1974). The fragmented and specialised division of labour, controlled by technocratic management practices, not only alienated the working class but also civil service professionals. In this regard, it is better to take a leaf from the avant-garde vision of Oppenheimer (1973), who reported nursing to be one of the *proletariat* professions, due to the bureaucratic frame of its scope of practice, and the oversupply and massification of graduates.

The impact of the economic crisis on the health-care sector has already been analysed in terms of the prevalence of certain diseases, hospital admissions and pharmaceutical consumption (van Gool & Pearson 2014). However, there is a scarcity of studies regarding the impact of austerity policies on the working conditions of the civil service professions (possible burnout, deficits in teamwork collaboration, scarcity of new professionals, workplace violence, wage reduction) and its effects on occupational commitment, career planning and emigration rates.

Nursing in Portugal

As in other countries, nurses are the most numerous group of health professionals in Portugal. In the last decade, there has been an annual increase in registered nurses, from 37,623 in 2000 to 64,535 in 2011, a rise of 53 per cent. The majority of nurses are generalists, but the number of specialised nurses, mainly working in rehabilitation and maternal health nursing and midwifery, reached 18 per cent in 2011 (OE 2012). Recognition of the specialty nurse as a staff category with its own job profile and jurisdiction is currently under debate in the

Portuguese Parliament, after a public petition was launched by the Nursing Council (OE).

Nursing is a young (in 2012, 52 per cent of registered nurses were under 40 years old) and predominantly female profession (in 2012, 81 per cent were women) (OE 2013). With regard to the division of labour in nursing, there is an internal segmentation along gender, with the managerial functions being performed mostly by men (Carvalho 2009). The central and district hospitals employ around 74 per cent of nurses, the primary care services 20 per cent and psychiatric services 3 per cent (Barros et al. 2011).

The number of nurses per 100,000 inhabitants has increased in the last 15 years, but the ratio of nurses to physicians has remained stable (at 1.5), one of the lowest in Europe (OECD 2013). However, it is important to regard this indicator with caution, especially after the implementation of the austerity measures. For instance, in Portugal the overall population growth could slow in the next four or five decades, due to emigration and low birth rates (Buchan et al. 2013a).

Despite the shortage question being a direct concern for the Nursing Trade Union (SEP) and the Nursing Council with regard to securing quality health-care provision,[2] there is unemployment among nurses because of the strict employment policies imposed since the economic crisis. In 2012, the Nursing Council estimated that there were between 7,000 and 9,000 unemployed nurses (Conceição et al. 2012).

A survey of nurses who graduated in 2008, 2009 and 2010, conducted by the Nursing Council (Fernandes 2011), revealed the difficulties of the transition period between graduating and finding work. The fact is that the time it takes to find employment is getting longer: 20 per cent of nurses are not employed in the nursing profession, and 5 per cent of those are working in another job; 70 per cent of unemployed nurses have never had a nursing practice job offer; 873 nurses went abroad for work (with Spain and the United Kingdom being the main host countries). The north of Portugal is the region where unemployment is most severe, with 66 per cent of nurses either without work or with poor job security; 14 per cent of nurses have already worked free of charge; 42 per cent of nurses have been discriminated against regarding access to employment; and 40 per cent of nurses plan or, at one time, planned, to leave the nursing profession. After Lisbon and Porto, 'work abroad' is one of the most popular answer given as first choice for place of work.

Regarding the emigration flow of health-care professionals, currently there is no monitoring procedure (Ribeiro et al. 2014). However, some studies provide data about Portuguese inflows to specific receiving countries. In 2006, there were 277 nurses of Portuguese origin in France (Delamaire & Schweyer 2010); between 2002 and 2007, 221 Portuguese nurses were registered in Spain (Lopez-Valcarcel et al. 2011); and in 2008, 544 in Germany (Ognyanova & Busse 2011). The number of Portuguese nurses admitted to the United Kingdom has grown from 20 in 2006/2007 to more than 550 in 2011/2012, according to data from the UK Nursing and Midwifery Council (Buchan & Seccombe 2012). Additionally, the number of nurses that requested the EU directives document (a document that ensures free mobility among EU countries) has increased almost fourfold (from 609 in 2009 to more than 2,300 in 2012) (OE 2012).

In addition, external recruitment agencies, mainly looking for nurses and specialist physicians, are becoming increasingly active in Portugal. The main nursing demands are from Germany, the United Kingdom, the Netherlands and Switzerland.

Besides being a source country for nurses, Portugal has received foreign health-care professionals since the early 1990s. Numbers of these reached a peak in 2004 (35 per thousand). In 2013, there were 612 nurses of foreign origin, which corresponds to 26 per cent of the total number of foreign staff in the public health sector (ACSS 2014).

Between 2004 and 2013, however, the number of foreign nurses in the NHS dropped by around 65 per cent (Table 5.1), mainly due to the exit of Spanish nurses,[3] who made up the majority of foreign nurses in Portugal at that time. The improvement of working conditions and better job opportunities in Spain could explain this trend. Simultaneously, short-term individual contracts increasingly became the norm in Portugal.

Professionalisation in the making

According to Carapinheiro and Rodrigues (1998), there is a need for research on professionalisation, legitimacy strategies and the closure of professional groups in Portugal.

In the Portuguese nursing profession, this process is strongly connected to the expansion of nursing education, the emergence of professional associations and the rationalisation of nursing practices (Carvalho 2009).

The first schools of nursing were created in the final years of the 19th century, and were directly dependent on central hospitals and thus on medical schools. The training provided, open to both men and women,

Table 5.1 Number of foreign nurses and total of foreign human resources in the NHS, by country groups, 2004 to 2013

Group of countries/ Country		2004	2005	2006	2007	2008	2009	2010	2011	2012	2013	Variation (%) (2004 to 2013)
EU	Total	2,679	2,478	1,937	1,647	1,389	1,314	1,339	1,252	1,259	1,283	−52.1
	Nurses	1,355	1,135	718	526	399	417	406	78	111	95	−93.0
Spain	Total	2,390	2,179	1,689	1,356	1,140	1,037	1,031	969	910	929	−61.1
	Nurses	1,238	1,013	630	431	319	328	310	289	274	264	−78.7
PALOP	Total	1,160	1,088	891	877	743	816	753	653	807	706	−39.1
	Nurses	235	220	179	169	116	130	115	116	173	135	−42.6
Brazil	Total	348	374	343	363	405	457	475	397	395	362	4.0
	Nurses	96	97	84	75	66	78	77	61	56	49	−49.0
Other countries	Total	303	365	384	372	404	494	494	623	605	596	96.7
	Nurses	44	74	73	66	66	102	92	86	89	69	56.8
Total	Nurses	1,730	1,526	1,054	836	647	727	690	630	703	612	−64.6
	Total	4,490	4,305	3,555	3,259	2,941	3,081	3,061	2,302	2,339	2,327	−48.2

Notes: EU – European Union; PALOP – Países Africanos de Língua Oficial Portuguesa, African Countries with Portuguese as Official Language.
Source: Health System Central Administration (ACSS) 2014, *Boletim Informativo: Recursos Humanos Estrangeiros no Ministério da Saúde – Actualização 2011/2013*, Health System Central Administration, Lisbon. [Table elaborated by the author.]

was limited to the basic skills necessary for performing auxiliary roles for physicians.

However, in the 1940s, the totalitarian regime explicitly favoured single or widowed female applicants for nursing studies. In the course of the 1960s, nursing education progressively became the responsibility of the nurses, which ensured their autonomy from the medical schools. The creation of the Portuguese Nursing Association represented an important step towards the professionalisation process.

The Portuguese Revolution of April 1974 also brought about important changes in the nursing profession. A nursing career demanded a single training level aimed at providing general health care. Nursing auxiliary training was scrapped, and existing auxiliary nurses were granted opportunities to retrain so as to equip them to perform nursing duties.

A turning point in nursing career empowerment came about in the 1980s, when a new career progression was established which defined roles and tasks for specific grades (nurses' salaries are linked to the civil service pay-scale). Moreover, nursing education was integrated in the technical education system, and job performance evaluation became the nurses' responsibility, instead of the responsibility of physicians.

Ten years later, the level of nursing self-regulation increased: a nurses' trade union was created (SEP – Sindicato dos Enfermeiros Portugueses) and the career trajectory of nurses was reviewed. The regulation for nursing practice was issued (REPE – Regulamento do Exercício Profissional dos Enfermeiros), the Nursing Council was approved and nursing schools began to provide university degrees.

In this way, greater public recognition of the nursing profession was progressively achieved. In the European context, Portugal was a pioneer in terms of this upgrade to degree level, which has consequences even today with regard to the international recognition of the Portuguese nursing training. All nursing schools (47, of which 20 are private) have a first cycle programme of 240 ECTS, following the Bologna norms, and PhD nursing programmes have been available since 2002. Therefore, the investment in higher education is one of the main dimensions of the nursing professionalisation, as the importance of credentials reveals (Larson 1977).

Currently, a model of professional development (MDP – Modelo de Desenvolvimento Profissional) is being launched, with the aim of achieving a certified licensure for nursing practice to protect the quality of care provision and to guarantee appropriate training in clinical services (as a period of subordinate practice is established). In this way, the power of the self-regulatory professional body will be preserved, as this regulatory closure strategy was implemented in name of public interest. Implementation of this certification procedure is being developed within the framework of revised Nursing Council statutes.[4] The purpose is to guarantee compliance with EU single-market rules, namely those concerning the free flow of services, admission and license to professional practice. In addition, it ensures the regulation of educational and working mobility paths at a European level.

Bearing in mind the definition of professionalisation – stated by Larson (1977) and Abbott (1988) to be an open-ended process to guarantee the monopoly protection of the occupational jurisdiction – it is crucial to pay close attention to the effects of adopting some austerity measures as a requirement of health spending efficiency. One such measure was the compulsory reuse of surgical material, of which the Portuguese Association of Nurses in Operating Rooms complained, arguing against it in defence of patient safety. Since it calls into question the professionals' autonomous decision-making, one might anticipate that this regulation could cause considerable tension.

The current economic and financial crisis tends also to be an opportunity to open the debate about the skill mix among different professionals and the process of functions delegation, the task-shifting process (Buchan et al. 2013b; OECD 2013), as, for example, between nurses and pharmacists (by, for instance, extending vaccine delivery provision to pharmacists); between nurses and health auxiliaries (by, for instance, replacing nurses with health auxiliaries in the operating room); and between nurses and physicians (by, for instance, the possibility of nurses following up on women's maternity health status or prescribing pills for patients with chronic diseases). Regarding the latter, there is another recent example. The Ministry of Health, at first with the resistance of the Physicians' Council (*Ordem dos Médicos*), authorised the prescription of supplementary diagnostic exams by nurses, during the screening process in the emergency services. This task-shifting was introduced in February 2015, in order to reduce the waiting time in the emergency services, in part; a consequence of the financial budget cuts in the health care sector, which caused restrictions on new personnel contracts.

Considering the above examples, the structural changes introduced by the austerity policy could have an impact on either the de-professionalisation process of the nursing profession, either on its 're-professionalisation'. Indeed, some trends enhance the de-professionalisation dimension, namely with regard to restricting its jurisdiction, such as losing the monopoly on duties, losing the monopoly on leadership positions and the fragmentation of tasks. Simultaneously, advanced roles are performed by nursing, replacing physicians in its occupation's jurisdiction, which can be considered a 're-professionalisation' trend. In both cases, the focus is on the interprofessional competition (Larson 1977) and on the rearrangements of interprofessional autonomy, which proves that the general picture is only provided by the interprofessional relationships analysis. The knowledge interaction between the users of health services and professionals, stated by Haug (1973) in her notion of losing of monopoly over a specific body of knowledge, doesn't explain the entire process of devaluation of specialisation. Indeed, in this case, the de-professionalisation argument outlined by Abbott (1988) – occurring when a certain occupation's jurisdiction or area of responsibility is reduced and the occupational duties become less specialised – is more appropriate, requiring an integrative analysis of the professions. De-professionalisation and 're-professionalisation' are two faces of the same phenomenon, occurring in a time of cost-effectiveness of health care resources, including the human resources ones, and under an increase of health care needs.

To sum up, the internationalisation of labour markets, the Bologna education system and the marketisation of the health-care system constitute new challenges for nursing professionalisation, which may cause tension between national and supranational regulation. However, these power asymmetries are in line with Siegrist's argument (Siegrist 1990) of discontinuities in professionalisation processes, a trend to which the nursing profession is not immune, namely in a period of austerity, such as the current one.

(De)nationalising professional projects: A case study of foreign nurses in the Portuguese NHS[5]

The right to mobility and free circulation of general care nurses within the scope of the European Union (EU) are protected by directives dating from the mid-1970s. However, some studies (Jinks et al. 2000; Peixoto 2001) draw attention to the fact that, compared with other regional areas, intra-European mobility is still fairly low. The liberalisation of labour markets and the mutual recognition of qualifications are necessary, but not sufficient, to stimulate mobility.

As can be seen 'from the analysis in the following section "Spanish nurses in Portugal" ', professional mobility constraints are explained by the persistence of cultural and institutional barriers, even with regard to EU nursing professionals.

Spanish nurses in Portugal

Since the late 1990s, Portugal had been a receiving country for Spanish nurses for several reasons. Besides being a country with which Spain has linguistic and cultural affinities, years worked in Portugal count towards time served in the Spanish health-care institutions. Furthermore, Portugal provided an opportunity to upgrade academic skills, since nursing degree courses were of a higher level in Portugal than in Spain at that time.

Nevertheless, skilled intra-EU movers had to face certain difficulties, mainly to do with recognition of postgraduate credentials. Indeed, obtaining recognition of a nursing specialty is a time-consuming process, which is not helped by the lack of information surrounding the required procedures.

This could explain the fact that the majority of the Spanish nurses interviewed are newly qualified and have been working for a relatively short time – generally three or four months. Some of them had even been out of work for a short time in their country of origin. Social networks formed by Spanish colleagues played a key role in the migration decision process and in the choice of Portugal as a destination country. These networks minimise the absence of institutional support for mobility like, for instance, the provision of language training courses. To overcome this language skills problem, an internal segmentation of nursing was developed. The recently arrived nurses were often set to work in the operating theatre where patients are silent.

The integration period, when there is one, is used as an excuse for more precarious forms of work arrangements – short-term contracts – instead of being used for local training in areas such as organisational culture and clinical procedures. Differences in occupational structure between Portugal and Spain (namely the absence of nursing assistants in Portugal) contribute to the perception of occupational segregation among Spanish nurses. Indeed, some of these professionals are often called upon to perform tasks that involve activities they perceive as unskilled, such as washing patients.

East European nurses in Portugal

In the beginning of the 2000s, Portugal received another significant migration flow, in this case from some East European countries. It is estimated that these immigrants were overqualified for the jobs they were expected to perform in Portugal.

In the case of the interviewed East European nurses, they suffered a downward process of occupational mobility and thus a professional identity change. Their insertion in the secondary labour market was mainly in the construction sector (in the case of men) and in domestic service (in the case of women).

Settling in Portugal depends on the success of getting credentials recognised, because without that recognition, nurses are not permitted to perform nursing duties. To be able to register as a nurse involves a process of reaccreditation, which includes overcoming systemic barriers and fulfilling the requirements of several institutions – nursing schools, embassies or consulates, the Borders and Foreign Bureau (SEF), the Health Ministry and employers' organisations –, to name the principal ones. The process is time-consuming, bureaucratic and expensive.

In 2005, a non-governmental organisation (Serviço Jesuíta aos Refugiados) and a foundation (Fundação Calouste Gulbenkian) began a reskilling programme to promote the recognition of nursing study credentials for those from countries with which Portugal does not have any automatic diploma recognition. Being registered on this programme entitles the applicant to a monthly grant, a place on a Portuguese language course and financial support for nursing school fees and document translation.

During the training period, other foreign colleagues – particularly Spanish nurses – routinely discriminated against East European nurses. This can be explained by the fact that the reskilling programme began at a time when the labour market was already saturated, in part due to the emergence of private nursing schools. There were also reports of communication problems due to the Spanish nurses' accent, which complicated the teamwork collaboration in a culturally and language-diverse work environment.

Additionally, monopoly control of work (Larson 1977) is not interpreted in the same way in Portugal as it is in East European countries; in their countries of origin, East European nurses are more subordinate to doctors.

Despite that, the presence of East European nurses can be considered as a strategic recruitment option, in part because they are motivated to work in medicine services usually neglected by Portuguese nurses and which also require certain soft skills: holistic care, empathy, interaction with the patients and clinical intuition.

Moreover, there is a mismatch between the labour contract and the functions actually performed. Despite not being formally recognised as specialist nurses, and thus not recruited as such, the job they perform corresponds closely to their previous specialist qualifications.

Joana Sousa Ribeiro 113

The presented case study sheds light on how regulatory frameworks (for instance, the professional associations, the academic institutions, the EU directives) and non-state institutional actors are key factors in the development of more inclusive (or exclusive) regulatory mechanisms working towards the governance of a diversified health workforce. This is even more important in the nursing profession where intersections between different lines of division – gender, citizenship status, place of graduation and level of specialisation – shape selective inclusion, and/or exclusion, dynamics (Larson 1977; Parkin 1979; Witz 1992; Saks & Kuhlmann 2006; Carvalho 2009) and differentiated occupational integration paths (Ribeiro 2008).

Towards a crisis of professionalism (or not)?

The questions presented in this chapter are fundamental to the debate on the following trends, which occur simultaneously and even head in the same direction: overproduction of graduates and disqualification, precarious nursing labour conditions and proletarianisation, interference in the monopoly control of work and de-professionalisation, international recruitment of agency nurses versus deskilling/reskilling of international graduate nurses and deregulation/re-regulation processes.

Beyond an evaluation of the extent to which the devaluation of professional power and its consequences affects the debate on de-professionalisation/proletarianisation (Haug 1973; Oppenheimer 1973), the analysis of the nurses' profile, nursing process of professionalisation and transnational professional projects reinstates the question of how different power pressures are being negotiated in the governance system – self-regulation (professional governance), public regulation (state governance) and market regulation (private governance).

The discourse aimed at promoting and facilitating rationalisation – managerial and organisational objectives, budgetary restrictions, standardisation of work practices, performance targets, accountability measures, financial control, and commodification – can be considered a disciplinary mechanism for exercising 'the appropriate conduct', which resembles Foucault's analysis of surveillance power, social control and governmentality (Foucault 1979).

Managerialist approaches can contribute to an imbalance between 'occupational professionalism' (or within professionalism) and 'organizational professionalism' (or professionalism 'from above'), with increased relevance of the latter (Evetts 2005). This is not a new issue, as Larson (1977) and Freidson (1994, 2001) have already considered professionalism as a means of ideological control exercised from above. However, in line with Evans (2008), it is important to consider the meshing of external ('demanded/requested professionalism' or 'prescribed professionalism') and internal ('enacted professionalism') conceptions of professionalism.

In this regard, the concept of 'pragmatic professionalism', applied by Andreas Liljegren (2012) to social workers, clearly translates the present moment – 'where the professionals claim to stand for one form of professionalism but, at times, fall back on the opposing form' (p. 309). In our view, it is precisely the internal and external control mechanisms, which may intersect in different ways and produce this back-and-forth movement that it is essential to analyse. At what point is the inferential decision process the main driver responsible for answering complex societal transformations? Or, on the contrary, is reflexive control – the core of 'hybrid professionalism' (Noordegraaf 2007) – the only way to maintain the notion of professionalism? And, if that is the case, how does it interact with self-control and organisational control?

Therefore, a central issue to highlight would be how health-care reforms, as part of a larger reform of the civil service, are producing inclusive, or exclusive, dynamics on the state professions' occupational structure, professional collaboration and internal division of labour in health care; along, for instance, lines of gender, citizenship status, place of graduation and level of specialisation.

This debate should be addressed, bearing in mind not only the 'public interest' domain, which, as Mike Saks (2005) underlined, is not necessarily the opposite of self-interest, but also the 'citizen professionals' purpose (Kuhlmann 2013a). In doing so, it reinstates the mediating role of professions and the blurring of dichotomies, such as professionalism/managerialism; self-control/organisational control; private interest/public interest.

Rather than just finding out whether professionalism is in crisis, it is essential to understand the internal and external mechanisms that are (re)producing professionalism in its multiple forms, and take into account not only a relational and comprehensive approach, but also the specific-context frame, which is increasingly transnational and neo-liberal in its scale and scope of action. This chapter contributes to this discussion, but further studies are needed in the future.

Notes

1. An exception to this are the following supranational initiatives, launched by supranational institutions, such as the European Commission (*EU Level Collaboration on Forecasting Health Workforce Needs, Workforce Planning and Health Workforce Trends: A Feasibility Study* and a Joint Action on *Health Workforce Planning and Forecasting*); the OECD (*Health Workforce Planning in OECD Countries: A Review of 26 Projection Models from 18 Countries*); and the WHO and Global Health Workforce Alliance (*A Universal Truth: No Health without a Workforce*).
2. The Nursing Trade Union (SEP) estimates that 5,000 and 20,000 nurses are lacking, respectively, in health centres and in hospitals.
3. The emergence of Spanish nurses in Portuguese NHS institutions occurred during a period when public hospitals with semi-private management and greater autonomy in contracting a workforce were established. This, in turn, led to active recruitment policies, such as advertisements in Spanish hospitals, contacts with Spanish nursing schools and with Spanish nurses' trade unions, and use of informal networks with professional peers.
4. A demand of the EU for the proper transposition of the EU Directive regarding the recognition of professional qualifications (Directive 2005/36/EC and its amendment – Directive 2013/55/EC) and of the memorandum agreement made in 2011 with three international supranational institutions – the European Commission, the European Central Bank and the International Monetary Fund.
5. This section is based on PhD research about the social mobility process of foreign nurses and physicians. For the purpose of this chapter, 26 interviews were analysed (12 nurses who had come from Spain to Portugal and 14 nurses from some Eastern European countries – Ukraine, Russia and Moldavia – to Portugal).

References

Abbott, A. 1988. *The System of Professions: An Essay on the Division of Expert Labor*, University of Chicago Press, Chicago.
ACSS (Health System Central Administration). 2014. *Boletim Informativo: Recursos Humanos Estrangeiros no Ministério da Saúde – Actualização 2011/2013*, Health System Central Administration, Lisbon.
Barros, P., Machado, S. & Simões, J. 2011. 'Portugal: Health system review', *HIT*, Vol. 13, No. 4, pp. 1–156.
Braverman, H. 1974. *Labor and Monopoly Capital: The Degradation of Work in the Twentieth Century*, Monthly Review Press, New York.
Buchan, J. & Seccombe, I. 2012. *Overstretched. Under-Resourced: The UK Nursing Labour Market Review*, Royal College of Nursing, London.
Buchan, J., O'May, F. & Dussault, G. 2013a. 'Nursing Workforce Policy and the Economic Crisis: A Global Overview', *Journal of Nursing Scholarship*, Vol. 45, No. 3, pp. 298–307.
Buchan, J., Temido, M., Fronteira, I., Lapão, L. & Dussault, G. 2013b. 'Nurses in advanced roles: A review of acceptability in Portugal' *Revista Latino-Americana de Enfermagem*, Vol. 21, January–February (Spec.), pp. 38–46.

Carapinheiro, G. & Rodrigues, M. 1998, 'Profissões: Protagonismos e Estratégias', in J. Viegas & A. Costa (eds.), *Portugal, que Modernidade?*, Celta Editora, Oeiras.
Carpenter, M. 1993. 'The subordination of nurses in health care: Towards a social division approach', in E. Riska & K. Wegar (eds.), *Gender, Work and Medicine: Women and the Medical Division of Labour*, Sage Publications, London.
Carvalho, T. 2009. *Nova Gestão Pública e Reformas da Saúde*, Edições Sílabo, Lisbon.
Conceição, C., Ribeiro, J., Pereira, J. & Dussault, G. 2012. *Mobility of Health Professionals in Portugal* (unpublished report for MoHProf project), ADMT/IHMT-UNL, Lisbon.
Delamaire, M. C. & Schweyer, F. 2010. 'Nationally moderate, locally significant: France and health professional mobility from far and near' in W. Wismar, C. Maier, I. Glinos, G. Dussault & J. Figueras (eds.), *Health Professional Mobility and Health Systems: Evidence from 17 European Countries*, WHO Regional Office for Europe, the European Observatory on Health Systems and Policies, Copenhagen.
Evans, L. 2008. 'Professionalism, professionality and the development of education professionals', *British Journal of Educational Studies*, Vol. 56, No. 1, pp. 20–38.
Evetts, J. 2005. 'The management of professionalism: A contemporary paradox', in *Changing Teacher Roles, Identities and Professionalism*, Conference, Kings College, London.
Fernandes, R. (ed.) 2011. *Situação Profissional dos Jovens Enfermeiros em Portugal*, OE-Portuguese Nursing Council, Lisbon.
Foucault, M. 1979. 'Governmentality', *Ideology and Consciousness*, Vol. 6, pp. 5–21.
Freidson, E. 1994. *Professionalism Reborn: Theory, Prophecy and Policy*, University of Chicago Press, Chicago.
Freidson, E. 2001. *Professionalism, the Third Logic*, Polity Press, Cambridge.
Fronteira, I., Conceição, C. & Biscaia, A. 2008. 'Políticas de saúde e enfermagem em Portugal: Perspectivas evolucionistas para um futuro (in)certo', in J. Lima & H. Pereira (eds.), *Políticas Públicas e Conhecimento Profissional: a educação e a enfermagem em reestruturação*, Legis Editora, Porto.
Halford, S., Savage, M. & Witz, A. 1997. *Gender, Careers, and Organisations*, Palgrave Macmillan, Basingstoke & New York.
Haug, M. 1973. 'Deprofessionalization: An alternative hypothesis for the future'. *Sociological Review Monographs*, Vol. 20, No. S1, pp. 195–211.
Jinks, C., Ong, B. N. & Paton, C. 2000. 'Mobile medics? The mobility of doctors in the European economic area', *Health Policy*, Vol. 54, No. 1, pp. 45–54.
Kuhlmann, E. 2013a. "'Riders in the Storm": The professions and healthcare governance', *Saúde and Tecnologia*, Suppl., pp. 6–10.
Kuhlmann, E., Batenburg, R., Groenewegen, P. P. & Larsen, C. 2013b. 'Bringing a European perspective to the health human resources debate: A scoping study', *Health Policy*, Vol. 110, No. 1, pp. 6–13.
Larson, M. 1977. *The Rise of Professionalism: A Sociological Analysis*, University of California Press, Berkeley.
Liljegren, A. 2012. 'Pragmatic professionalism: Micro-level discourse in social work', *European Journal of Social Work*, Vol. 15, No. 3, pp. 295–312.

Lopez-Valcarcel, B., Pérez, P. & Quintana, C. 2011. 'Opportunities in an expanding health service: Spain between Latin America and Europe', in M. Wismar, C. Maier, I. Glinos, G. Dussault & J. Figueras (eds.), *Health Professional Mobility and Health Systems: Evidence from 17 European Countries*, WHO Regional Office for Europe, the European Observatory on Health Systems and Policies, Copenhagen.
Noordegraaf, M. 2007. 'From "pure" to "hybrid" professionalism present-day professionalism in ambiguous public domains', *Administration and Society*, Vol. 39, No. 6, pp. 761–785.
OE (Ordem dos Enfermeiros). 2012. *Nursing Council Statistic Data* (unpublished), OE, Lisbon.
OE (Ordem dos Enfermeiros). 2013. *Nursing Council Statistic Data* (unpublished), OE, Lisbon.
OE (Ordem dos Enfermeiros). 2014. *Nursing Council Statistic Data* (unpublished) OE, Lisbon.
OECD (Organisation of Economic Co-operation and Development). 2013. *Health at a Glance*, OECD Publishing, Paris.
Ognyanova, D. & Busse, R. 2011. 'Germany: A destination and a source country: Managing regional disparities in the health workforce by drawing upon foreign physicians', in M. Wismar, C. Maier, I. Glinos, G. Dussault & J. Figueras (eds.), *Health Professional Mobility and Health Systems: Evidence from 17 European Countries*, WHO Regional Office for Europe, the European Observatory on Health Systems and Policies, Copenhagen.
Oppenheimer, M. 1973. 'The proletarianization of the professional', in P. Halmos (ed.), *The Sociological Review Monograph (Professionalisation and Social Change)*, University of Keele, Keele.
Parkin, F. 1979. *Marxism and Class Theory: A Bourgeois Critique*, Tavistock, London.
Peixoto, J. 2001. 'Migrações e políticas migratórias na União Europeia: Livre circulação e reconhecimento de diplomas', *Análise Social*, Vol. 36, Nos. 158 and 159, pp. 153–183.
Ribeiro, J. S. 2008. 'Gendering migration flows: Physicians and nurses in Portugal', *Equal Opportunities International*, Vol. 27, No. 1, pp. 77–87.
Ribeiro, J. S., Conceição, C., Pereira, J., Leone, C., Mendonça, P., Temido, M., Vieira, C. P. & Dussault, G. 2014. 'Health professionals moving to...and from Portugal', *Health Policy*, Vol. 114, Nos. 2 and 3, pp. 97–108.
Saks, M. 2005. *Professions and the Public Interest*, Routledge, London.
Saks, M. & Kuhlmann, E. 2006. *Modernising Health Care: Reinventing Professions, the State and the Public*, Policy Press, Bristol.
Siegrist, H. 1990. 'Professionalization as a process: Patterns, progression and discontinuity', in M. Burrage & R. Torstendahl (eds.), *Profession in Theory and History: Rethinking the Study of the Professions*, Sage Publications, London.
Van Gool, K. & Pearson, M. 2014. 'Health, austerity and economic crisis: Assessing the short-term impact in OECD countries', *OECD Health Working Papers*, Issue 76, OECD Publishing, Paris.
Walby, S., Greenwell, J., Mackay, L. & Soothill, K. 1994. *Medicine and Nursing: Professions in a Changing Health Service*, Sage Publications, London.
WHO (World Health Organization). 2000. *Munich Declaration: Nurses and Midwives: A Force for Health, 2000*, WHO Regional Office for Europe, Copenhagen.

Wismar, M., Glinos, I., Maier, C., Dussault, G., Palm, W. & Bremner, J. 2011. *Health Professional Mobility and Health Systems: Evidence from 17 European Countries*, WHO Regional Office for Europe on behalf of the European Observatory on Health Systems and Policies, Copenhagen.

Witz, A. 1992. *Professions and Patriarchy*, Routledge, London.

6
Managing the Medics in Britain
Mike Dent

Introduction

This chapter examines the impact of the various waves of new public management (NPM) and governance on hospital doctors in Britain – and more recently in England. NHS England became a separate entity in April 2013, and while much of the material discussed here will also apply to Wales, Northern Ireland and Scotland, there are differences which would take too long to properly look into here. I have chosen to concentrate on the acute hospital sector on the grounds that, historically, this is where professional power and dominance been concentrated. There is also an important and interesting story to be told about doctors working in general practice, but there the dynamic of the new managerialism and governance followed a different trajectory (Pollock 2005, pp. 132–164). General practitioners (GPs) are generally independent contractors, who see themselves often as 'partners with the state' in delivering health services (Harrison 2004, pp. 52–53), although this situation has changed somewhat with 'an increasing number of both salaried GPs and GPs who have specific (Personal Medical Services) contracts' (p. 54). Nevertheless, this contrasts with the status of hospital specialists who are – albeit well paid – technically employees. Whereas many employees are directly under the control of managers, skilled, professional employees have been able to make even greater claims to autonomy – and even dominance – within the work organisation. This is based on their education, training and the trust-based characteristic of their relations with patients, in addition to any complexity in the work activities themselves.

Until the introduction of general management in the early 1980s managers were not even called managers, they were administrators, whose responsibility was largely one of coordinating activities and providing support for professionals; as a consequence, their role was far more that of the *diplomat* rather than the *manager* (see Harrison & Pollitt 1994, p. 36). This began to change in the 1980s, and it is here that this chapter will begin. I will discuss why the managerialist movement emerged at that time, and why the medical profession saw NPM as a particular challenge. It will be necessary to then explain why the managerialist focus then shifted from NPM to a new public governance approach (Ferlie 2012, pp. 240–242) as well as considering the emergence of the 'hybrid' doctor-cum-manager. Underlying much of the sociological interest in the phenomena is the question of doctors' professional dominance (Freidson 1970), and while it is not the intention here to revisit the questions of putative medical 'proletarianisation' or 'de-professionalisation' in any detail (see Freidson 1994, pp. 128–146) some conclusions are drawn. As will be seen, medical status and control within hospitals is not a zero-sum game, but one that, within the English NHS, has experienced some turbulence under NPM and its aftermath. Strangely perhaps, the profession seems to have suffered less than might have first been expected *except* in having to learn to live with managerialism and adapt to it.

Drawing on new institutionalism

The chapter is organised as follows: first, is an account of how we might best understand the dynamics of the managerialist changes within the English NHS, drawing on a path-dependency approach; second, a description of the NPM and the later new governance, their implementation and the response of the medical profession; third, the emergence of the 'hybrid' medical manager; fourth, I apply the logic of Barley and Tolbert's (1997) new institutionalist analysis of innovation to better understand the dynamics of the shift to the new managerialism and governance. The chapter closes with a concluding discussion.

Managing hospital doctors in the English NHS

For a long time – up until the 1980s – the implicit arrangement within the British NHS was one in which the politicians, and more particularly the Minister and the Department for Health, provided the overall direction – and resources – albeit accepting that the medical profession within the local hospitals would dominate how the policy would be implemented – and the funding spent (Greener 2009, pp. 80–81). This was a case of *realpolitik* from the outset, when Bevan – the Labour minister responsible for implementing the NHS in 1948 – accepted that the medical profession were too powerful for the government to be able to bring about all the changes they had envisaged. Bevan is quoted as saying '[f]rankly, I do not consider the battle worthwhile' (cited in Klein 2001, p. 38). In the years that followed 1948 a culture emerged that provided the normative 'glue' that underpinned the doctors in their ascendant position in relation to other health professions and the hospital administration (Klein 1990). It was they who could technically determine what patients needed, and therefore their work also significantly shaped the work of the other health professionals. At the same time, the medical profession were able to exploit their jurisdictional powers to leverage considerable 'occupational control', for example, the right to private practice (Harrison & Pollitt 1994, p. 2; Evetts 2003). This settlement between profession and politicians started to break down in the 1980s – for reasons I will explain in the next section, 'The rise of NPM' – and, perhaps surprisingly, it was the then Conservative government who instigated the assault on the doctors' autonomy and dominance within hospitals. But first let us address the question as to why had it taken so long from Bevan's pragmatic settlement with the doctors before these radical changes came about.

The answer lies in the peculiar inertia of large complex systems and organisations, including health care. These reflect strongly their contextual as well as organisational cultures, and these provide a certain stability within the institutions of any health-care system (Wilsford 1994; Rochaix & Wilsford 2005, pp. 106–107). Professional dominance of hospital doctors (Freidson 1970, 1994, pp. 30–45), moreover, is a widespread phenomenon – although it does takes different forms in different countries (Dent 2003) – and it too has been highly resistant to major change, reflecting, as it does, the organisational culture and practices within which it is embedded. This is a situation that can be described as a 'sticky stasis' (Rochaix & Wilsford 2005, p. 107; see also Pierson 2000, p. 490) and a cause of 'entropy' within any health-care system (Greener 2002, p. 164). Paradoxically, this institutional approach of path dependency can also provide us with a means of explaining change as well as stasis.

Wilsford (1994, p. 257), in his classic analysis of the French healthcare system, suggested that change can be the outcome of specific but rare 'conjunctures', defined as the 'fleeting coming together of a number of diverse elements into a new, single combination' (p. 257), or 'the distinctive short-term mixes of fluid contingencies with sticky structures' (Rochaix & Wilsford 2005, p. 106). In other words, they are the result of exogenous shocks to the system, whose consequences that are difficult to predict or control. Such jolts to the system make continuation of the status quo impossible, and will force the pre-existing institutional arrangements onto a new trajectory and bring about major change within a system and its organisations. The welfare state had been faced with at least two sets of challenges for some time (Esping-Andersen 1996, pp. 6–7), and, in the case of health, this meant, first, the exponential rising costs due to an aging population, new drugs and technology, and people's expectations. More generally, the tax take that would be needed to fund such an NHS was politically too high. No political party was prepared to stand for an election with higher taxes as part of its manifesto, because they knew that while British public liked their NHS they disliked paying higher rates of tax even more. The general answer to this conundrum was the neo-liberal one, with the policies advocated by radical right-wing Conservative Thatcher government of the 1980s. The specific solution applied to the NHS was the introduction of what came to be known as NPM.

The rise of NPM

It was the tenets of neo-liberalism that provided the underlying rationale for the new managerial arrangements that came to radically change the way doctors' work was organised and controlled. The pressure for the changes, as already suggested, was not purely ideological. As elsewhere in the West, welfare state health provision is confronted by patient demand outstripping the available supply. The problem with doctors, from the government's perspective, was that they were the major spenders of the health-care budget, yet they were not directly accountable nor responsible for their spending.

What was needed, so the argument ran, was a strong injection of management. It was the Griffiths Report (1983) that provided the initial model for this new approach. The report advocated, first, that doctors had to take into account the cost as well as the clinical effectiveness of their actions. Second, a new breed of general managers needed to be introduced to provide direction, in order to establish a cost-conscious organisational culture within hospitals and across the NHS (Salter 2004, p. 71). This policy saw a rise in the numbers of senior management from about 1,000 in 1986 to 20,842 in 1995 (Pollock 2005, p. 39). This managerial cadre was intended to provide a 'tighter measurement and control of clinicians work' than was previously the case (p. 107). Attempts to engage doctors directly in management were miscalculated and according to one senior hospital doctor, '[this was] one of the serious fallacies of Griffiths' (Harrison et al. 1989, p. 11), although later some headway was made in engaging doctors in management (see the discussion in the section 'Leadership and "hybrids"'). Moreover, despite the reforms, doctors remained 'conspicuously autonomous' (Harrison et al. 1992, p. 146). Nevertheless, the new managerialism did gradually take root. It became part of the broader NPM movement. This had its attraction in the claim that it could deliver more efficient public services, including health care, whilst empowering both the employees and users of the services. The key initiative here was the introduction of the quasi-market. This was first spelt out in the White Paper, *Working for Patients* (Department of Health (DoH) 1989), a document much informed by Enthoven's reflections on the management of the NHS (1985). Enthoven was a strong advocate of the approach based on the health maintenance organisation (HMO) model from the United States. The 'reflections' recommendations were for the NHS to become more like a US HMO, something that has remained implicit as well as explicit within NHS reforms ever since (Light & Dixon 2004).

These reforms were certainly attractive to senior public servants (Pollitt 1990, pp. 171–172), who were increasing being challenged by the rigidities of the welfare states' 'bureau-professional regime' (Clarke & Newman 1997, pp. 12–13). It appeared to provide the possibility for a degree of operational control not previously achievable, for much of what constitutes NPM was directly derived from the managerial techniques long established in the private sector, which were rooted in scientific management and human relations approaches (Pollitt 1990, pp. 11–27 and 187; Ranade 1997, pp. 121–126), and the proponents of the new approach promised to provide a whole new toolkit for running hospitals. But the reforms were a direct challenge to the doctors, for the medical profession had previously been recognised as 'their own managers...accountable to their patients...and...cannot be held accountable to the NHS authorities' (DHSS 1972, para. 1.18, quoted in Stacey 1984). The document did add that doctors should 'act within...policy for the use of resources' (para. 1.18), but, sadly in some ways doctors were unable to control their spending within this voluntaristic approach. This was not unique to the English NHS; it is found generally across Europe and is one of the reasons for the widespread introduction of costing frameworks based on the US Diagnostic Related Groups (DRG) model (see Dent 2003).

But, to return to the historical thrust of this account, within the United Kingdom it was Christopher Hood (1991, 1995, pp. 95–97) who distilled the essentials of NPM and presented them in what essentially became a set of protocols, the 'building blocks' for the new managerialism:

1. Greater 'disaggregation' of public sector organisations into separately managed units;
2. enhanced competition and application of private sector managerial techniques;
3. an emphasis on 'discipline and parsimony' in resource use;
4. greater 'hands-on management';
5. adoption of measurable standards of performance;
6. use of 'pre-set output measures'.

This led to a process-driven approach with a sometimes over-anxious concern with measureable performance and 'star ratings', and a 'dashboard'-driven management culture. Later in the 1990s, Hood – with others (1999, pp. 191–193) – observed that NPM had become much more concerned with surveillance (increased 'oversight') and regulation, rather than directly controlling through the mechanisms such as audit and inspection – a shift that was to characterise the new governance regime within the NHS. None of this contradicted the HMO model (based on *not-for-profit* organisations), although much of the critical response to developments came much more from the perceived threat that parts of the NHS would be sold off to *for-profit* corporations (e.g. Pollock 2004).

Within NHS hospitals, perhaps the key development was the introduction of clinical directorates (Llewellyn 2001, p. 597). It was the one that most immediately and directly affected the doctors. Clinical directors were introduced early in the 1990s as were the new breed of medical directors, who were now advisors to the hospital boards on medical matters, as well as providing a linkage between management and doctors (Kirkpatrick et al. 2007). This was in marked contrast to the previous 'consensus model', where the medical director was the chair of the hospital 'medical executive committee'. Then the medical director would commonly take the role of the doctors' professional representative on the hospital board. Thus, the new model for medical directors seriously undermined the profession's influence on this senior management board. On the issue of clinical directorates, the organised profession, in the form of the British Medical Association (BMA) and Royal College of Physicians (RCP), were not opposed to them in principle (Kitchener 2000, p. 138), so doctors came to accept the new clinical director roles, and, in the process, became the first generation of hybrid doctor-managers (Fitzgerald et al. 2006).

It was these clinical directors who 'enable[d] cost consciousness, performance review, standardisation and evidence-based practice' to become established within English hospitals (Llewellyn 2001, pp. 618–619). Some doctors even 'actively pursued a management opportunity as an alternative to clinical medicine' (Forbes et al. 2004, p. 167), although they were in the minority; most doctors had no desire to become clinical directors (Kitchener 2000, p. 739; Hoque et al. 2004; Kirkpatrick et al. 2007) as they find clinical practice more rewarding – extrinsically as well as intrinsically. So even where doctors appeared to be acquiescing to the new regime, it is probable that they were only doing so 'on the surface', being more strongly wedded to the pre-existing arrangements in a way paralleling Cooper and colleagues' (1996) sedimentation argument.

Managerialism and the new governance

Initially, NPM had given rise to the 'Audit Society' (Power 1997), but under New Labour it transmuted more into a system of 'enforced self-regulation' (Hood et al. 2000). This emphasis changed to one that encouraged the internalisation of the rules and protocols, because compliance meant the hospital might avoid the direct intervention of the external regulator. It combined the 'iron fist of Draconian central intervention with the velvet glove of self-regulation' (p. 284) – it threatened 'interven[tion] in inverse proportion to success' (Cabinet Office 1999, para. 4.6). This can be seen as the introduction of 'soft bureaucracy' (Courpasson 2000) into the NHS, in which central control is strongly exerted but more by protocols and guidelines than edict.

The general shift from NPM to this 'soft bureaucracy' of the new governance was a gradual one, as the role of the regulatory governance structures evolved within health care, as elsewhere in the public sector (e.g. Rhodes 1997, 2000; Stoker 1999, 2000; Bevir & Rhodes 2003, p. 41; Flynn 2004). Nevertheless, a key moment was when the Labour administration came to power in 1997, for they did not see the containment of health costs as only achievable through the introduction of quasi-market techniques or privatisation (Hood et al. 2000; Dent et al. 2007, pp. 2–3). Nevertheless, they did see the need to moderate the medical profession's dominant 'countervailing powers' (Light 1995, 2010), and were keen to outmanoeuvre what came to be thought of as doctors' 'knavish' behaviour (Le Grand 2003). It needs to be pointed out that NPM was part of this problem, for it was its emphasis on performance and output measures that encouraged such 'knavish' game playing, for example, finding ways of meeting targets without necessarily meeting patients' needs. Or discharging patients too early to meet a target (but then being faced with the problem of higher levels of readmissions) in order to enhance the standing of a hospital.

Overall, neither hospital managers nor doctors were happy with the new arrangements. In general, the new managerialism and governance were viewed as 'anti-patient, anti-clinical freedom and a threat to...autonomy and values' (Jacobs 2005, p. 137). Despite Labour's rhetoric that they were moving away from the market model, the general perception was that they remained very much preoccupied with the financial 'bottom line'. Crilly and Le Grand (2004), for example, in a survey of over 1,500 managers and consultants, reported a general dissatisfaction with what was seen as 'the single-minded pursuit of financial targets' (p. 1809), while other studies reported similar findings too, including Rundall, Davies and Hodges (2004), and Degeling and colleagues (2006). Yet there were differences, the introduction of independent sector treatment centres (ISTCs) (DoH 2005), for example, were intended to ensure 'contestability' rather than 'market competition'. The distinction, however, is a fine one, which was normatively defined as follows:

> [P]lanning and competition should be used together...[to ensure the] possibility that contracts will move [between providers]...rather than the actual movement.
> (Ham 1996, p. 70)

More simply put, private sector provision would be employed to enhance public sector efficiency rather than replacing it. Similarly, the introduction of 'patient choice' was, in part, intended to have the same effect (Appleby & Dixon 2004; Dent 2006). But it was the emphasis on evidence-based medicine (EBM) that really opened up the profession's quality of care to external inspection and control (Harrison & Macdonald 2003, p. 117). This underpinned the clinical governance of medical work within hospitals, as the criteria for assessing clinical quality are based on scientific and medical evidence, *but* clinical governance was now the responsibility of the chief executives of hospitals (p. 117), whereas previously the profession would have had the power not to have allowed that to happen.

Leadership and 'hybrids'

As we have already seen in the earlier section entitled 'The rise of NPM', doctors have not been keen to engage in management, and even though the clinical directorates are now ubiquitous, and medical directors well established on hospital boards, on the whole hospital specialists do not see either responsibilities as attractive or rewarding. Moreover, it would be bad economics to employ highly skilled specialists to spend a significant part of their working week in management for which they have not been trained or – for the most part – in which they have little interest. On the other hand, unless hospital specialists are engaged in management it is difficult for the hospital to provide as fully efficient and integrated service as they might, because this service needs the technical expertise and detailed knowledge of the specialists. Moreover, if these same specialists have some knowledge of budgets and finances they may be more prepared to work with management to improve the service the hospital can deliver. This is why there has been a growing interest in the possibilities of engaging doctors more directly, by them taking on a *hybrid* medical-management role within hospitals (Fitzgerald et al. 2006, pp. 16–17). Yet, in England, most management training and support for doctors 'tended to be ad hoc and episodic' (Clark 2006, p. 14). This is hardly surprising given that doctors' careers will be focused on their clinical work. This is what they trained for, and what potentially will provide them with the greater material rewards. Management, for them, is a distraction. This is further compounded by the traditional focus of the medical education, training and socialisation of doctors. Within the English NHS, medics moving into management are often considered, jokingly, by their colleagues as going over to the 'dark side' (a reference to Darth Vader in the *Star Wars* films). Nevertheless, some progress has been made in countering the generally ambivalent attitude doctors have towards management. One important initiative has been the Academy of Medical Royal Colleges and NHS Institute for Innovation and Improvement programme: 'Enhancing Engagement in Medical Leadership'. The aim here has been 'to develop an integrated medical management and leadership competency, education and assessment framework for doctors throughout the UK' (Clark & Armit 2008, p. 36).

Darzi, in his report (2008), was particularly influential in emphasising the need for more and better medical training in management and leadership. There are now a considerable number of postgraduate courses in place. These appear to attract, predominantly, registrars (equivalent to residents in the United States), although it is too early yet to know whether this will lead to any sea change in medics' general attitudes towards engaging with management. Nevertheless, the intent to engage the new generation of hospital doctors unambiguously in management – more in line, perhaps, with the Danish model – and, in the process, overcome the long-established hostility within the profession towards management, is there (Kirkpatrick et al. 2009, p. 648). A key message within the Darzi Report is that doctors should not be treated solely as skilled artisans, instead they need to fully participate in the management of service delivery and take on senior leadership roles within the hospital (Darzi 2008, pp. 4–5, para. 4).

Rewriting the management of hospital medics

How are we to make sense of this narrative of managerialism and doctors in the English NHS? We can usefully analyse the processes by drawing on Barley and Tolbert's (1997) new institutionalist notion of 'scripts'. This will enable us to account for the organisation-level changes that have taken place since the earlier period – when the hospital doctors had professional dominance within the workplace and when they believed themselves to be fully autonomous in their clinical practice – to the periods of NPM and the new governance, and on to the current period; that is, the putative 'hybrid' medic directly engaged in management and interested in re-establishing their leadership role within the organisation.

Meyer and Rowan (1991, p. 41) suggested that the 'formal structures of many organizations... reflect the myths of their institutional environments instead of the demands of their work activities'. This could be true of the professional dominance of hospital doctors and some aspects of their clinical autonomy. There is, according to this argument, a 'decoupling' of the formal organisation 'myth' from the reality, which acts as an uncertainty-absorbing arrangement, as well as underpinning the legitimacy of an organisation and its survival. Clinical autonomy would be a good example of 'decoupling', for it is separate and discrete from the formal organisational rules. But it is not simply another way of classifying the 'informal organisation', instead it provides the license for the application of professional, or specialist, judgement (discretion) in clinical care. Meyer and Rowan (1991) argue that 'decoupling' is the means by which complex organisations effectively and legitimately function, which would otherwise be impossible. While insightful, the argument is a little too simple. In the case of hospital doctors, for example, they will commonly have an allegiance to their profession, and an interest in their patients and the hospital within which they work, but these interests can and do conflict, as we have seen in the case of NPM. This is where the analysis of Barley and Tolbert (1997, p. 98) is useful. They suggest that a new institutionalist approach can be usefully combined with structuration theory (Giddens 1984) to provide a toolkit for understanding the process of change. In the present case, how professionals gradually come to adopt, and modify, new working and management practices. Key to this argument is the concept of 'scripts' (Barley 1986). These are *'observable, recurrent activities and patterns of interaction characteristic of a particular setting'* (p. 98; emphasis in original), and they underpin the 'four moments' of the institutionalisation process (Barley & Tolbert 1997, pp. 100–103):

1. 'encoding of institutional principles in the scripts used in specific settings' (a process of socialisation and internalisation);
2. enactment of the 'scripts that encode institutional principles' (which 'may or may not entail conscious choice');
3. revising or replicating scripts (intentional alteration 'is more likely to lead to institutional change' than those which are made unconsciously); and
4. 'objectification and externalisation of the patterned behaviours and interactions produced during the period in question'.

Set out like this, one can see how NPM may be 'encoded' and 'enacted', and how hospital doctors may play an active role in the 'revising' of such scripts – along with other social actors engaged in the process, such as managers, civil servants, politicians and so on. Thus, the early developments of the NPM initiated new scripts that had great impact, while the longer-term evolution of the new managerialism led the emphasis to switch more to governance and regulation that is informed by EBM. All of this provided the rationale for the medical profession to adapt – however reluctantly – to the new regime, for it reflected a certain continuity, in keeping with path dependency, where clinical autonomy has been reconfigured and there is the possibility of a new medical ascendancy – under the rubric of 'leadership'. This contrasts markedly with the early vision of the Thatcher administration to firmly subordinate hospital doctors to management, or even the later Labour administration that constructed its hospital governance arrangements on the principle that doctors were not to be trusted, that 'knavish' game-playing behaviour was to be assumed. This reflects Barley's (1986, p. 107) argument that social interaction within an organisational field is 'constrained by histories and ritualistic patterning' very similar to the logic of path dependency, but which, nevertheless, can lead to the cumulative structuring and hence institutionalisation of new arrangements. This is an ongoing, iterative process of institutionalisation that 'is a continuous process whose operation can be observed only through time' (Barley & Tolbert 1997, p. 100). In the case of NPM, and later the new governance, there were a sequence of 'scripts' that turned from political rhetoric to organisational practice and substantially reconfigured the work situation of hospital doctors, but in the end failed to remove them from their ascendant position within the health-care division of labour within hospitals. Moreover, in the end, the process has also seen doctors as providing a key role in the leadership of these organisations.

Concluding discussion: Reflections on medicine, management and leadership

In this chapter I have reviewed the impact of NPM and governance on hospital doctors in Britain, and more especially within England. The account started with the managerialist movement in the 1980s and the roots of what became known as NPM. The approach, as we have seen, had its own limitations, for it alienated many within the profession as a result of what was seen as managerialist overemphasis on metrics and costs and perceived devaluing of the role of the hospital doctors. All of this gave rise to a culture of 'gaming' within NHS hospitals, whereby managers and doctors were thought to be more interested in 'playing the system', that is, more concerned with formally meeting their performance targets than actually delivering good-quality patient care. This reached its managerial nadir with the Mid-Staffordshire Hospital scandal (Francis 2013), but long before then there had been a shift of emphasis to the new governance model, in part to avoid this unintended consequence of the new managerialism.

At the same time, there has been renewed effort in finding ways of more fully engaging doctors in the management process. This has created some interest in the possibility of establishing the medical hybrid role within English hospitals. While this had proved to be very difficult in the early years of NPM (see Harrison & Pollitt 1994), some progress has been made, particularly following the Darzi Report (2008). This has been, in part, achieved by emphasising that the role is a leadership one rather than managerial, the rhetoric here being as important as the actuality (O'Reilly & Reed 2012). Nevertheless, there does appear to be a

Mike Dent 131

realisation among some sections within the profession that to have a successful medical career as a hospital doctor and specialist will mean actively engaging in management in order to better achieve objectives. Involvement in management, to be successful, has to be seen by the profession as not signifying an erosion of autonomy and influence within health care. However, it is likely to mean further changes to the roles and relations within the hospital organisation, that is, a move away from physicians' sense of separateness and towards a more corporate involvement within hospital management. It is a process that has generally been resisted, but, perhaps because there is no sign that managerialism is going to go away any time soon, there are signs that hospital doctors have come to accept the necessity of genuine engagement.

References

Appleby, J. and Dixon, J. 2004. 'Patient choice in the NHS: Having choice may not improve outcomes', *British Medical Journal (BMJ)*, Vol. 329, No. 7457, pp. 61–62.
Barley, S. 1986. 'Technology as an occasion for structuring: Evidence from observations of CT scanners and the social order of radiology departments', *Administrative Science Quarterly*, Vol. 31, pp. 78–108.
Barley, S. & Tolbert, S. 1997 'Institutionalization and structuration: Studying the links between action and institution', *Organization Studies*, Vol. 18, No.1, pp. 93–117.
Bevir, M. & Rhodes, R. 2003. 'Searching for civil society: Changing patterns of governance in Britain', *Public Administration*, Vol. 81, No. 1, pp. 41–62.
Cabinet Office. 1999. *Modernising Government (Cm. 4310)*, HMSO, London.
Clark, J. 2006. 'Enhancing medical engagement in leadership', *Innovate/Improve/In View*, Vol. 10 (June), pp. 14–15.
Clark, J. & Armit, K. 2008. 'Attainment of competency in management and leadership: No longer an optional extra for doctors', *Clinical Governance*, Vol. 13, No. 1, pp. 35–42.
Clarke, J. & Newman, J. 1997. *The Managerial State*, Sage, London.
Cooper, D., Hinings, B., Greenwood R. & Brown, J. 1996. 'Sedimentation and transformation in organizational change: The case of Canadian law partnerships', *Organization Studies*, Vol. 17, No. 4, pp. 623–647.
Courpasson, D. 2000. 'Managerial strategies of domination: Power in soft bureaucracies', *Organization Studies*, Vol. 21, No. 1, pp. 141–162.
Crilly, T. & Le Grand, J. 2004. 'The motivation and behaviour of hospital trusts', *Social Science & Medicine*, Vol. 58, No. 10, pp. 1809–1823.
Darzi, A. 2008. *High Quality Care for All, Cm 7432*, HMSO, London.
Degeling, P., Zhang, K., Coyle, B., Xu, L., Meng, Q., Qu, J. & Hill, M. 2006. 'Clinicians and the governance of hospitals: A cross-cultural perspective on relations between profession and management', *Social Science & Medicine*, Vol. 63, No. 3, pp. 757–775.
Dent, M. 2003. *Remodelling Hospitals and Health Professions in Europe: Medicine, Nursing and the State*, Palgrave Macmillan, Basingstoke.

Dent, M. 2006. 'Patient choice and medicine in health care: Responsibilisation, governance and proto-professionalisation', *Public Management Review*, Vol. 8, No. 3, pp. 451–464.

Dent, M., van Gestel, N. & Teelken, C. 2007. 'Symposium on changing modes of governance in public sector organizations: Action and rhetoric', *Public Administration*, Vol. 85, No. 1, pp. 1–8.

DHSS (Department of Health and Social Security). 1972. *Management Arrangements for the Reorganized Health Service*, HMSO, London.

DoH (Department of Health). 1989. *Working for Patients (Cmnd 555)*, HMSO, London.

DoH (Department of Health). 2005. *Treatment Centres: Delivering Faster, Quality Care and Choice for Patients*, TSO, London.

Enthoven, A. 1985. *Reflections on the Management of the National Health Service: An American Looks at Incentives to Efficiency in the Health Services Management in the UK*, Nuffield Provincial Hospitals, London.

Esping-Andersen, G. 1996. 'After the golden age? Welfare state dilemmas in a global economy', in G. Esping-Andersen (ed.), *Welfare States in Transition*, Sage, London.

Evetts, J. 2003. 'The sociological analysis of professionalism: Occupational change in the modern world', *International Sociology*, Vol. 18, No. 2, pp. 395–415.

Ferlie, E. 2012. 'Paradigms and instruments of public management reform – the question of agency', in C. Teelken, E. Ferlie and M. Dent (eds.) *Leadership in the Public Sector: Promises and Pitfalls*, Routledge, London.

Fitzgerald, L., Lilley, C., Ferlie, E. & Buchanan, D. 2006. *Managing Change and Role Enactment in the Professionalised Organisation*, Report to the National Co-ordinating Centre for the NHS Service Delivery and Organisation R&D, London.

Flynn, R. 2004. ' "Soft Bureaucracy", governmentality and clinical governance: Theoretical approaches to emergent policy', in A. Gray & S. Harrison (eds.), *Governing Medicine: Theory and Practice*, Open University Press, Maidenhead.

Forbes, T., Hallier, J. & Kelly, L. 2004. 'Doctors as managers: Investors and reluctants in a dual role', *Health Services Management Research*, Vol. 17, pp. 167–176.

Francis, R. 2013. *Report of the Mid Staffordshire NHS Foundation Trust Public Inquiry*, The Stationery Office, London. Available online at http://www.midstaffspublicinquiry.com/report (accessed 26 March 2015).

Freidson, E. 1970. *Professional Dominance: The Social Structure of Medical Care*, Atherton Press, New York.

Freidson, E. 1994. *Professionalism Reborn: Theory, Prophecy and Policy*, Polity, Cambridge.

Giddens, A. 1984. *The Constitution of Society*, Polity, Cambridge.

Greener, I. 2002. 'Understanding NHS reform: The policy transfer, social learning and path dependency perspectives', *Governance*, Vol. 15, No. 2, pp. 161–183.

Greener, I. 2009. *Healthcare in the UK: Understanding Continuity and Change*, Policy Press, Bristol.

Griffiths, R. 1983. *National Health Service Management Inquiry*, 6 October, Department of Health and Social Security, London.

Ham, C. 1996. 'Contestability: A middle path for health care', *British Medical Journal*, Vol. 312, pp. 70–71.

Harrison, S. 2004. 'Medicine and management: Autonomy and authority in the National Health Service', in A. Gray & S. Harrison (eds.), *Governing Medicine: Theory and Practice*, Open University Press, Maidenhead.
Harrison, S. & Macdonald, R. 2003. 'Science, consumerism and bureaucracy: New legitimations of medical professionalism', *International Journal of Public Sector Management (IJPSM)*, Vol. 16, No. 2, pp. 110–121.
Harrison, S. & Pollitt, C. 1994. *Controlling Health Professionals: The Future of Work and Organization in the NHS*, Open University Press, Buckingham.
Harrison, S., Hunter, D. J., Marnoch, G. & Pollitt, C. 1989. *The Impact of General Management in the NHS*, Nuffield Institute, Leeds.
Harrison, S., Hunter, D. J., Marnoch, G. & Pollitt, C. 1992. *Just Managing: Power and Culture in the National Health Service*, Palgrave Macmillan, London.
Hood, C. 1991. 'A public management for all seasons?', *Public Administration*, Vol. 69, pp. 3–19.
Hood, C. 1995. "The "New Public Management" in the 1980s: Variations on a theme, *Accounting, Organizations and Society*, Vol. 20, No. 2/3, pp. 93–109.
Hood, C., James, O. & Scott, C. 2000. 'Regulation of government: Has it increased, is it increasing, should it be diminished?', *Public Administration Review*, Vol. 78, No. 2, pp. 283–304.
Hoque, K., Davis, S. & Humphreys, M. 2004. 'Freedom to do what you are told: Senior management team autonomy in an NHS acute trust', *Public Administration*, Vol. 82, No. 2, pp. 355–375.
Jacobs, K. 2005. 'Hybridisation or polarisation: Doctors and accounting in the UK, Germany and Italy', *Financial Accountability & Management*, Vol. 21, No. 2, pp. 135–161.
Kirkpatrick, I., Jespersen, P. K., Dent, M. & Neogy, I. 2009. 'Medicine and management in a comparative perspective: The case of Denmark and England', *Sociology of Health & Illness*, Vol. 31, No. 5, pp. 642–658.
Kirkpatrick, I., Maltby, B., Dent, M., Neogy, I. & Mascie-Taylor, H. 2007. *National Inquiry into Management and Medicine: Final Report*, Centre for Innovation and Health Management, University of Leeds, January.
Kitchener, M. 2000. The 'bureaucratization' of professional roles: The cases of clinical directors in UK hospitals', *Organization*, Vol. 7, No. 1, pp. 129–154.
Klein, R. 1990. 'The state and the profession: The politics of the double bed', *British Medical Journal*, 3 October, pp. 700–702.
Klein, R. 2001. *The New Politics of the NHS* (4th edn), Prentice-Hall, London.
Le Grand, J. 2003. *Motivation, Agency and Public Policy: Knight and Knaves, Pawns and Queens*, Oxford University Press, Oxford.
Light, D. W. 1995. 'Countervailing powers: A framework for professions in transition', in T. Johnson, G. Larkin & M. Saks (eds.), *Health Professions and the State in Europe*, Routledge, London.
Light, D. W. 2010. 'Health professions, markets and countervailing powers', in C. Bird, P. Conrad, A. Fremont & S. Timmermans (eds.), *Handbook of Medical Sociology* (6th edn), Vanderbilt University Press, Nashville, TN.
Light, D. W. & Dixon, M. 2004. 'Making the NHS more like Kaiser Permanente', *British Medical Journal*, Vol. 328, No. 7442, pp. 763–765.
Llewellyn, S. 2001. '"Two-way windows": Clinicians as medical managers', *Organization Studies*, Vol. 22, No. 4, pp. 593–623.

Meyer, J. W. & Rowan, B. 1991. 'Institutionalized organizations: Formal structure as myth and ceremony', in W. W. Powell and P. J. DiMaggio (eds.) *The New Institutionalism in Organizational Analysis*, The University of Chicago Press, Chicago.
O'Reilly, D. & Reed, M. 2012. ' "Leaderism" and the discourse of leadership in the reformation of UK public services', in C. Teelken, E. Ferlie & M. Dent (eds.), *Leadership in the Public Sector: Promises and Pitfalls*, Routledge, London.
Pierson, P. 2000. 'The limits of design: Explaining institutional origins and change', *Governance*, Vol. 13, No. 4, pp. 475–499.
Pollitt, C. 1990. *Managerialism and the Public Services: The Anglo-American Experience*, Blackwell, Oxford.
Pollock, A. 2005. *NHS PLC: The Privatisation of Our Health Care* (2nd edn), Verso, London.
Power, M. 1997. *The Audit Society: The Rituals of Verification*, Oxford University Press, Oxford.
Ranade, W. 1997. *A Future for the NHS: Health Care in the Millennium* (2nd edn), Longman, London.
Rhodes, R. 1997. *Understanding Governance*, Open University Press, Buckingham.
Rhodes, R. 2000. 'Governance and public administration', in J. Pierre (ed.), *Debating Governance: Authority, Steering and Democracy*, Oxford University Press, Oxford.
Rochaix, L. & Wilsford, D. 2005. 'State autonomy, policy paralysis: Paradoxes of institutions and culture in the French health care system', *Journal of Health Politics, Policy and Law*, Vol. 30, No. 1–2, pp. 97–119.
Rundall, T., Davies, H. & Hodges, C. 2004. 'Doctor–manager relationships in the United States and the United Kingdom', *Journal of Healthcare Management*, Vol. 49, No. 4, pp. 251–268.
Salter, B. 2004. *The New Politics of Medicine*, Palgrave Macmillan, London.
Stacey, M. 1984. 'The general medical council and professional accountability', *Public Policy and Administration*, Vol. 4, No. 1, pp. 12–27.
Stoker, G. 1999. *The New Management of British Local Governance*, Palgrave Macmillan, London.
Stoker, G. 2000. *The New Politics of British Local Governance*, Palgrave Macmillan, London.
Wilsford, D. 1994. 'Path dependency, or why history makes it difficult but not impossible to reform health care systems in a big way', *Journal of Public Policy*, Vol. 14, No. 3, pp. 251–283.

7
The Changing Medical Profession in England

Mike Saks

Introduction

In contributing to the mainstream theme of the book on professionalism, managerialism and reform in higher education (HE) and the health services, this chapter focuses on the development of the English medical profession based on credentialism – from the pivotal achievement of state-supported exclusionary social closure in a relatively open field over 150 years ago to the present day. In so doing, it considers the ways in which the medical profession has changed in a shifting socio-political environment where there have been a multitude of challenges over time, including from the market, the state and users. Finally, the current position of doctors in England is examined in an international context, as well as being contrasted with that of academics in HE – a group which is also central to this book. However, before the analysis of the medical profession in England can begin, it is first necessary to sketch out the neo-Weberian theoretical framework for studying medicine as a profession on which this chapter is based.

The theoretical context for studying medicine as a profession

From the viewpoint of theory, professions are seen here as a knowledge-based group centred directly or indirectly on exclusionary social closure, a concept drawn from the seminal work of Max Weber (1968) – where legally enshrined boundaries create ranks of insiders and outsiders through the establishment of a state-supported register of eligibles (Saks 2012). Here doctors, along with lawyers, are regarded as archetypal professions in modern society underpinned by credentialism, with qualifications gained in HE underlining their privileged position in a competitive marketplace (Parkin 1979). However, it is recognised that the situation, achieved through the exercise of collective occupational interests, is complex. Internal hierarchies exist within professional groups despite the formal ideology of a community of equals – as illustrated in English medicine by the traditional split between specialists and generalists related to different levels of income, status and power (Saks 1995). Equally, while many occupations in the health and other fields do not achieve the standing of a profession, others are in the process of professionalisation, albeit governed by voluntary rather than statutory regulation.

There are also, of course, many different forms of social closure – not only in relation to the legal basis underpinning the position of 'top dog' professions but also in terms of the hierarchical position of professional occupations. Turner (1995), for instance, classically notes that orthodox health professions are divided into the following hierarchical categories: the dominant medical profession, which stands at the apex of health care in modern industrial societies; 'limited' health professions such as dentists and opticians, which are restricted to particular parts of the body; and 'subordinated' health professions like nurses and midwives, which are under the authority of doctors in the division of labour. These categories and their place in the pecking order are not static – neo-Weberians in fact typically see health and other occupational fields as highly contested, fluid arenas in which professional groups jockey with each other for position in line with their own group self-interests (Saks 2010). This picture also needs to be expanded holistically to include marginal groups who fall into the category of 'exclusion', bearing in mind that the unorthodoxy of one era can readily become the orthodoxy of the next, and vice-versa. This is highlighted in health care by those engaged in complementary and alternative medicine (CAM), who are normally excluded from orthodox health care as they lack official state backing – with all the implications that such inequalities of position carry for inequalities of public access to such therapies (Saks 2014a).

It is very important, however, to highlight that there are other theoretical perspectives on professions. These range from the structural functionalist and interactionist approach to Marxism and Foucauldianism. Functionalists view professions at a macro level, as based on esoteric knowledge of great importance for society, in which professional groups fulfil a crucial social function – that of protecting the public through codes of ethics in exchange for a privileged position in society (see, for example, Barber 1963). But if functionalists regard dominant and semi-professions as naturally placed in the pecking order, reflecting their knowledge base, symbolic interactionists are more critical; they see the notion of a 'profession' as an honorific symbol that is socially negotiated in the politics of work – thereby avoiding the reflexive adoption of legitimating professional ideologies (see, for instance, Becker 1962). Such micro-oriented work has acted as a platform for more critical macro contributions. Here, Marxist accounts view professions as being rewarded for carrying out surveillance and control functions to preserve the capitalist status quo (as illustrated by Navarro 1986), while Foucauldian analyses challenge the rationality of scientific progress associated with professional engagement in governmentality (as exemplified by Johnson 1995). These theories sit in opposition to the neo-Weberian social closure approach, as does the work of Evetts (2013), which argues that this approach is becoming less relevant since occupational professionalism is being replaced with organisational professionalism, as professions are increasingly being embedded in managerial bureaucracies.

Such challenges to neo-Weberian contributions based on exclusionary closure, though, are rather too assumptive. As Saks (2010) points out, the macro-functionalist approach takes a too glossy and uncritical view of the key features of a profession, while the more challenging micro-focused interactionist approach shares a failure to systematically adduce evidence for its claims, as well as giving too little attention to the wider structural and historical dynamics of professions. Moreover, Marxist thinking, like Foucauldianism, provides an unhelpful conceptual straitjacket for operationally and empirically considering claims about the professions. Arguments about organisational professionalism similarly fly in the face of recent empirical studies, which show that, even in face of audit, professional strategies still frequently outweigh organisational belonging in decision-making in the knowledge society (see, for example, Jonnergård & Erlingsdóttir 2012). Although neo-Weberianism is not without its difficulties, including the cavalier manner in which it has sometimes been applied, such an approach is felt to provide a more flexible framework for understanding both professional and non-professional groups in the division of labour, in which interest group politics is central in the health-care marketplace (Saks 1995). On this basis, the development of medicine as a profession in England – on which this chapter focuses – is charted following the achievement of exclusionary social closure in the mid-19th century in a relatively open health-care field.

The rise of the English medical profession and the turbulence of the counterculture

According to Porter (1995), pre-industrial health care in Britain was historically characterised by a comparatively undifferentiated, pluralistic field in which various practitioners plied their trade – with the absence of a national, enforceable legal monopoly of medicine and difficulties in distinguishing between practitioners in terms of their theories, practice, training and repute. However, Waddington (1984) notes that, from the early 19th century, the medical profession was forged against this backcloth from a situation in which there was considerable fragmentation amongst doctors themselves – with competing groups of apothecaries, surgeons and elite physicians operating alongside groups of 'irregulars'. This was achieved through a lobby for a unified profession led by the Provincial Medical and Surgical Association, which was later to become the British Medical Association. In its successful campaign to professionalise medicine, it was increasingly supported by the state in an evolving medical–Ministry alliance, as well as driven by its own attacks on rival health groups for engaging in 'quackery' through popular and medical media (Porter 2001). In an age where scientific knowledge was becoming increasingly significant, it was also sustained by the growth of programmes of medical education centred around biomedicine – even if, by the mid-19th century when exclusionary social closure was obtained, medicine was primarily classificatory rather than curative, hospitals were known as 'gateways to death', and asepsis and anaesthesia were still to be widely introduced (Saks 2005).

Nonetheless, following a series of bills, the 1858 Medical Act was finally passed; this led to the upward collective social mobility of doctors, raising their stock to that of a fullyfledged profession with an ensuing increase in their income, status and power (Parry & Parry 1976). The profession was to be based on a self-regulatory system, with entry limited through a national register maintained by the General Medical Council, which was also tasked with controlling standards of education and training and disciplinary matters related to its newly established code of ethics (Stacey 1992). Importantly, the medical profession in England became pivoted on a de facto monopoly, in that non-medical CAM outsiders like herbalists and homeopaths were not prevented from practising under the Common Law as long as, amongst other things, they did not represent themselves as qualified doctors (Saks 2003). This politically inspired monopoly thereby enabled doctors on the medical register to enhance their socio-economic opportunities in a highly competitive marketplace, especially since their rivals in the private sector were greatly disadvantaged, as state medical funding increased through the 1911 National Health Insurance Act and the 1946 National Health Service Act (Ham 2009). As a result, potential competitors were not only precluded from direct state financial support, but also prevented from, *inter alia*, signing death certificates and recovering unpaid medical charges – as well as inhibited from collaborating with non-medically qualified practitioners through restrictive codes of medical ethics (Saks 1996).

The ever wider state market shelter, backed up by growing paradigmatic unity around biomedicine, and an increasingly standardised and enhanced medical curriculum, served medical interests in neo-Weberian terms by placing the newly founded, initially all male, medical profession in a stronger position in the market (Parry & Parry 1976). Its position was further reinforced in the first half of the 20th century by the development of legislation supporting the state-sanctioned establishment of a range of limited and subordinated health professions which were heavily populated by women – from nursing and midwifery early in the 20th century to the aptly named 'professions supplementary to medicine', like occupational therapy and physiotherapy, by the early 1960s (Allsop and Saks 2002) – which allowed medicine to extend its dominance of orthodox health care still further. The rising influence of the medical profession also prompted legislation restricting the claims of rival CAM practitioners to treat conditions such as cancer and diabetes, while sidelining attempts to professionalise CAM therapies like chiropractic and osteopathy in the 1920s and 1930s through providing adverse medical advice to government (Larkin 1995). The loss of state legitimacy for CAM, together with internal controls over medical careers and ongoing attacks on the practice of outsiders through medical journals and other publications, meant that the employment of rival CAM therapies had gone into sharp decline by the mid-20th century (Saks 2003).

This had the effect of reinforcing the medical monopoly underpinned by exclusionary social closure in England – supported by a stream of scientific discoveries since its foundation in the mid-19th century which revolutionised medical theory and practice (Duffin 2010). This moved medicine from its one-to-one practice at the bedside, in which the fee-paying client shaped diagnosis and treatment in the 18th century, through classificatory hospital medicine in the 19th century, to laboratory medicine based on bacteriological research by the 20th century (Chamberlain 2012). However, it should not be imagined – with the consolidation of the medical profession following the introduction in the mid-20th century of the National Health Service (NHS) providing a state-funded service free at the point of access (Klein 2013) – that orthodox medicine had it all its own way. Paradoxically, despite growing medical specialisation and an array of medical innovations, from hip replacements and organ transplants to the use of antibiotics (Le Fanu 2011), the 1960s onwards were a time when medicine faced its greatest challenges – starting with the turbulent development of a counterculture, which acted as a catalyst for not only more critical theoretical analyses of the professions in general and the medical profession in particular, but also further substantive changes in the position of the medical profession in England.

The medical counterculture in the late 1960s and early 1970s in England was part of a broader backlash against 'scientific progress' in the West, as high technology biomedicine was disparaged as disempowering, depersonalising and counterproductive. Instead of technocratic solutions to issues, a desire for alternative lifestyles emerged, based on everything from mysticism to mind-expanding drugs – with an increasing critique of institutionalised professions, from schoolteachers to doctors (Saks 2000). Orthodox medicine was assailed for having distinct limits, including ineffectiveness, iatrogenesis and dehumanisation (see, for instance, Illich 1976). In this sense, the counterculture was associated with fast-rising popular interest in CAM and a commensurate growth in the number of its practitioners – as well as the professionalisation of osteopathy and chiropractic in the 1990s through exclusionary social closure with protection of title through private members' bills, albeit on restricted terms (Saks 2005). Such interest was underlined by powerful lobbies led by Prince Charles and others, and the generally supportive House of Lords Select Committee on Science and Technology (2000) Report on CAM. However, this potential threat to the income, status and power of the medical profession was largely countered by the selective medical incorporation of CAM practices within a biomedical frame of reference, and the increasing trend for doctors to employ CAM either directly or on a subcontracted basis (Cant 2009). The profession, though, was to face still stronger head-on challenges, especially from the state, from the late 20th century onwards.

Challenges by the state to the English medical profession

The subsequent more direct challenges by the state to the medical profession induced further changes; these included ensuring more market exposure, increased professional accountability and, notwithstanding medical resistance, greater patient and public involvement in health care in England (Tritter et al. 2010). This direction was particularly apparent with the incoming Conservative government in the late 1970s. Its policies were based on a desire to gain greater control over the medical profession through managerial reforms, in the face of pressure to reduce costs and rising consumer demand. Given its discomfort with independent self-regulation in medicine, the Conservative Party sought to introduce private sector management philosophies into the NHS by establishing general managers to increase the organisation's efficiency (Ham 2009). However, whilst this threatened the income, status and power of the profession, doctors largely neutralised this attempt at change by themselves filling such posts and limiting its impact on the ground (Harrison & Pollitt 1994). A similar fate awaited the desire of the government to bring an internal market into the NHS through a purchaser–provider split, which did not significantly shake medical professional dominance – even if it led to the enhancement of the relative position of fundholding general practitioners (GPs) (Saks 2003). Nor did the introduction of a Patients' Charter in the early 1990s give users much more of a voice, as the rights and standards set out were formalistic, limited and non-mandatory – at a time of rising class, gender and ethnic inequalities in health (Ham 2009).

The New Labour government that came into office in 1997 posed yet another threat to the interests of the medical profession, as it was intent on modernising the state health service. Nonetheless, the establishment of primary care groups with commissioning powers further increased the standing of GPs (Klein 2013), who formed approximately half of the medical profession relative to the burgeoning numbers and spread of hospital specialists (Larkin 2000). However, aside from the ongoing restratification of the medical profession as the balance swung from specialists to generalists (Calnan & Gabe 2009), New Labour showed its determination, in official publications like *The NHS Plan* (DoH 2000), to engage in such actions as reducing waiting times, increasing the employment of information technology, creating independent Foundation Trusts and encouraging a closer relationship with private providers in the NHS. It was also keen to extend user engagement in health care – as manifested by the founding of the Nursing and Midwifery Council to replace the United Kingdom Central Council and the English National Board for Nursing, Midwifery and Health Visiting, and the Health Professions Council to supplant the Council for the Professions Supplementary to Medicine, which both had greater lay representation

(Allsop & Saks 2002). The General Medical Council itself was also obliged to enhance its lay constituency, and was overseen, along with other health professions, by the new Council for Healthcare Regulatory Excellence, which was established to ensure consistency and good regulatory practice in the health arena (Ham 2009).

Such reforms were driven, at least in part, by growing concerns by the state regarding the abuse of self-regulatory powers in the health professions – not least in medicine, with the notorious case of Dr Harold Shipman, who killed over two hundred patients without detection by the regulatory mechanisms of the medical profession. The position was exacerbated by a range of other cases of medical abuse, from the removal of organs from the deceased without consent at Alder Hey Hospital in Liverpool, to heart surgery on children with excessively high mortality rates at Bristol Royal Infirmary (Allsop & Saks 2002). The result was the government-commissioned Donaldson Review, which aimed to improve medical procedures for patient safety, to ensure effective revalidation of practitioners, and to enhance the role, structure and function of the General Medical Council (DoH 2006a). This review was paralleled by the Foster Review, with a similar remit for other health-related professions (DoH 2006b). The result was *Trust, Assurance and Safety: The Regulation of Health Professionals in the 21st Century* (DoH 2007), a White Paper that included proposals designed to ensure more independent regulatory bodies, continuous fitness to practice, improvements to the educational function of regulators and an expanded information set about health professionals in the public domain. These precursors translated into the 2008 Health and Social Care Act, which variously enhanced medical transparency, significantly diminished the self-regulatory powers of medicine and amplified the public voice in relation to the medical profession.

But if the medical profession could be seen to be in retreat in relation to its interests following the implementation of New Labour policies, there were further changes after the Conservative and Liberal Democratic Coalition came to power in 2010, with a more deregulatory approach in the wake of its Big Society ideology (Ishkanian & Szreter 2012). The philosophy of the government was set out in the White Paper *Equality and Excellence: Liberating the NHS* (DoH 2010), which sought to cut management costs and foster devolved self-regulation to increase efficiency, using Monitor as a central economic regulator – while at the same time facilitating increased patient choice of healthcare professions, yet more public information in relation to medical performance and the growing commercialisation of the NHS. Needless

Mike Saks 143

to say, the medical profession opposed the more pronounced and challenging market approach (Klein 2013). However, following further consultation with stakeholders, the main reforms were put in place through the 2012 Health and Social Care Act. A key aspect of these reforms was to give major commissioning responsibility to GPs as chairs of new Clinical Commissioning Groups. Notwithstanding GPs' initial reluctance to engage, this further underwrote the rising star of general practice in the ongoing restratification of medicine – despite the subsequent top-down management from NHS England, and representation from hospital consultants and other health professions on such bodies (Speed & Gabe 2013).

One further aspect of the Coalition reforms (in terms of doctors) from a neo-Weberian viewpoint was the dissolution of a number of structural boundaries between health and social care. This built on the reforms of New Labour, which brought into being for the first time a social work profession based on exclusionary social closure early in its period of office (Rogowski 2010). As a result of the Coalition reform programme, social work became absorbed into a new Health and Care Professions Council that unified the regulation of the allied health and social care professions – along with broadening the remit of the National Institute of Clinical Excellence in its task of establishing national standards, reflected in its renaming as the National Institute for Health and Care Excellence (Klein 2013). Health and Wellbeing Boards were also established for health and care professions, including medicine, to enable them to work together locally. In turn, the Professional Standards Authority for Health and Social Care – previously entitled the Council for Healthcare Regulatory Excellence – came into existence to provide more inclusive oversight arrangements (Saks 2014b). In addition to these measures, which positively encouraged collaboration across previously silo-based professional boundaries founded on competing interests (Pollard et al. 2009), it was appropriate that – along with government enhancement of the standards of inspection of the Care Quality Commission – the General Medical Council implemented procedures in 2013 for revalidating doctors on a five-year cycle.

The English medical profession in comparative context

Overall, therefore, in the wake of the counterculture and subsequent Conservative, New Labour and Coalition health policies, there have been many changes to the medical profession, which can also be linked to the rise of the new public management (NPM) – especially with the ever growing emphasis on evidence-based medicine (EBM) and externally policed outcome measures (Speed & Gabe 2013). As such, the medical profession has been subject to increasing critical scrutiny in the face of rising market pressures and more bureaucratic monitoring, as well as the enhanced influence of users, all of which has impacted on medicine at the micro, meso and macro levels. While there have been claims about de-professionalisation, these do not stand up strongly, as such challenges – while eroding to some degree traditional professional autonomy – have largely been countered by the profession's own strategies in protecting its interests, such that it still plays a central role in deciding the form of both regulation and quality assurance in education and practice (Chamberlain 2012). In this sense, the medical profession has certainly retained its position of exclusionary social closure in the marketplace, albeit with important shifts. Light (2010) highlights the following main changes: from a training-and-licence accountability to a competency/performance model; from self-regulated embodied trust to enforceable, informed trust against external standards; and from individualistic forms of care to a team approach, with non-medical staff increasingly taking on work previously in the exclusive domain of doctors.

Arguments for this new professionalism in the continuing state shelter of the NHS in a liberal democratic society based on a form of welfare capitalism (Newton & van Deth 2010) are further underwritten by the restratification that has occurred within the medical profession – in which women are now much more strongly represented in an occupational group that has generally retained its dominance over other professions in the health-care division of labour (Chamberlain 2012). As has been seen, this has prompted the steadily increasing standing of GPs in the market in neo-Weberian terms, related to their growing role in commissioning health care under successive governments (see, for example, Calnan & Gabe 2009). In terms of restratification, this rise needs to be contrasted with the declining position of hospital specialists, who are themselves organised hierarchically in terms of income, status and power – from high-ranking fields like cardiology to Cinderella areas such as psychiatry (Saks 2014a). The claims about the general maintenance of medical professional standing as a result of its interest-based strategy in England – despite the challenges it has faced – are further thrown into relief by comparing the position of medicine in this country with that in other neo-liberal societies, in particular in the United States and elsewhere in Europe.

The United States is most akin to England in terms of professionalisation, especially in relation to medicine, where exclusionary social closure is also centred on accreditation, albeit in a more privatised, differentiated and marketised form of capitalism. As Starr (1982) notes, 18th- and 19th-centuries health care was similarly characterised by eclecticism, with a wide spectrum of 'regular' and 'irregular' practitioners in the market, who were difficult to distinguish in a more anti-corporatist system. This context helps to explain variations between the two societies in the timing and nature of professional closure, despite no less powerful lobbying by the American medical profession against 'quackery'. This may help to explain why – despite a parallel knowledge base – the initial professionalisation of American medicine occurred 50 years later in Britain (Stevens 1998). The American profession was also established on a less centralised, state-by-state, basis, with greater medical specialisation, in a manner resonant with a more strongly devolved laissez-faire political culture. The medical monopoly in the United States too was based on a de jure, rather than a de facto model as in Britain, as the ability to engage in health-care practice hinged on state licensure (Berlant 1975). Most significantly, though, there has been greater de-professionalisation of physicians in terms of conditions of service as compared to Britain, primarily because of the much larger impact of private corporations – providing both health care and health insurance – which have striven to drive down costs and exert greater control over physicians (Saks 2003).

Medical interests in the United States, as in Britain, were also threatened by the development of the 1960s and 1970s counterculture, and stronger associated legislative support for the professionalisation of CAM therapies such as osteopathy and chiropractic, as well as powerful consumer lobbies. However, these were, to some degree, countered through medical incorporationism and the ongoing, if shifting, dominance of medicine over other health professions (Saks 2003). Physicians managed too to capitalise on the fee-earning opportunities presented by Medicare and Medicaid when they materialised (Stevens 1998) – as they will doubtless do, alongside multinational corporations, through Obama's 2010 Affordable Care Act (Gibson & Singh 2012). This highlights the contrast with Europe, in many parts of which exclusionary social closure has not emerged in medicine in quite the same way as in the Anglo-American context (Kuhlmann & Saks 2008). This is most clearly exemplified by Soviet Russia, where the medical profession was disestablished after the Bolshevik Revolution, together with other professional groups, which were seen as a political threat to the regime and are only now beginning to re-emerge (Moskovskaya et al. 2013). However, even in Western Europe, medicine in welfare-focused nations such as Sweden (Brante 2010), and state-centrist countries like France (Rodwin 2011), has still proved largely to have been a creature of government, embedded in public service bureaucracies rather than acting as the relatively independent body it generally remains, particularly in England and, to a lesser degree, in the United States.

Nonetheless, even though there is a stronger history of 'professionalisation from within' in the Anglo-American context, as compared to the more pervasive European model of 'professionalisation from above' (McClelland 1991), the picture is by no means straightforward. While, in neo-Weberian terms, there is a weaker tradition of autonomous professions in Continental Europe, the pattern followed in different European countries lies more on a continuum than at polar ends of the spectrum (Collins 1990). It is also subject to change. Thus, professional exclusionary social closure is now more fully established in medicine and elsewhere in some European societies like Germany – although its prevalence in health care is not as great as in England (Kuhlmann et al. 2009). Moreover, medicine and other professions have recently undergone significant transformations in the wider European welfare state, following the example of England. Svensson and Evetts (2010), for instance, observe that, as a result of economic drivers, there has been more of a convergence with that of the Anglo-American context in the form professionalisation has taken in Continental Europe over recent decades.

This sheds interesting comparative light on academics in HE in England who – notwithstanding their own role in credentialism on courses leading to professional qualifications (Parkin 1979) – do not themselves possess the archetypal professional closure extant in medicine in this country. To be sure, bodies such as the University and College Union act on their behalf, and the Higher Education Academy is striving to enhance professional development. However, specific forms of accreditation are not typically required at a national level for recruitment to academic posts, except in the particular professional fields to which they minister, and at the local discretion of lecturers and their professors at the universities concerned. This situation too is changing, with the greater influence of managerialism in English universities and wider government scrutiny, as the nature of HE is reshaped in an era of increasing marketisation (Brown 2013). In this context, there has recently been a strong desire to protect academic autonomy as these agendas have promoted feelings of de-professionalisation amongst academics (Kolsaker 2008). In this sense, just as with the medical profession in England on which this chapter has focused, the past few decades have been times of substantial change in an increasingly neo-liberal privatised knowledge-based society.

Conclusions

In summary, then, as has been seen in this chapter through the lens of a neo-Weberian approach, the fully fledged professionalisation of medicine was introduced from the mid-19th century in England. What has been most striking, though, is the way in which this form of state-supported medical professionalisation has changed in subsequent decades – related to increased market pressures, external monitoring and user demands. Such trends have not so much led to the de-professionalisation of medicine in England, but rather to a restratification of the medical profession. Looked at from an international comparative perspective, the exclusionary social closure gained by the English medical profession is clearly an exemplar, like that of its counterpart in the United States, of 'professionalisation from within' – in contrast to the 'professionalisation from above' that has been more characteristic of some parts of the rest of Europe. As noted in the foregoing, this picture itself is by no means static. In the change agenda involved, the distinction from the position of academics in HE in England is salutary, highlighting the diverse ways in which different knowledge-oriented occupational groups have evolved, even in the same socio-political setting.

References

Allsop, J. & Saks, M. (eds.) 2002. *Regulating the Health Professions*, Sage, London.
Barber, B. 1963. 'Some problems in the sociology of professions', *Daedalus*, Vol. 92, pp. 669–688.
Becker, H. 1962. 'The nature of a profession', in National Society for the Study of Education (ed.) *Education for the Professions*, The University of Chicago Press, Chicago.
Berlant, J. 1975. *Profession and Monopoly: A Study of Medicine in the United States and Great Britain*, University of California Press, Berkeley.
Brante, T. 2010. 'State formation and the historical take-off of Continental professional types: The case of Sweden', in L. Svensson & J. Evetts (eds.) *Sociology of Professions: Continental and Anglo-Saxon Traditions*, Daidalos, Gothenburg.
Brown, R. (ed.) 2013. *Everything for Sale? The Marketisation of UK Higher Education*, Routledge, Abingdon.

Calnan, M. & Gabe, J. 2009. 'The restratification of primary care in England? A sociological analysis', in J. Gabe & M. Calnan (eds.), *The New Sociology of the Health Service*, Routledge, Abingdon.

Cant, S. 2009. 'Mainstream marginality: "Non-orthodox" medicine in an "orthodox" health service', in J. Gabe & M. Calnan (eds.), *The New Sociology of the Health Service*, Routledge, Abingdon.

Chamberlain, J. 2012. *The Sociology of Medical Regulation*, Springer, London.

Collins, R. 1990. 'Market closure and the conflict theory of the professions', in M. Burrage & R. Torstendahl (eds.), *Professions in Theory and History: Rethinking The Study of the Professions*, Sage, London.

DoH (Department of Health). 2000. *The NHS Plan*, The Stationery Office, London.

DoH (Department of Health). 2006a. *Good Doctors, Safer Patients: Proposals to Strengthen the System to Assure and Improve the Performance of Doctors and to Protect the Safety of Patients*, The Stationery Office, London.

DoH (Department of Health). 2006b. *The Regulation of the Non-Medical Healthcare Professions: A Review by the Department of Health*, The Stationery Office, London.

DoH (Department of Health). 2007. *Trust, Assurance and Safety: The Regulation of Health Professionals in the 21st Century*, The Stationery Office, London.

DoH (Department of Health). 2010. *Equality and Excellence: Liberating the NHS*, The Stationery Office, London.

Duffin, J. 2010. *History of Medicine* (2nd edn) University of Toronto Press, Toronto.

Evetts, J. 2013. 'Professionalism: Value and ideology', *Current Sociology*, Vol. 61, No. 5/6, pp. 778–796.

Gibson, R. & Singh, J. 2012. *The Battle over Health Care: What Obama's Reform Means for America's Future*, Rowman & Littlefield, Lanham, MD.

Ham, C. 2009. *Health Policy in Britain* (6th edn), Palgrave Macmillan, Basingstoke.

Harrison, S. & Pollitt, C. 1994. *Controlling Health Professionals: The Future of Work and Organization in the National Health Service*, Open University Press, Buckingham.

House of Lords Select Committee on Science and Technology. 2000. *Report on Complementary and Alternative Medicine*, The Stationery Office, London.

Illich, I. 1976. *Limits to Medicine*, Penguin, Harmondsworth.

Ishkanian, A. & Szreter, S. 2012. *The Big Society Debate: A New Agenda for Social Policy?*, Edward Elgar, Cheltenham.

Johnson, T. 1995. 'Governmentality and the institutionalization of expertise', in T. Johnson, G. Larkin & M. Saks (eds.), *Health Professions and the State in Europe*, Routledge, London.

Jonnergård, K. & Erlingsdóttir, G. 2012. 'Variations in professions' adoption of quality reforms: The cases of doctors and auditors in Sweden', *Current Sociology*, Vol. 60, No. 5, pp. 672–689.

Klein, R. 2013. *The New Politics of the NHS: From Creation to Reinvention* (7th edn), Radcliffe Publishing, London.

Kolsaker, A. 2008. 'Academic professionalism in the managerialist era: A study of English universities', *Studies in Higher Education*, Vol. 33, No. 5, pp. 513–525.

Kuhlmann, E. & Saks, M. (eds.) 2008, *Rethinking Professional Governance: International Directions in Healthcare*, Bristol, Policy Press.

Kuhlmann, E., Allsop, J. & Saks, M. 2009. 'Professional governance and public control: A comparison of medicine in the United Kingdom and Germany', *Current Sociology*, Vol. 57, No. 4, pp. 511–528.

Larkin, G. 1995. 'State control and the health professions in the United Kingdom: Historical perspectives', in T. Johnson, G. Larkin & M. Saks (eds.), *Health Professions and the State in Europe*, Routledge, London.
Larkin, G. 2000. 'Health workers', in R. Cooter & J. Pickstone (eds.), *Medicine in the Twentieth Century*, Harwood Academic Publishers, Amsterdam.
Le Fanu, J. 2011. *The Rise and Fall of Modern Medicine* (2nd edn), Abacus, London.
Light, D. 2010. 'Health care professions, markets, and countervailing powers', in C. Bird, P. Conrad, A. Fremont & S. Timmermans (eds.), *Handbook of Medical Sociology*, Vanderbilt University Press, Nashville, TN.
McClelland, C. 1991. *The German Experience of Professionalization: Modern Learned Professions and Their Organizations from the Early Nineteenth Century to the Hitler Era*, Cambridge University Press, Cambridge.
Moskovskaya, A., Oberemko, O., Silaeva, V., Popova, I., Nazarova, I., Peshkova, O. & Chernysheva, M. 2013. *Development of Professional Associations in Russia: Research into Institutional Framework, Self-Regulation Activity, and Barriers to Professionalization*, Moscow, Higher School of Economics Research Paper No. WP BRP 26/SOC/2013.
Navarro, V. 1986. *Crisis, Health and Medicine: A Social Critique*, Tavistock, London.
Newton, K. & van Deth, J. 2010. *Foundations of Comparative Politics* (2nd edn), Cambridge University Press, Cambridge.
Parkin, F. 1979. *Marxism and Class Theory: A Bourgeois Critique*, Tavistock, London.
Parry, N. & Parry, J. 1976. *The Rise of the Medical Profession*, Croom Helm, London.
Pollard, K., Thomas, J. & Miers, M. 2009. *Understanding Interprofessional Working in Health and Social Care: Theory and Practice*, Palgrave Macmillan, Basingstoke.
Porter, R. 1995. *Disease, Medicine and Society, 1550–1860* (2nd edn), Cambridge University Press, Cambridge.
Porter, R. 2001. *Quacks: Fakers and Charlatans in English Medicine*, Tempus Publishing, Stroud.
Rodwin, M. 2011. *Conflicts of Interest and the Future of Medicine: The United States, France and Japan*, Oxford University Press, New York.
Rogowski, S. 2010. *Social Work: The Rise and Fall of a Profession?*, Policy Press, Bristol.
Saks, M. 1995. *Professions and the Public Interest: Medical Power, Altruism and Alternative Medicine*, Routledge, London.
Saks, M. 1996. 'From quackery to complementary medicine: The shifting boundaries between orthodox and unorthodox medical knowledge', in S. Cant & U. Sharma (eds.), *Complementary and Alternative Medicines: Knowledge in Practice*, Free Association Books, London.
Saks, M. 2000. 'Medicine and the counter culture', in R. Cooter & J. Pickstone (eds.), *Medicine in the Twentieth Century*, Harwood Academic Publishers, Amsterdam.
Saks, M. 2003. *Orthodox and Alternative Medicine: Politics, Professionalization and Health Care*, Sage, London.
Saks, M. 2005. 'Political and historical perspectives', in T. Heller, G. Lee-Treweek, J. Katz, J. Stone & S. Spurr (eds.), *Perspectives on Complementary and Alternative Medicine*, Routledge, Abingdon.
Saks, M. 2010. 'Analyzing the professions: The case for the neo-Weberian approach,' *Comparative Sociology*, Vol. 9, No. 6, pp. 887–915.
Saks, M. 2012. 'Defining a profession: The role of knowledge and expertise', *Professions and Professionalism*, Vol. 2, No. 1, pp. 1–10.

Saks, M. 2014a. 'Professions, marginality and inequalities', *Sociopedia*, Available online at http://www.isa-sociology.org/publ/sociopedia-isa/ (accessed 15 March 2015).
Saks, M. 2014b. 'The regulation of the English health professions: Zoos, circuses or safari parks?', *Journal of Professions and Organization*, Vol. 1, pp. 84–98.
Speed, E. & Gabe, J. 2013. 'The health and social care act for England 2012: The extension of "new professionalism"', *Critical Social Policy*, Vol. 33, No. 3, pp. 564–574.
Stacey, M. 1992. *Regulating British Medicine: The General Medical Council*, Wiley & Sons, Chichester.
Starr, P. 1982. *The Social Transformation of American Medicine*, Basic Books, New York.
Stevens, R. 1998. *American Medicine and the Public Interest*, University of California Press, Berkeley.
Svensson, L. & Evetts, J. 2010. 'Introduction', in L. Svensson & J. Evetts (eds.), *Sociology of Professions: Continental and Anglo-Saxon Traditions*, Daidalos, Gothenburg.
Tritter, J., Koivusalo, M., Ollila, E. & Dorfman, P. 2010. *Globalisation, Markets and Healthcare Policy: Redrawing the Patient as Consumer*, Routledge, Abingdon.
Turner, B. 1995. *Medical Power and Social Knowledge* (2nd edn), Sage, London.
Waddington, I. 1984. *The Medical Profession in the Industrial Revolution*, Gill & Macmillan, London.
Weber, M. 1968. *Economy and Society: An Outline of Interpretive Sociology*, Bedminster Press, New York.

8
The State and Medicine in the Governance of Health Care in Portugal

Tiago Correia, Graça Carapinheiro and Helena Serra

Introduction

According to Newman (2005), the way the state, public and private stakeholders, the health professions and the market connect with each other determines the structure of governance in health care in each particular country. This concept stresses a more complex and diversified set of regulatory mechanisms and practices than those provided by the broad typologies that divide Western health-care systems into national health services (the Beveridge model), social security systems (the Bismarck model) and private health insurance systems (the market model) (see van der Zee & Kroneman 2007 for a synthesis). Countries sharing the same typology may actually reflect different governance arrangements, depending on the threefold articulation between the state, the professions and the market. In some cases, network-based governance has pride of place (the Netherlands or Norway); in others that key position is taken either by the state (the United Kingdom) or health professionals (in which case medicine may stand alone (Germany) or be obliged to negotiate with other health professions (Denmark)) (Burau & Vrangbæk 2008).

As regards Portugal, the place of medicine and its relationship with the state is still poorly understood, in particular in comparison with countries sharing the Beveridge model. In those, it is well known that tighter regulation of accountability and performance has become the main policy to reform the governance of health care (Kuhlmann & Saks 2008). Such policies must be rooted in broader processes and not exclusively in the health sector – an issue that is highlighted by other contributions to this book. Such process is connected with the knowledge society but in a way that affects well-established professions. Like medicine in its professionalisation (Freidson 1970), health management and other health professions nowadays make use of the status of their scientific knowledge to claim authority over new professional jurisdictions or compete for established jurisdictions in health care. Another of those processes is linked to the disengagement of the welfare state from areas traditionally under its protection, for example, the health sector, as competition and marketisation increase within the public administration in most European countries (Burau & Vrangbæk 2008). The latter process is what is commonly known as the new public management (NPM), which originated in public-choice theory and managerialism (Gruening 2001).

Of particular relevance for Portugal is the key position the medical profession continues to play in health care as against other stakeholders, including the state and other health professions (see Lopes 2006; Carvalho 2012, 2014). Moreover, according to a recent enquiry, the Portuguese continue to rely more on physicians than any other health professionals or patients' associations (Espanha et al. 2013). In sum, the place and role of medicine in Portugal apparently fails to confirm the evidence pointing towards increasing criticism of medical authority, the sharing of power with other health professions and the lack of trust in medical autonomy by better-informed citizens. While these transformations are taking place, and are also expected to expand in the future in Portugal, our standpoint here is that processes of change should be perceived as cumulative rather than a break with the past. National dynamics profoundly affect how broader trends, such as those described, turn out in each country. In relation to Portugal, after the dictatorship fell in 1974 and the transition of the Social Security System to the National Health Service (NHS) was legally accomplished in 1979, neither health professionals and the population in general, nor the politicians and regulators, were really more detached institutionally from previous ways of working, in particular with regard to the place given to physicians as the centrepiece in the governance of the health-care system (Carapinheiro 2006).

With this background in mind, this chapter brings together the evidence of three pieces of medical sociology research in Portugal, conducted 20 years apart (Carapinheiro 1993; Serra 2008; Correia 2012a). Each of these followed qualitative, in-depth methods focusing on specific features of the medical profession. Here, they are joined together and reinterpreted from a specific angle: the capacity of physicians to influence the way health policies are applied at the workplace level in public hospitals. The dimensions on which this examination is based are as follows:

(i) the aim and scope of NPM;
(ii) the colonization of management tools by medical professionals; and
(iii) the medical control of technologies in health care.

From the past to the present in health policy

In most countries, NPM has led the state to tighten its control over the national regulatory frameworks for health care, in order to achieve greater predictability and a reduction in the waste of resources. However, there are three ideas about health policy that are often mistaken. These are, firstly, that health policies resulted from the regulation of medicine; secondly, that ethical/moral issues underpinned the emergence of health policies; thirdly, that health policies were established after the Second World War.

The spread of health policies in Western countries registered differences both in speed and in motives. As Foucault (1979) describes, the first type of modern health policy was originally pursued in Germany in the early 18th century, as part of the state strategy to manage demography in the context of ongoing wars. Medical training and practice became partially subject to state regulation, which gave rise to national-level health plans and the creation of medical policies aimed at supervising and controlling populations. The second type was visible in late 18th-century France. In this case, the concerns of the increasingly influential urban bourgeoisie were behind the rise of health policies. These were centred, in particular, on the collectivisation of urban spaces, such as cemeteries, sewers and basements, which were perceived as threatening public health. Sanitary policies, including quarantine against the plague, emerged at that time. In this case, medicine did not serve as a means for the state to control the population, as in Germany, but rather to identify, group, delimit and oversee outbreaks of disease ('sanitary medicine'). A third type of health policy was particularly visible in England in the second half of the 19th century, when diseases became statistically correlated with poverty and unemployment in the industrial era. State health-care policies sought to provide social assistance for the poor through the control of vaccination, the specification of housing conditions and clinical registration.

In short, these three points in European history reveal differences in health policy: this was implemented according to specific political and economic demands that, in turn, created differences in the interplay between the state and medicine. On the other hand, regardless of such differences, the interdependence between these two players became common in Western countries. The more medical knowledge was regarded as the sole basis to define and defeat diseases, the more medical and state regulation overlapped. Scientifically tested allopathic medicine became one of the expert systems that states most needed to expand their administrative rationale. This eventually boosted the autonomy and authority of medicine throughout the various countries, producing the so-called golden era of medicine (Turner 2006).

In sum, with reference to health policies in Western societies, the following should be considered:

(i) The processes through which the body, health and illness became collective issues, and thus a matter of public concern and surveillance.
(ii) The different aims encompassed by medical knowledge, involving both dependence on and independence from the state (that is, the aim of assistance for the poor and the control and protection of workers, the sanitary aim for the population at large, and the liberal aim for the richer, according to the rules of the market) (Herzlich & Pierret 1987).

At present, further changes in the interplay between the state and medicine are reigniting this discussion. Not only have different players emerged, such as pharmacologists, biotechnologists (Clarke et al. 2010) and private investors in increasingly liberalised markets (Mirowski & Plehwe 2009), but financial constraints have also led the states to increase their control over medical procedures. Today's public policies are shaped by NPM rationale and thus aim to introduce the 3Es into public organisations: economics, effectiveness and efficiency (Rhodes 1994). Generally speaking, the public sector is run and funded, like private corporations (Ferlie et al. 1996; du Gay 2000), through the strengthening of bureaucratic procedures. It is expected that greater objectivity and predictability will be achieved when dealing with uncertainty and the lack of transparency by the discretionary use of scientific knowledge (Slater 2001; Gabe 2004; Chamberlain 2009). This issue has been addressed, in particular, with regard to medical autonomy and authority. Cross-country analyses converge in showing the states involved as generally pursuing strategies that enhance their position in the governance of health-care systems. However, the consequences for medicine seem contradictory, given that the results vary between continued autonomy and greater accountability (Davies 2004).

Sociological perspectives of the governance of health care in Portugal

The Portuguese health-care system has undergone comprehensive reforms, just like its Western counterparts. Although the underlying reasons are similar, the outcomes diverge, notably in the influence of medical professionals on shaping regulatory mechanisms and practices. In other words, despite the strengthening of hierarchical control over professional autonomy, which has made medical professionals more accountable and has led to an evaluation of their procedures and performance, a number of studies in Portugal have noted strategies of medical professionals within the organisations that protect occupational professionalism (e.g. values based on trust, competence, identity and cooperation; see Evetts 2005). It is therefore important to shed light on how medical professionals maintain, almost intact, self-regulation over procedures and performance, by either bypassing tighter state regulation, or bringing it within their own jurisdiction.

Readers who are not familiar with the Portuguese situation should be aware of the gap commonly identified in Southern European countries between how institutional policies are presented and how they are implemented (Gough 1996). This issue reveals the contrast between the analyses by medical sociologists and those of health economists and policy analysts. Whereas the latter draw their conclusions from institutional features, the former pay attention to the processes taking place within organisational spaces. Fundamentally, the conclusions sociologists have managed to reach remain invisible to the eyes of other disciplines in Portugal.

By following qualitative and intensive data collection techniques, Portuguese medical sociologists have sought to provide a comprehensive explanation of precisely how the legal transformations in the health-care system impact on the micro-level relationships that exist in health organisations. This includes the study of internal differences in the medical profession, as well as the interplay of physicians with other health professionals, and with managers and patients. The evidence presented in this chapter draws on the conclusions of three of these studies (Carapinheiro 1993; Serra 2008; Correia 2012a), which

156 *Professionals in Health*

related, in particular, to the relationship between the state and medicine within public hospitals. We intend here to provide a schematic and longitudinal reading of the interplay between state regulation and professional self-regulation in Portugal, regarding the medical professionals' strategies to bypass, react to and in some cases control the constraints externally imposed by hospital administrators. It is important to mention that, despite the internal hierarchies in the medical profession, which are important to reaching an understanding of the strategies medical professionals can or cannot employ, they are not analysed in this discussion. They involve a more comprehensive reading of the medical profession in Portugal, which remains to be conducted. For the moment, the intention is to shed light on certain conditions that help us to understand how medical professionals succeed in resisting pressures introduced externally by the state within the framework of NPM. The market also remained outside the analysis, given that its implications for the medical profession have only recently started to be grasped in greater detail.

The aim and scope of NPM in the Portuguese NHS

In classical studies, terms such as advisory bureaucracy (Goss 1963) and professional bureaucracy (Bucher & Stelling 1969) are used to describe the organisational structure of hospitals, given the effects of the authority exerted by medical professionals. Essentially, this reflects the role of expertise in defining bureaucratic procedures.

In publicly funded and managed hospitals in particular, the state hierarchy necessarily encounters medical self-regulation. On the one hand, the NHS model presumes a single voice of command in the provision of and access to health care. Historically, on the other hand, the development of hospitals has overlapped with the professionalisation of medicine (Coe 1984).

According to recent studies, the maintenance of self-regulated medical spaces in hospitals has no general pattern in Western countries, in view of the differences in the roles of nurses, management and users in the arrangements for hospital governance (see examples in Kuhlmann et al. 2013). The evidence relating to Portugal demonstrates that the medical professionals have always played a key position in governing hospitals, by either unsettling or replacing managerial authority. Not only do the independent interests of those in charge of a ward usually prevail over those of the hospital's board of directors, but medical rationale outweighs administrative logic in arranging organisational spaces:

To a certain extent, the wards are not organised to offer the assistance, teaching and research (...) that the country needs. They are moulded much more in line with the personal interests of the medical directors who run them and work in them. (...) In a teaching hospital like this, which still has an almost medieval tradition, in some ways this is felt much more strongly.

(Physician 1988)

The hospital administrators might have the support of a clinical director and a nursing director... but they aren't physicians (...) In practice, have they altered the way I work? No, they haven't. Despite all the changes that have taken place more recently [in the direction of the NPM rationale], the physicians still have muscle. Even the administrators who dare to pressure us directly and threaten us are afraid of the consequences. A physician can say before a judge, 'That patient died because of the administrator's decision.' That is hell and can end up in a court case. So the physicians are very strong. They have a lot of power and they sometimes forget this. And so that's another reason why I say that I am not afraid of anything or anyone in my daily professional life (...).

(Physician 2010)

Even though these two statements were made over twenty years apart, they point towards the same issue: the medical professional's authority underpinned by the use of 'discretion'. Apparently, this has not been limited over time, either formally, by the regulators, or informally, by increasingly demanding users. In fact, discretion has consistently been the medical professionals' main strategy to fight back external pressures, even in the context of managerialism, for example, where non-clinical administrators are formally accountable for running hospital organisations.

Shaping how health care is organised and delivered is one of the cornerstones of the NPM rationale in Portugal. Generally speaking, it means non-clinical administrators are given the authority to define the nature, content and form of the professionals' work organisation. However, the changes in the way organisations function fall far below expectations:

Governments insist on hospitals having more and more rules and greater compliance with them by medical professionals (...) as they can't have everything their own way. However, it's very hard working with them. They go against us [administrators] and want no interference in their work. It is very difficult to change the way medical professionals organise their own and the nurses' work; information is not shared with administrators. Besides, it is virtually impossible to understand their minds from a rational point of view.

(Administrator 2010)

What this evidence shows is that medical professionalism continues to shape the hospital space and processes. The issue is to understand how medical professionals succeed in resisting the changes imposed by administrators if administrators are legally charged with controlling the hospitals' administrative processes and procedures. This explanation must be sought in the aim and scope of the policies implementing NPM in Portugal. Firstly, NPM should be understood as a normative conception that depends on each country's institutional features and right- and left-wing parties' ideologies (Gruening 2001). In the United Kingdom, NPM has turned into national-level policies aiming at the structural control of medical knowledge (e.g. regulatory institutions providing standard specifications, inspection of performance and the reconfirmation of physicians' registration (see Harrison 2003)). In contrast, NPM in Portugal has restricted itself more to the financial control of organisations (Correia 2012a). On this evidence, alongside the hospital-centred configuration of the Portuguese NHS, conclusions may be drawn as to medical professionals' ongoing power in relation to other health professions, hospital administrators and the state, due to their control of medical knowledge (Carapinheiro & Page 2001; Correia 2012a). Decisions on what to do, and when and how to do it, remain under medicine's jurisdiction.

The colonisation of hospital management by medical professionals

The arguments set out in the section 'The aim and scope of NPM in the Portuguese NHS' seem to show that medical professionals stand in opposition to administrators. Yet what the evidence really suggests is a hybrid position between them, as they may oppose as much as cooperate. More importantly, the data also suggests that some medical professionals have colonised the managerial instruments in hospital organisations. By colonisation we mean the process by which professionals on a more individual basis, or professions in more structural terms, make use of other professions' tasks, knowledge and rationale in order to strengthen their own professionalism. In this case, we refer to surgeons selecting, appropriating and making use of administrative instruments as a means of protecting their own positions within hospitals. Although this process is not common among medical specialties, discussing it in the context of stricter managerial rules is meaningful. Against the background of recent debates on the interplay between managerialism and professionalism, this evidence suggests not only that professionals are willing to accept new organisational orders (Exworthy & Halford 1999), but that hybrid professionalisms are arising within professions (Noordegraaf 2007; Correia 2013). It also underlines the fact that professionals undertake individual strategies to strengthen their positions within bureaucracies (Faulconbridge & Muzio 2008).

In 2002, Law 27/2002 was passed by the Portuguese parliament, with the aim of redesigning hospital governance, in particular by turning public hospitals into public corporations. This transformation, usually referred as 'corporatisation', can also be seen in other NHS countries subject to NPM rationale. Broadly speaking, it means aligning the rules for funding and human resources in the public administration with the rules prevailing in the private sector. For this reason, administrators are given stronger powers to enhance efficiency and control over professional discretion (see Correia 2011 for a detailed description).

That law, with other pieces of legislation that followed, was intended to centralise hospital governance under the administrators' control. In particular, this involved financial matters (drawing up hospital and ward budgets and setting and controlling performance targets) and quality (controlling technological tools, auditing clinical procedures, setting quality targets and clinical guidelines, monitoring patient safety programmes, evaluating malpractice, rewarding best practices, defining staff qualifications).

The empirical research conducted on the corporatisation of public hospitals in Portugal (Correia 2012a) suggests that a managerial/bureaucratic hierarchy coexists with well-established medical power that is exerted from the bottom up by medical professionals in wards. Administrative changes on the top level of the hospitals have taken place, although their influence is poorly established at the different levels of the organisation. Accordingly, professionals have continued to control some of the tools that administrators were expected to secure more firmly after the reforms were put into practice. Forms of partnership between physicians and other health professionals such as nurses, and even patient involvement in hospital governance have also been poorly developed. Moreover, as a result of the fragmented and limited power that administrators were able to exert over the physicians' self-governance, managerial governance itself lacks transparency and, more importantly, the outcomes vary in different hospitals. One of the cases that best illustrate the tensions and intersections between hospital administration and medical professionals in Portugal, specifically regarding the latters' colonisation of managerial tools, relates to the integrated responsibility centres (IRCs). These units were created within public hospitals exclusively for medical specialties with a high level of technical specialisation, technological dependence and patient turnover. They are fully independent with regard to their assets, finances and human resources (see Correia 2014):

> An IRC represents financial and administrative independence, which is ideal for us. It would allow us [surgeons] to hire in line with the head of ward's specific targets; we could invoice our work and then pay our salaries. Part of the profits we [surgeons] brought to the hospital would ultimately be distributed in the unit [IRC] for investment and staff.
>
> (Surgeon 2010)

> Transplants play a huge role in the hospital's financing as they increase its case mix index. We [administrators] have found a totally different structure there from other wards so we choose not to interfere. The surgeons are the ones who must take the decisions there! We generally know how they are organised and the way they distribute their own financial incentives, though without interfering in the process. We are not even worried about trying to implement other criteria there.
>
> (Administrator, 2010)

First, these excerpts demonstrate that professionalism and managerialism do not necessarily conflict. This argument has also found support in recent debates drawing attention to hybrid interests linking medicine and management (Noordegraaf 2007; Jespersen & Wrede 2009; Goodall 2011; Saltman et al. 2011; Reich 2012; Kuhlmann et al. 2013). In this case, medical and managerial values meet with regard to the standardisation of procedures, greater efficiency and predictability, greater productivity, and economy in the use of resources. The more procedures are performed, the more money comes into the hospital through the surgeons. If we look back in time, similar trends were visible in physicians' concerns with being more profitable and productive 20 years ago (Carapinheiro 1993):

There are pros and cons to choosing to specialise. The advantage is that with the same resources we produce much more protocols and better structures are created. This is a huge advantage for patients, the hospital and the interns (...) I think that the move of this department towards specialisation is a must. There are more advantages than disadvantages!

(Physician 1988)

Second, the excerpts point out the medical control of managerial tools in hiring professionals and staff, defining salaries, distributing profits, defining teams and so on. The very establishment of IRCs implied the need for professionals to make use of bureaucratic tools. Given that IRCs have been created by the government in order to enhance the quality of highly specialised medical expertise within the NHS, medical colonisation of managerial tools is ultimately strengthened by the state. As the most innovative managerial event in health care in Portugal, IRCs can only be run more effectively if new and strengthened managerial tools and procedures are defined and assessed on the basis of medical criteria. Otherwise, surgeons will not be interested in getting involved, nor will administrators know how to meet professionals' needs.

Medical control over health technologies

The control of health technologies is the third example of the intersection between the state and medical regulation. As noted, the setting of the quality of medical procedures in countries where health care is publicly funded creates a paradox: the need for public investment in technologies coexists with the inability to control them. That is to say, in the context of the knowledge society, expertise is not only secured by traditional professions such as medicine, but the expertise itself is perceived as a threat to public security (Nowotny et al. 2001) – and yet the state continues to rely on medicine's discretionary expertise for the selection and use of technical procedures in health care. Moreover, access to technology gives rise to competition among hospitals, medical specialties, wards and patients. Regarding hospitals and medical specialties more particularly, the control of technologies allows them to attract public and private investment as much as it boosts professionals' self-regulation. The study by Serra (2008) shows that cutting-edge wards are defined as such not only due to the technical expertise involved, but also for allowing other hospital areas to develop, which, in turn, stimulates the development of the organisation as a whole. The excerpt below provides evidence from a liver transplant unit (TU):

> It doesn't just involve the whole hospital; in fact, a hospital that has a transplant unit has to be one with excellent services, it has to have a blood service... our blood service is exceptional in transplants and I think it is one of the best I have ever seen. So it really draws the best out of what there is. Some wards were started because of the transplants, the liver transplants. This kind of surgery is really a driving force for every area of a hospital.
>
> (Surgeon 2002)

Actually, this technical rationale reveals more than the interdependence of wards. It indicates the key position of cutting-edge wards in a hierarchy of priorities and funding, making them the driving force of the hospital. Given the scarcity of resources in public administration and the highly differentiated knowledge applied in these units, professionals working there enjoy economic and strategic advantages over other wards, even in the same hospital. Serra (2008) also noted that, to some extent, these wards are immune to unfavourable opinions from the hospital board of directors. One of the surgeon states:

> In comparison to other wards, my impression is that the board of directors gives us preference. For instance, the previous board was 100% for us and we are grateful to them. With other wards things get stuck, work any which way (...) compared to the other wards, we seem to be given preference. Even if there was ill feeling towards the TU, administrators would not be able to openly undermine us. The procedures we perform here are what make this hospital stand out from other hospitals. Therefore, administrators can't say anything against the transplant unit. There has never been any open hostility, never. So, all the boards that have run the hospital have supported us. We are a kind of flagship for the hospital, and administrators do everything in their power to ensure the ward works as well as possible.
>
> (Surgeon 2002)

Other opinions in the hospital regarding the ward are ambiguous. Physicians and nurses often use expressions like 'it's an elitist ward' or 'they are seen with a certain exoticism' (field notes); whatever the standpoint, other professionals' comments testify to the exceptional nature of the cutting-edge ward and the hierarchies it causes within medicine. Though the ward is seen as bringing prestige to the hospital, the other wards consider that they are disadvantaged in relation to it. On the side of the hospital board of directors, the dominance given to cutting-edge wards over other hospital wards is also confirmed. Transplant surgeons have priority over all other surgeons in access to operating theatres. In sum, the administrators do everything possible to allow the transplant surgeons to do their work as well and as quickly as possible. According to one of the administrators:

> The outcome for the hospital is positive, very positive... I mean, look at the situations the patients find themselves in – they are almost dying when they are admitted, but they leave alive and well – that makes the work 'enjoyable'. It's highly gratifying for health professionals to see the fruits of their labour, isn't it? On the other hand, the infrastructure has recently been renewed and well equipped. All this attracts people, particularly the best. The kind of patients admitted there also makes the professionals treat them very carefully; they are very vulnerable and that makes us take great care.
>
> (Administrator 2002)

These findings are enlightening, particularly if we go back to the early 1990s. At that time, Carapinheiro (1993) found the beginning of the strengthening of bureaucratic/managerial procedures inside hospitals that, years later, gave rise to the corporatisation process described in the section entitled 'The aim and scope of NPM in the Portuguese NHS'. According to those initial findings, the formal hierarchical rules continued to be informally bent by medical professionals, up to the point where this affected the bureaucratic functioning of the medical specialties and activities performed in different wards:

> There are early signs that something is growing there [reference to the doctors' attempt to create new wards in the hospital]. We have to be very careful to understand whether it fits in with the rationale of the hospital or if it's just in one man's interest.
>
> (Administrator 1988)

Despite the new principles linked to the 3Es – economy, effectiveness and efficiency (Rhodes 1994) – that are reshaping the governance of hospitals nowadays, the capacity of medical professionals to control organisations scientifically and technologically has remained almost unchanged, a fact that, consequently, determines the financial control. Professionals still have autonomy to decide what technologies are used, when they are used and for whom. The dependence on technology is defined as 'technocracy' (Serra 2010, 2011), which means that medical procedures converge with the managerial rationale insofar as this boosts professional power. To a certain extent, NPM allows medical technocracy to grow stronger. Medical procedures using technologies are viewed as being 'more scientific' than other medical knowledge, besides creating order and certainty in chaos and uncertainty. Technology justifies itself as safe, neutral and objective knowledge. Moreover, according to Nettleton (1995), medicine mobilises public opinion and the state, as long as it controls the use and application of technology.

Not even the rise in Portugal of new health professions related to the use of technological procedures has threatened medical dominance (Lopes 2006). In fact, the strategies of professionalisation, supported by legal recognition through the academic training carried out by professions such as cardiopneumology and radiology, have not changed the medical domination of the social division of hospital work. What has happened has been a mismatch between the skills taught in these new health professions and those that medical professionals allow their members to perform in health organisations. For this reason, the professional independence of these professions is far from being achieved. In contrast to the established form of medicine, the knowledge in these professions means standardisation is controlled from the outside by another profession, thus limiting their recognition in the eyes of the state and users.

The state and medical regulation in Portugal: The ebbs and flows of power

The more health turned into an issue of a public right, the more difficult it became to clearly define state and medical regulation in the governance of health care. Though related, these forms of regulation should remain distinct. In the light of the three studies, we will now discuss the ebb and flow of power between the state and medicine in the governance of health care in Portugal.

The thread linking these studies is that, both formally and informally, medical professionals have managed to employ strategies in workplace contexts that bypass policies imposed externally by the state – thus protecting specific, profession-related interests. These two parties should not be viewed as separate players standing against each other as countervailing forces. Rather, the situation indicates the complex nature of this interplay. The state is as dependent on medical discretion as medicine is on state policies to boost occupational professionalism – hence what we term the ebb and flow of power. This interdependence has arisen from three features encountered in the Portuguese NHS: the aim and scope of NPM, the NHS's strengthened managerial tools and the NHS's technological investment. In particular, the medical professionals' control of managerial tools reveals changes in medical knowledge. More importantly, possession of the control of knowledge is the best strategy for a profession to protect its occupational professionalism. This is precisely what has happened with medicine in Portugal in relation to the strengthening of NPM. Additionally, we have been able to show the extent to which policies formally controlled by the state hierarchy are filtered and reshaped in workplace contexts by those responsible for undertaking them in their daily practice. The issue is that hospital reform has had little impact on the structure of governance of public hospitals. To help the reader grasp the argument more easily, we may summarise the salient features as follows:

(i) The definition of public policies: by legislative or executive bodies that may or may not listen to the regulatory bodies of the medical profession (the National Association, unions or advisory panels).
(ii) The implementation of public policies: in a fragmented manner due to the medical professionals' possession of control within organisational spaces. The governance structure of hospitals has remained almost intact, as the legally required changes at the workplace level have not been fully implemented.
(iii) The monitoring and assessment of public policies at the workplace level: ineffective plans for monitoring and evaluating malpractice, poor performance or non-compliance with the state's regulations.

Previously, we mentioned the contrast between the analyses by medical sociologists and those of health economists and policy analysts. While the latter tend to analyse the ebb of power from the state to the medical profession, with the focus more on institutional processes (point (i)), the former includes in the analysis the flow of power from the medical profession to the state, with the focus on processes taking place within organisations (points (ii) and (iii)). By this we mean that one should not disregard the fact that the mechanisms set out by the state to define an organisation's funding and quality are continuously shaped by professionals in ways that allow them to boost their professional power inside organisations. Two of the strategies identified were the colonisation of professional jurisdictions and the control of instruments (e.g. technologies) that are key to the success or failure of public policies. As a result, medical professionals protect their autonomy and authority inside organisations by:

(i) setting professional jurisdictions;
(ii) influencing organisational models in the NHS (the definition of hospital versus non-hospital care);
(iii) defining how care is provided and evaluated (the control of financial and clinical instruments).

We also argue that the strengthened position of medical professionals within organisations is somehow transposed to macro-level dynamics. If physicians and surgeons control and define how national policies on specialisation, research and education are applied at the workplace level, then the structural legitimacy of medicine in society is reinforced even in the context of NPM.

In sum, organisational change should be perceived as more complex than the application of policies set out at a national level. Rather, those who control knowledge are the key players in determining how institutional reforms in the health-care sector turn out. It is important to mention that medical teaching and training is still restricted to public universities, and mostly defined and assessed by the medical profession itself. This gives it the capacity to gate-keep bureaucratic processes such as the division of labour and access to technologies.

As a consequence, the non-linearity between the regulatory and normative elements of institutions becomes visible (Burau & Vrangbæk 2008). The governance of institutions is as dependent on hierarchy-based regulation as on values not necessarily aligned with those regulatory institutions. This is precisely the space enjoyed by medicine. The increasing control imposed externally by public opinion and the state may be true. However, certain features may favour partial, self-regulated norms and values in order to continue blocking those pressures. Burau (2005) suggests the notion of 'actor-centred governance' as a step forward in conceptualising governance as comprising both institutional and normative dimensions that may or may not overlap. Similarly, our standpoint is that the effectiveness of reforms results less in institutional change itself and should include symbolic dimensions. Otherwise it will be difficult to grasp:

(i) how the medical profession continues to control organisational procedures under the jurisdiction of non-clinical administrators;
(ii) why regulation by the state is not effectively assessed at the workplace level; and
(iii) why the state is ambiguous in strengthening public accountability while allowing medical professionals effective control over the funding and quality of organisations.

These arguments should not underrate the increasing role of the state in the governance of health care in Portugal too. More than ever, these procedures allow the monitoring of performance more accurately; for example, skilled non-clinical managers have been hired for hospitals, information flows have been computerised and so on. Nevertheless, health-care reform has been more effective on the issue of accountability in relation to users and other health professionals than doctors. In the case of users, Correia (2012b) discusses the growing individualisation of access to health care in Portugal. The author means the process by which the state shifts a growing proportion of NHS funding onto the citizens, in addition to the taxes and contributions already paid. According to Organisation for Economic Co-operation and Development (OECD) data for 2011, Portugal was one of the countries where the percentage of co-payments has risen most sharply over the last decade. Portuguese families are now funding twice as much of their access to the NHS, which coexists, in some cases, with third-party funding for voluntary private health insurance. In the case of other health professions, studies have shown not only the dominance of the medical profession over these professions, but also the growing and effective control by the state through the use of those managerial tools that the medical profession has succeeded in controlling or bypassing (Serra 2008; Carvalho 2014). Nursing and other health professions are now under far more external constraints than before.

Final notes

Current analyses of the binomial relationship of state/medicine in the governance of health-care systems highlight different experiences, not only between Europe and North America, but also among European countries. These differences allow us to formulate two ideas: firstly, that comparative analyses of health policies must take contextual variables into account in order to ensure a detailed understanding of the arrangements linking the state, medicine and other health professions within organisations; secondly, that the mechanisms in the regulation of health care are not necessarily the same, despite shared financial constraints and pressures regarding NPM. This explains our concern to make the Portuguese case more visible within the debate. Despite the introduction of measures seeking the rationalisation of public resources, as in many other countries, public regulation has struggled to change the dominant position of medical professionals within health organisations, particularly in the light of the empirical evidence from the early 1990s. More importantly, 20 years later, studies show complex dynamics taking place, in particular with what we termed here the medical colonisation of management tools and the medical control of health technologies. Both cases suggest the strengthening of medical professionalism, even though extensive evidence is still required for the different medical specialties.

Studies in sociology often stand out from those in health economics and policy analysis. Our emphasis is that any discussion about health policies cannot underestimate informal, workplace dynamics in favour of biased institutional analyses. The state has been able to introduce normative changes at the macro level, although the consequences are not similarly transposed into organisations. To better grasp the reasons for this gap, we need to pay attention to the interplay between medicine, the state, management, other health professions and citizens.

In sum, the governance of health care in Portugal indicates interdependence rather than conflict between the state and the medical profession. Accordingly, we refer to the ebbs and flows of power: whereas the power of medicine builds on public policies by the state, the state depends on medicine to ensure the protection of health as a public right.

References

Bucher, R. & Stelling, J. G. 1969. 'Characteristics of professional organizations', *Journal of Health and Social Behavior*, Vol. 10, No. 1, pp. 3–15.

Burau, V. 2005. 'Comparing professions through actor-centred governance: Community nursing in Britain and Germany', *Sociology of Health and Illness*, Vol. 27, No. 1, pp. 114–137.

Burau, V. & Vrangbæk, K. 2008. 'Global markets and national pathways of medical re-regulation', in E. Kuhlmann & M. Saks (eds.), *Rethinking Professional Governance*, Policy Press, Bristol.

Carapinheiro, G. 1993. *Saberes e poderes no hospital [Knowledge and Powers in Hospitals]*, Afrontamento, Porto.
Carapinheiro, G. (ed.) 2006. *Sociologia da saúde: Estudos e perspectivas [Sociology of Health: Studies and Perspectives]*, Editores Pé de Página, Coimbra.
Carapinheiro, G. & Page, P. 2001. 'As determinantes globais do sistema de saúde português [The global determinants of the Portuguese health-care system]', in G. Carapinheiro & P. Hespanha (eds.), *Risco Social e incerteza: pode o Estado Social recuar mais*, Afrontamento, Porto.
Carvalho, T. 2012. 'Adapting to a managerial environment: A case from nurses in Portugal', *Journal of Health Organisation and Management*, Vol. 26, No. 4, pp. 524–541.
Carvalho, T. 2014. 'Changing connections between professionalism and managerialism: A case study of nursing in Portugal', *Journal of Professions and Organization*, Vol. 1, No. 2, pp. 176–190.
Chamberlain, J. M. 2009. 'The changing medical regulatory context: Focusing on doctor's educational practices', *Medical Sociology Online*, Vol. 4, No. 2, pp. 26–34.
Clarke, A., Shim, J., Mamo, L., Fosket, J. & Fishman, J. 2010. 'Biomedicalization: A theoretical and substantive introduction', in A. Clarke, L. Mamo, J. Fosket, J. Fishman & J. Shim (eds.), *Biomedicalization: Technoscience, Health, and Illness in the US*, Duke University Press, Durham.
Coe, R. 1984. 'Development of the modern hospital', in R. Coe (ed.), *Sociology of Medicine*, McGraw-Hill, New York.
Correia, T. 2011. 'New public management in the Portuguese health sector: A comprehensive reading', *Sociologia Online*, No. 2, pp. 573–598.
Correia, T. 2012a. *Medicina: o agir numa saúde em mudança [Medicine: Acting in a Changing Health]*, Mundos Sociais, Lisboa.
Correia, T. 2012b. 'Debating the comprehensive basis of Western healthcare systems in the light of neo-liberalism', *CIES e-Working Paper*, No. 124/2012.
Correia, T. 2013. 'The interplay between managerialism and medical professionalism in hospital organizations from the doctors' perspective: A comparison of two distinctive medical units', *Health Sociology Review*, Vol. 22, No. 3, pp. 255–267.
Correia, T. 2014. 'Connecting medical professionalism and large bureaucracies in the changing hospital governance', *European Journal of Public Health*, Vol. 24, Suppl. 2, pp. 181–181.
Davies, C. 2004. 'Regulating the health care workforce: Next steps for research', *Journal of Health Services Research & Policy*, Vol. 9, No. 1, pp. 55–61.
Du Gay, P. 2000. 'Enterprise and its futures: A response to Fournier and Grey', *Organisation*, Vol. 7, No. 1, pp. 165–183.
Espanha, R., Mendes, R. V., Fonseca, R. B. & Correia, T. 2013. 'The place and the role of internet use in health: The Portuguese case', *Health by Numbers Portugal*, No. 1, pp. 102–110.
Evetts, J. 2005. *The Management of Professionalism: A Contemporary Paradox*, in *Changing Teacher Roles, Identities and Professionalism*, Kings College, London.
Exworthy, M. & Halford, S. 1999. 'Assessment and conclusions', in M. Exworthy & S. Halford (eds.), *Professionals and the New Managerialism in the Public Sector*, Open University Press, Buckingham.
Faulconbridge, J. & Muzio, D. 2008. 'Organizational professionalism in globalizing law firms', *Work, Employment and Society*, Vol. 22, No. 1, pp. 7–25.

Ferlie, E., Pettigrew, A., Ashburner, L. & Fitzgerald, L. 1996. *The New Public Management in Action*, Oxford University Press, Oxford.
Foucault, M. 1979. 'La politique de santé au XVIIIe siècle', in M. Foucault, B. B. Kriegel, A. Thalamy, F. Beguin & B. Fortier (eds.), *Les Machines à Guérir. Aux origines de l'hôpital moderne*, Mardaga, Brussels.
Freidson, E. 1970. *Professional Dominance: The Social Structure of Medical Care*, Transaction Publishers, New Jersey.
Gabe, J. 2004. 'Risk', in J. Gabe, M. Bury & M. A. Elston (eds.), *Key Concepts in Medical Sociology*, Sage, London.
Goodall, H. 2011. 'Physician-leaders and hospital performance: Is there an association?', *Social Science & Medicine*, Vol. 43, No. 4, pp. 535–539.
Goss, M. 1963. 'Patterns of bureaucracy among hospital physicians', in E. Freidson (ed.), *The Hospital in Modern Society*, Free Press, New York.
Gough, I. 1996. 'Social assistance in Southern Europe', *South European Society and Politics*, Vol. 1, No. 1, pp. 1–23.
Gruening, G. 2001. 'Origin and theoretical basis of New Public Management', *International Public Management Journal*, Vol. 4, No. 1, pp. 1–25.
Harrison, S. 2003. 'Governing medicine: Governance, science and practice', in A. Gray & S. Harrison (eds.), *Governing Medicine: Theory and Practice*, Open University Press, Berkshire.
Herzlich, C. & Pierret, J. 1987. *Illness and Self in Society*, Johns Hopkins University Press, Baltimore.
Jespersen, P. & Wrede, S. 2009. 'The changing autonomy of the Nordic medical professions', in J. Magnussen, C. Vrangbæk & R. B. Saltman (eds.), *Nordic Health Care Systems*, Open University Press/McGraw-Hill Education, London.
Kuhlmann, E. & Saks, M. 2008. 'Changing patterns of health professional governance', in E. Kuhlmann & M. Saks (eds.), *Rethinking Professional Governance*, Policy Press, Bristol.
Kuhlmann, E., Burau, V., Correia, T., Lewandowski, R., Lionis, C., Noordegraaf, M. & Repullo, J. 2013. ' "A manager in the minds of doctors": A comparison of new modes of control in European hospitals', *BMC Health Services Research*, No. 13, 246.
Lopes, N. 2006. 'Tecnologias da saúde e novas dinâmicas de profissionalização [Health technologies and new patterns of professionalization]', in G. Carapinheiro (ed.), *Sociologia da Saúde: Estudos e Perspectivas*, Pé de Página, Coimbra.
Mirowski, P. & Plehwe, D. (eds.) 2009. *The Road from Mont Pélerin: The Making of the Neoliberal Thought Collective*, Harvard University Press, Cambridge, MA.
Nettleton, S. 1995. *The Sociology of Health and Illness*, Polity Press, Oxford.
Newman, J. 2005. *Modernising Governance: New Labour, Policy and Society*, Sage, London.
Noordegraaf, M. 2007. 'From "pure" to "hybrid" professionalism: Present-day professionalism in ambiguous public domains', *Administration Society*, Vol. 39, No. 6, pp. 761–785.
Nowotny, H., Scott, P. & Gibbons, M. 2001. *Re-Thinking Science: Knowledge and the Public in the Age of Uncertainty*, Polity Press, Cambridge.
Reich, A. 2012. 'Disciplined doctors: The electronic medical record and physicians' changing relationship to medical knowledge', *Social Science & Medicine*, Vol. 74, No. 7, pp. 1021–1028.

Rhodes, R. 1994. 'The hollowing out of the state: The changing nature of public services in Britain', *Political Quarterly*, Vol. 65, No. 2, pp. 138–151.
Saltman, R. B., Dubois, H. F. & Durán, A. 2011. 'Mapping new governance models for public hospitals', in R. B. Saltman, A. Durán & H. F. Dubois (eds.), *Governing Public Hospitals: Reform Strategies and the Movement towards Institutional Autonomy*, WHO on behalf of the European Observatory on Health Systems and Policies, Copenhagen.
Serra, H. 2008. *Médicos e poder: Transplantação hepática e tecnocracias [Doctors and Power: Liver Transplantation and Technocracies]*, Fundação Económicas/Almedina, Lisbon.
Serra, S. 2010. 'Medical technocracies in liver transplantation: Drawing boundaries in medical practices', *Health*, Vol. 14, No. 2, pp. 162–177.
Serra, H. 2011. 'Das tecnologias às tecnocracias: Novos protagonismos emergentes em saúde [From technology to technocracy: New and emerging protagonisms in health]', in A. Barbosa & J. Silva (eds.), *Economia, gestão e saúde*, Edições Colibri, Lisbon.
Slater, B. 2001. 'Who rules? The new politics of medical regulation', *Social Science and Medicine*, Vol. 52, No. 3, pp. 871–883.
Turner, B. S. 2006. 'Hospital', *Theory, Culture and Society*, Vol. 23, No. 2–3, pp. 573–579.
Van der Zee, J. & Kroneman, M. 2007. 'Bismarck or Beveridge: A beauty contest between dinosaurs', *BMC Health Services Research*, available online at http://www.biomedcentral.com/1472-6963/7/94 (accessed 17 March 2015).

Conclusions
Cross-Country and Inter-Professional Convergences and Divergences in Changes in Professions and Professionalism

Teresa Carvalho and Rui Santiago

Overall background

Professions in the European Union (EU) have faced significant and radical challenges since the beginning of the 1980s. The sources of such challenges are multiple and can be found at the macro, meso and micro levels. At the macro level it is undeniable that the advanced capitalism trajectory has permeated social institutions, which are framed by a new economic rationality that also reaches public institutions (Polanyi 2001; Dardot & Laval 2010; Ward 2012). The spread of this rationality throughout the public sector was supported by the criticism against welfare state 'interventionism' developed by Public Choice Theory. For instance, Hayek (2001) defends that welfare state politics produce a lack of consumer-informed choices, social and economic inefficiency, and, particularly, dependency on professionals' collective and individual corporatist self-interests. However, other authors, such as Foucault, sustain that what is at a stake is a real 'anthropological project' (Foucault 2004) that intends to align 'minds' and 'markets'. This means that changes in the welfare state may not be restricted only to its institutions, but are expected to transform individual and collective systems of beliefs and values, as well as ways of interpreting society's organisation and function (Fournier 1999). In fact, the traditional notions of citizen rights, collectivised well-being, and social responsibilities and socialised risk (Ward 2012) have been presented in some countries' public systems as outdated values that used to characterise 'modernity' but are not adequate for modern times.

In this context, the power of the professional groups – viewed, in its essence, as the expression of a collective corporatism – was elected as a key problem and obstacle to the disengagement of the welfare state from the social areas traditionally under its protection; or, at least, as an obstacle to an in-depth recomposition of these areas towards their realignment with the new logic of economic rationality. In this perspective, professionals are viewed more as self-interested economic agents, or as individual producers of welfare services, targeted to individual expectations and choices of consumers (Freidson 2001) in the marketplace, rather than as self-oriented public agents serving collective and community needs. To some extent, the increasing public scandals on professional bad practices also contributed to this view. As a consequence, the traditional welfare trust in professionals is being replaced by distrust. Professional knowledge is also under pressure, as it is expected that it can become more useful to the market if framed by the so-called knowledge society. To approach potential changes in the professions' institutional and organisational landscapes, it is also essential to understand how far the global and hegemonic tendencies emerging in this field affect the professionals' power and social status, as well as their professional beliefs, values and ideologies.

At the meso level, changes in professions and professionalism can be also connected with the reconfiguration of professional bureaucracies. These, to an increasing degree, are today captured by managerialism and aligned with priorities, practices and norms derived from firm-based or entrepreneurial models. This alignment, renamed as new public management (NPM) in the public sector, supposes the organic (re)construction of bureaucracies, towards more unitary (Carvalho & Santiago 2010) or 'complete organisations' (Enders et al. 2008), aimed at generating a new 'organisational identity' based on an expected self-renovated commitment of professionals to the mission, objectives and values of the organisations. In these attempts to create a new identity, it is expected that organisations will gain competencies and capacities to manage market opportunities in a more rational way, as well as to put forward more efficient mechanisms in order to better allocate their financial and human resources. At least in the public sector, these reconstruction dynamics of organisations as more organic entities translate attempts to deconstruct the 'professional bureaucracies' (Mintzberg 1979), or, in other words, to break the linkage nexus between bureaucracy and professionalism (Bleiklie & Michelsen 2008). Bureaucratic rules and professional power and autonomy, legitimated by expert knowledge, were associated with sustaining the division of professional work. This association has been questioned by the market and NPM assumptions and values. The split between the two is expected to result

174 *Conclusions*

in a decrease in the scope of traditional professional organisational power and autonomy.

Finally, at the micro level, the ways professionals develop their working practices and use their technical autonomy are also under pressure. Strong tendencies to standardise working processes through the introduction of technologies of micro control of the professional practices – as those embodied, for instance, by the quality assurance, performance evaluation and audit systems, which translate new templates to guide professionals' 'technical' decisions – arise. Potentially, this can imply limitations in the discretionary (Evetts 2002) or prudential (Champy 2011) practices, through an increased interference of professionals' judgement by organisational managerial and hierarchical control.

What we have learnt from this book

This book is based on the assumption that the way professions face these set of challenges can be better approached if developed in a comparative way. In fact, it is expected that, due to different professional identities, cultures, ethics, histories and national contexts, professional groups interpret, evaluate and respond differently to similar global principles. Starting from these theoretical and empirical assumptions, three distinct professions – academics (or academia), medical doctors and nurses – were analysed through a cross-national perspective of Portugal, Finland and the United Kingdom. The three countries' social systems embody distinct global models of welfare state.

Changes in state policies and roles

Changes in the welfare state, and their impact on professions, professionalism and professionalisation processes, were analysed within the eight book chapters, which drew their theoretical/conceptual and empirical proposals from the health and higher education (HE) sectors. The offered contents reveal that, in spite of some differences, the transformations promoted by the market, NPM and the knowledge society/economy are actually recognised as being inspired by similar principles and logics; or, at least, as following the same wider tendencies of reform in the European landscape. Referring to both sectors, all the book chapters concede that there is a trend that connects increased efficiency, quality improvement and the orientation of services to the 'citizens/consumers' as the leitmotif of the reforms' legitimacy. There is also a trend across countries, and sectors, to promote services delivery under a dominant managerial and economic logic of rationality. In Portugal, the United Kingdom and Finland, what is clearly identified by the book chapters in the health field is a 'movement' to institutionalise market coordination mechanisms in the National Health Service (NHS). But, in addition, the marketisation tendencies seem to also clearly emerge in HE. Referring to this sector, the authors state that there has been an in-depth reinterpretation of the universities' purposes. According to Guy Neave, universities are being transformed from 'a vehicle for redistributing wealth' into a way of 'creating wealth' (Chapter 1). Helena Hirvonen, arguing on changes in the Nordic welfare system, particularly in respect to the health sector, expresses a view that is not so far from Neave's reasoning. She emphasises, for instance, the fact that the Finland reforms attempted to rationalise the state by cutting public expenditure and introducing new private-like management models. This has resulted in a recalibration of the universalistic ideals that characterised the Nordic welfare state model.

These transformations, in the way states reinterpret how health and HE public goods can be distributed in society, are particularly relevant for the professional groups under analysis, since their professionalisation process has been supported by the state. Taking the example of academics, even if important differences in the way they have been represented in the American, British and Continental European contexts are recognised, Guy Neave's identification of 'its formal status as a state service; that is, a service provided by the state' (Chapter 1) is one of the particularities of academics in the European context. Mike Saks also claims there is strong state support for the medical profession in the British context, identifying the existence of an 'evolving medical–Ministry alliance' (Chapter 7). For the Finnish case, Timo Aarrevaara, reflecting on academics within the context of the Nordic countries, confirms this particularity, arguing that, traditionally, university staff were considered to be 'civil servants' (Chapter 3).

In spite of the transversal character of these transformations, which allows them to be classified as 'travelling ideologies', their impact may not be similar, taking the different national contexts and the specific characteristics of the different professional groups into account. In fact, despite shared financial constraints and ideological pressures regarding NPM, the mechanisms of the state control and regulation of the health and HE sectors and professional groups are not the same.

Convergence and divergence on changing professions and professionalism

Another aim of the comparative analyses presented in this book is also to understand the extent to which these trends threatened the traditional status and power of the three professions. From the analysis presented in the eight chapters it seems clear that NPM-informed policies and technologies on running systems and their institutions, as well as the widespread and hegemonic narratives on the knowledge society, do not have the same effect in the three professional groups. In the specific case of the health professions, there is a cross-country tendency for nurses being more affected than doctors. In the Portuguese context, Tiago Correia, Graça Carapinheiro and Helena Serra, based on a longitudinal analysis developed since the 1980s, demonstrate that medicine has dealt better with transformations and, during this time, its capacity to reshape professional jurisdictions and to influence organisational models in the workplace has not weakened. On the opposite side, Joana Sousa Ribeiro pointed out the highly negative effects of the new political and social institutional framework over nurses. She endorses the hypothesis that, in Portugal, this framework is assisting in nurses' de-professionalisation, and even proletarisation, process. In fact, in recent years, nurses' work conditions have worsened in this country.

These same tendencies, and differences between professional groups, seem to be in place in other national contexts. Mike Saks analyses the doctors' context in England and, based on a historical perspective, contests the idea of the presence of a de-professionalisation process. Although he recognises that important changes have been put in place, with the potential to erode, to some degree, doctors' traditional professional autonomy, he argues that doctors are still able to play a central role in deciding the form of both regulation and quality assurance in medical education and practice. In this sense, they have successfully managed to retain their position of exclusionary social closure in the marketplace. Mike Dent, in analysing the way doctors' face the different types of NPM influence in Britain (primarily in England), presents the same tendencies.

Conversely, presenting a case study of nurses in Finland, Helena Hirvonen refers not only to the perverse effects of the new state policies and forms of control and regulation over structures and the operation of health institutions, but especially in the practices of care and in the cultural understanding of care professionalism. According to her, within this new context professionalism is redefined, with professionals leaving behind traditional universal values and assuming instead the goals, ideals and efficiency targets of their workplaces. And this has even meant these changes in professional subjectivities apparently have disembodied 'traditional' nurses professionalism and replaced it by technical professionalism, which reproduces the gendered representations of care. This new institutional and professional scenario translates what Helena designates as a 'hybrid form of disembodied care professionalism' (Chapter 4).

The similarities found in the different health professional groups across these countries reveals that, in spite of the national and organisational contextual differences, similar tendencies emerge in the way professional groups interpret and respond to external pressures. The tendency for nurses to see their working conditions, status and power more fragile when compared with doctors may signify that the more institutionalised and powerful a professional group is, the more it is able to better 'resist' the pressures of changes in the state and society. Borrowing Bourdieu's (1997) terms, one can raise the hypothesis that professional fields of action, in their roles as mediators of external pressures, have different refractory characteristics: the more autonomous a professional field is, the greater will be its refractory power and, by this argument, the more external impositions can be transformed. Thus, doctors' margins of negotiation and of influence increased, not only over the definition of the new control and regulation rules, employment terms and work conditions, but also over their implementation in the organisations.

Nevertheless, the analysis based on academics identifies the same tendencies for the existence of threats to the traditional power and status of this profession. According to Guy Neave, changes in HE are profound. In fact, they assert that: 'few periods in the history of the universities in Europe have witnessed so many changes across so many dimensions as has been the lot of higher education over the course of the past two decades' (Chapter 1). In their perspective, envisaging these changes in the state and in the knowledge society context, academics are being transformed from an estate into a constituency, serving the market rather than the state. Timo Aarrevaara identified similar trends for the Finish context, where the de-professionalisation process seems to have been carried with the introduction of the New Universities Act (2009), which changed academics' contractual statute from state civil servants to direct employees of the universities.

The attempts to compare the three professional groups presented by Teresa Carvalho and Rui Santiago (Chapter 2) also sustain the identified inter-professional differences with nurses, once again revealing their more fragile position in the system. However, Chapter 2 also highlights relevant intra-professional differences. Specifically, when referring to professional autonomy within the same group some surveyed professionals emphasised losses in autonomy, while others mentioned gains. The authors claim that this may be the result of bilingualism, surface compliance or non-consent, but that it can also be interpreted as the result of distinct power relations based on emerging intra-group professional elites and hierarchies, and/or the competence and recognition of individuals' expertise.

Actually other results, in the cross-country and cross-professional comparative analyses developed throughout the book, also reveal intraprofessional group differences as an important dimension of the impact of NPM, managerialism and the knowledge society over professions. For instance, Mike Saks claims 'internal hierarchies exist within professional groups despite the formal ideology of a community of equals' (Chapter 7). In analysing the same professional group, Tiago Correia, Graça Carapinheiro and Helena Serra argue that even if a strengthening of medical professionalism is identified as a result of changes in health governance, differences arise between medical specialties. Following the authors' reasoning, the internal stratification and, subsequently, the new emerging hierarchy of the medical profession are concerns that should be grasped in further research. Looking now to the case of the academic profession in Finland, Timo Aarrevaara's chapter also highlights the appearance in the system of this internal stratification phenomenon. It is revealed not only when comparing academics in general with those from health disciplines, but also between different academic generational groups.

Open tracks for further research

Following the book chapters' analytical and conceptual proposals, it is our conviction that this book represents an important contribution to the development of the sociology of professions. In fact, this cross-national and cross-professional comparative analysis reveals that the potential impact of NPM and the knowledge society over professional groups can only be fully understood if analysed both from the theoretical/conceptual and empirical perspectives. This encompasses the idea that the analysis undertaken needs to be framed, in general terms, by both the structure and the agency. More specifically, this means that attention has to be given to the co-determination dynamics between the state and social changes and the capacity professional groups have to interpret, evaluate, respond and influence these dynamics. Simultaneously, professional groups cannot be seen as homogeneous entities, since intra-professional dynamics of differentiation, towards stratifying, fragmenting and hierarchising, seem to be a relevant phenomenon nowadays with regard to the panorama of professional groups' positioning in their market labour enclosures. Furthermore, an inter-professional analytical approach needs also to be undertaken, based on an examination of the situation of one group by comparison with another, with similar or opposite conditions. Convergences and divergences resulting from this examination are key insights in understanding how far the transformations in the political, social, economic and cultural environment surrounding professions are deskilling and de-professionalising or, on the contrary, are simply reframing professions. Reciprocally, from an agency perspective, it is also key to give attention to the professional groups' positioning in these processes, namely through strategising and making decisions regarding their responses and actions taken in the face of changes in their wider institutional and closer organisational environments.

References

Bleiklie, I. & Michelsen, S. 2008. 'The university as enterprise and academic co-determination', in A. Amaral, I. Bleiklie & C. Musselin (eds.), *From Governance to Identity: A Festschrift for Mary Henkel*, Springer, Dordrecht.
Bourdieu, P. 1997. *Les usages sociaux de la science: Pour une sociologie Clinique du champ scientific*, Institute Nationale de la Research Agronomic (INRA), Paris.
Carvalho, T. & Santiago, R. 2010. 'Still academics after all', *Higher Education Policy*, Vol. 23, No. 3, pp. 397–411.
Champy, F. 2011. *Nouvelle théorie sociologique des professions*, Presses Universitaires de France, PUF, Paris.
Dardot, P. & Laval, C. 2010. *La nouvelle raison du monde. Essai sur la société néolibérale*, La Découverte/Poche, Paris.
Enders, J., de Boer, H. & Leisyte, L. 2008. 'On striking the right notes: Shifts in governance and the organisational transformation of universities', in A. Amaral, I. Bleiklie & C. Musselin (eds.), *From Governance to Identity: A Festschrift for Mary Henkel*, Springer, Dordrecht.
Evetts, J. 2002. 'New directions in state and international professional occupations: discretionary decision-making and acquired regulation', *Work, Employment and Society*, Vol. 16, No. 2, pp. 341–353.
Foucault, M. 2004. *Naissance de la biopolitique. Cours au collège de France (1978–1979)*, Seuil/Gallimard, Paris.
Fournier, V. 1999. 'The appeal to "professionalism" as a disciplinary mechanism', *Social Review*, Vol. 47, No. 2, pp. 280–307.
Freidson, E. 2001. *Professionalism, the Third Logic*, Polity Press, Cambridge.
Hayek, F. 2001. *The Road to Serfdom*, Routledge, London.

Mintzberg, H. 1979. *The Structuring of Organizations: A Synthetics of Research*, Prentice Hall, Englewood Cliffs, NJ.
Polanyi, K. 2001. *The Great Transformation: The Political and Economic Origin of Our Time*, Beacon Press, Boston.
Ward, S. 2012. *Neoliberalism and the Global Restructuring of Knowledge and Education*, Routledge, New York & London.

Index

Aarrevaara, T., 8, 64, 65, 66, 68, 69, 76, 77, 175, 177, 178
Abbott, A., 1, 11, 37, 59, 102, 109, 110, 115
academic constituency, 8, 24, 25, 26, 27
academic estate, 7, 8, 15, 16, 18, 21, 22, 23, 24, 26
academic guild, 7, 20
academics, 1, 5, 6, 8, 11, 32, 36, 38, 39, 40, 44, 45, 46, 47, 48, 49, 50, 52, 55, 56, 57, 58, 60, 63, 67, 69, 73, 75, 76, 77, 135, 146, 147, 174, 175, 177, 178, 179
accountability, 10, 16, 17, 25, 37, 38, 44, 48, 53, 73, 81, 82, 83, 85, 86, 88, 89, 90, 91, 92, 93, 96, 97, 98, 100, 113, 133, 134, 141, 144, 151, 155, 167
Ackroyd, S., 12, 36, 61, 100
administration, 15, 19, 20, 24, 25, 39, 49, 52, 54, 61, 62, 67, 68, 69, 70, 71, 72, 75, 78, 98, 100, 107, 115, 117, 121, 125, 129, 131–3, 152, 159, 160, 162, 170
administrators, 73, 119, 156, 157, 158, 159, 160–3, 174
Allsop, J., 139, 142, 147, 148
Amaral, A., 11, 12, 15, 17, 23, 28, 29, 59, 60, 61, 62, 179
Anttonen, A., 83, 85, 98
assessment, 8, 12, 23, 25, 48, 53, 62, 87, 89, 127, 165, 169
audit, 9, 37, 38, 81, 89, 90–2, 98, 100, 124, 125, 134, 137, 148, 159, 174
austerity, 9, 81, 83, 98, 104, 105, 109, 110, 117
autonomy, 1–3, 8, 12, 28, 31–7, 41, 44–7, 50, 51, 53–9, 61, 62, 64, 65, 66, 68, 69, 73, 74, 84, 101, 108, 110, 115, 119, 121, 126, 131, 133, 134, 146, 152, 154, 155, 164, 166, 170–1, 173–4

autonomy of practice, 8, 36, 41, 42, 53–9
clinical autonomy, 55, 128
organisational autonomy, 8, 34, 35, 41, 42, 44–7, 50, 53, 57
professional autonomy, 1, 7, 8, 9, 10, 30, 31–2, 34, 36, 37, 42, 43, 46–9, 57, 144, 155, 176, 178
structural autonomy, 8, 34, 42, 43, 45, 46, 53, 57, 58

Barley, S., 120, 128, 129, 130, 131
Bourdieu, P., 6, 11, 31, 59, 177, 179
Brint, S., 1, 11, 33, 37, 53, 60
Buchan, J., 105, 106, 109, 115
Burau, V., 30, 59, 61, 151, 152, 166, 168, 170
bureaucracy, 1, 22, 34, 35, 42, 43, 74, 77, 125, 156, 173
bureaucratic, 2, 5, 6, 10, 34, 35, 43, 55, 57, 64, 68, 92, 104, 112, 144, 156, 159, 161, 163, 166, 173

Calnan, M., 85, 86, 95, 98, 141, 144, 148
Carapinheiro, G., 10, 106, 116, 151, 152, 155, 158, 160, 163, 169, 170, 176, 178
care, 9, 38, 40, 50, 67, 81–9, 90–8, 102, 103–6, 109, 111, 114, 121, 126, 128, 130, 131, 141, 143, 144, 145, 146, 151, 163, 166, 176, 177
care work, 9, 81–9, 90–8
career, 18, 19, 27, 38, 40, 41, 42, 45, 46, 47, 57, 58, 66, 71, 76, 83, 104, 108, 127, 131, 139
Carvalho, T., 1, 4, 5, 8, 11, 12, 30, 32, 36–9, 44, 47, 50, 51, 53, 56, 60, 62, 77, 90, 96, 97, 98, 99, 105, 106, 113, 116, 152, 167, 169, 172, 173, 177, 179

Chamberlain, J., 139, 144, 148, 156, 169
Champy, F., 1, 11, 37, 50, 53, 60, 174, 179
Chandler, J., 94, 98, 99
citizen(s), 2, 23, 64, 66, 82, 92, 152, 167, 168, 174
citizenship, 113, 114
Clark, J., 127, 131, 154, 169
Clark, R., 15, 23, 28, 127
Clegg, S., 35, 36, 60
Comparative, 5, 7, 11, 17, 27, 29, 30, 32, 59, 62, 68, 77, 78, 99, 100, 132, 138, 143, 146, 147, 149, 168, 174, 176, 178
Conceição, C., 106, 116, 117
consumer(s), 2, 28, 42, 72, 92, 133, 141, 145, 150, 172, 173, 174
Continental Europe, 18, 23, 146, 175
control, 1–4, 7, 9, 10, 18, 21, 24, 31, 33–6, 42, 43–5, 47–8, 51, 53–4, 57–8, 61, 65, 69, 71, 73, 85, 86, 89, 100, 104, 112, 113, 114, 119, 120–6, 133, 137, 138, 139, 141, 145, 148, 149, 153, 154–6, 158, 159, 161, 163, 164–8, 170, 174–7
Correia, T., 10, 32, 50, 60, 151, 152, 155, 158, 159, 160, 167, 169, 170, 176, 178
council, 39, 66, 72, 141, 143
  nurses' council, 103, 105, 106, 108, 109, 116, 117, 141
  physicians' council, 109, 134, 138, 142, 143, 150
credentialism, 6, 34, 38, 135, 146

Dahl, H., 84, 99, 101
Davies, 87, 94, 96, 99, 101, 124, 155, 169
de Boer, H., 60, 179
Dent, M., 9, 10, 38, 60, 90, 99, 119, 121, 123, 125, 126, 131, 132, 133, 134, 176
de-professionalisation, 4, 9, 10, 31, 36, 46, 109, 110, 113, 120, 144, 145, 146, 147, 176, 177
Di Luzio, G., 85, 86, 99
Diefenbach, T., 4, 11, 36, 60

Dingwall, R., 38, 60, 61
Discretion, 1, 37, 128, 146, 157, 159, 165
discretionary, 1, 11, 37, 53, 60, 154, 161, 174, 179
disembodied care, 9, 85, 97, 177
disembodied professionalism, 9, 87, 92, 93
doctors, 1, 5, 6, 7, 8, 9, 10, 11, 32, 33, 36, 39, 40, 46, 47, 48, 49, 50–8, 84, 112, 119, 120–9, 130, 132, 135, 136, 138, 140, 141, 143, 144, 163, 167, 174, 176, 177

empowerment, 47, 95, 108
Enders, J., 47, 60, 69, 77, 173, 179
entrepreneurial, 2, 24, 25, 30, 64, 72, 173
Evetts, J., 1, 3, 11, 12, 31, 36, 37, 53, 60, 86, 99, 114, 116, 121, 132, 137, 146, 147, 148, 150, 155, 169, 174
exclusionary, 10, 135, 137, 138, 139, 140, 143, 144, 145, 146, 147, 176
expertise, 3, 4, 33, 34, 35, 37, 54, 56, 59, 82, 86, 102, 127, 156, 161, 178

Ferlie, E., 36, 56, 60, 120, 132, 134, 154, 170
Foucault, M., 2, 4, 12, 113, 116, 153, 170, 172, 179
Fournier, V., 3, 12, 61, 169, 172, 179
Freidson, E., 1, 4, 12, 31, 33, 34, 36, 42, 53, 60, 61, 114, 116, 120, 121, 132, 152, 170, 173, 179

gender, 9, 27, 67, 85, 88, 95, 97, 98, 99, 100, 101, 105, 113, 114, 116, 141
Governance, 3, 9, 11, 12, 15, 18, 20, 25, 36, 38, 39, 43, 47, 54, 56, 58, 59, 60–2, 65, 66, 69, 70, 77, 88, 102, 113, 116, 119, 120, 124–6, 128, 129, 130–2, 134, 148, 151, 152, 155, 156, 159, 160, 163–9, 170, 171, 178–9
Greenwood, R., 2, 12, 121
Gruening, G., 152, 158, 170

Index 183

Häikiö, L., 83, 85, 98
Halford, S., 102, 116, 159, 169
Ham, C., 126, 129, 132, 141, 142, 148
Harrison, S., 119, 120, 121, 123, 126, 130, 132, 133, 141, 148, 158, 170
Haug, M., 110, 113, 116
health, 1, 6, 7, 8, 9, 10, 32, 37, 38, 40, 43, 45–7, 49, 50–2, 56, 57, 59, 60, 61, 67–9, 70, 74–7, 79, 81–6, 89, 90, 93–8, 100–3, 109, 112, 113, 115, 116, 117, 118, 120, 121–3, 136, 139, 141, 142, 143, 151, 156–9, 161, 162, 164, 165, 174, 175, 176–8
health-care, 6, 9, 50, 87, 102, 103, 105, 106, 108, 111, 114, 121, 130–2, 136, 137–9, 141, 142, 144, 145, 151–3, 155, 161, 164, 166, 167
health policy, 103, 153, 154, 168
health-related sciences, 65, 67
health services, 64, 86, 102, 119, 135, 139, 151, 152
National Health Service, 38, 102, 139, 140, 141, 152, 175
Henriksson, L., 81, 83, 84, 85, 92, 97, 99
higher education, 1, 5, 13, 15, 16, 17, 19, 21, 22, 23, 24, 25, 27, 32, 54, 64, 108, 135, 146, 174, 177
higher Education policy, 17
Hirvonen, H., 9, 81, 83, 87, 88, 89, 95, 99, 100, 175, 176
hospital, 5, 6, 8, 10, 38, 39, 40, 43, 46, 53, 54, 56, 57, 70, 86, 87, 103, 104, 105, 106, 119, 120–9, 130, 131, 138, 139, 141–4, 153, 156–9, 160–7
Hunter, D., 36, 49, 61, 133
hybrid, 9, 10, 89, 97, 114, 120, 123, 127, 128, 130, 158, 159, 160, 177
hybrid doctors, 10, 120, 125

identity, 4, 18, 22, 23, 25, 27, 37, 95, 104, 112, 155, 173
internal hierarchies, 136, 156, 178
inter-professional, 50, 57, 172, 178, 179
intra-professional, 50, 178, 179

Johnson, T., 1, 12, 33, 61, 133, 137, 148, 149
jurisdiction, 1, 2, 4, 10, 42, 43, 102, 104, 109, 110, 121, 152, 155, 158, 166, 167, 176

Kitchener, M., 36, 61, 124, 125, 133
Klein, R., 121, 133, 140, 141, 143, 148
knowledge, 1, 4, 5, 6, 11, 24, 30, 31, 33, 34, 35, 36, 37, 41, 42, 43, 51, 53, 54, 55, 59, 88, 94, 96, 110, 127, 135, 136, 137, 138, 145, 152, 154, 158, 162, 164, 165, 166, 173
knowledge economy, 3, 5, 27, 30
knowledge production, 3, 57, 86
knowledge society, 3, 4, 5, 8, 9, 10, 81, 82, 85, 86, 92, 96, 97, 137, 147, 152, 161, 173, 174, 176–8
Kuhlmann, E., 4, 12, 30, 36, 50, 61, 84, 86, 87, 100, 102, 113, 114, 116, 117, 145, 146, 148, 151, 156, 160, 168, 170

labour, 1, 17, 42, 93, 102, 104, 105, 113, 114, 120, 125, 126, 129, 130, 136, 137, 141–4, 163, 166, 179
labour market, 9, 33, 34, 64, 68, 74, 97, 102, 103, 104, 110, 112
Larkin, G., 133, 139, 141, 148, 149
Larson, M., 1, 30, 33, 35, 36, 57, 61, 108, 109, 110, 112, 113, 116
leadership, 26, 40, 69, 70, 71, 87, 110, 123, 127, 128, 129, 130
Light, D., 123, 125, 133, 144, 149

management, 1, 2, 3, 6, 8, 10, 15, 30, 34, 36, 38, 39, 40, 41, 43, 45, 47, 49, 51, 52, 54, 57, 58, 59, 66, 69, 70, 71, 74, 81, 84, 86, 88, 90, 91, 92, 93, 94–7, 103, 104, 122, 123, 124, 125, 127, 128, 129, 130, 131, 141, 142, 143, 152, 156, 158, 160, 168, 175

Index

management – *continued*
manager(s), 10, 36, 39, 41, 49, 57, 59, 69, 70, 73, 81, 85, 86, 90, 98, 103, 119, 120, 122, 123, 125, 126, 129, 155, 156, 167
managerialism, 2, 25, 34, 36, 49, 51, 52, 88, 90, 114, 119, 120, 123, 124, 125, 126, 128, 129, 130, 131, 135, 141, 146, 152, 157, 159, 160, 173, 178
new public management, 24, 30, 56, 81, 119, 144, 152, 173
market, 1, 3, 4, 6, 7, 9, 10, 24, 25, 30, 31, 33, 34, 36, 43, 45, 52, 56, 59, 64, 68, 71, 74, 77, 88, 92, 97, 102, 103, 109, 110, 112, 113, 123, 125, 126, 135, 139, 140, 141, 143, 144, 145, 147, 151, 154, 156, 172, 173, 174, 175, 177, 179
medics, 119, 127, 128
medical profession, 16, 38, 59, 102, 120, 121, 123, 125, 129, 135, 136, 138, 139, 140–5, 147, 152, 153, 155, 156, 157, 158, 159, 160, 163, 164–8, 175, 176
medicine, 16, 19, 67, 70, 125, 126, 130, 135–9, 140–7, 151–6, 158, 160, 161, 163–8, 176
midwifery, 104, 106, 139, 141
migration, 9, 102, 105, 111
Mintzberg, H., 2, 12, 35, 42, 43, 61, 173, 180
monopoly, 1, 9, 33, 109, 110, 112, 113, 138, 139, 145

National Health Service, 38, 102, 139, 140, 141, 152, 175
Neave, G., 5, 7, 11, 12, 15, 17, 18, 20, 23, 24, 25, 26, 28, 29, 44, 60, 61, 62, 175, 177
Noordegraaf, M., 35, 62, 84, 92, 94, 100, 114, 117, 159, 160, 170
nurses, 1, 5, 6, 7, 9, 11, 32, 36, 40, 46, 47, 48, 50, 51, 53, 54, 55, 56, 57, 58, 73, 82, 83, 84, 87, 89, 92, 95, 102, 103, 104, 105, 106, 107, 108, 109, 110, 111, 112, 113, 136, 156, 158, 159, 162, 174, 176, 177, 178
nursing, 9, 16, 24, 38, 40, 45, 46, 57, 67, 82, 84, 85, 90, 94, 95, 96, 102, 103, 104, 106, 108, 109, 110–11, 112, 113, 115, 139, 141, 157, 167

occupational groups, 1, 4, 30, 84, 147

Parkin, F., 33, 62, 113, 117, 136, 146, 149
patient, 40, 49, 54, 56, 91, 92, 94, 109, 111, 112, 119, 121, 122, 123, 126, 129, 130, 141, 142, 155, 157, 159, 160, 161, 163
patient choice, 88, 142, 152
physician, 40, 102, 105, 106, 108, 109, 110, 124, 131, 138, 145, 152, 155, 157, 158, 159, 160, 161, 162, 166
Pollitt, C., 24, 29, 30, 36, 62, 81, 86, 100, 120, 121, 123, 130, 133, 134, 141, 148
power, 1, 2, 4, 8, 10, 18, 20, 22, 25, 30, 32, 33, 34, 35, 36, 39, 43, 48, 50, 51, 54, 57, 58, 59, 69, 70, 81, 82, 84, 85, 87, 92, 95, 97, 109, 110, 113, 119, 121, 125, 126, 136, 138, 140, 141, 142, 144, 152, 157, 158, 159, 162, 164, 165, 166, 168, 172, 173, 174, 176, 177, 178
Power, M., 82, 100, 125, 134
precarious, 9, 55, 111, 113
privatisation, 30, 83, 103, 125
professional bureaucracy, 35, 42, 43, 156
professionalisation, 1, 4, 9, 10, 33, 35, 57, 59, 70, 83, 84, 106, 108, 110, 136, 140, 146, 147, 152, 156, 164, 174, 175
de-professionalisation, 31, 36, 46, 109, 110, 113, 120, 144, 146, 147, 176, 177
professionalization, 103, 109, 110
professions, 1–8, 19, 24, 27, 30–3, 36, 37, 40, 43, 45, 58, 83, 85, 89, 104, 110, 114, 121, 135, 136, 139, 140–6, 151, 152, 158, 159, 161, 164, 167, 168, 172–4, 176, 178, 179

professionalism, 1–5, 9, 23, 30, 31, 33, 34, 43, 49, 50, 51, 56, 59, 81, 84, 85, 86–9, 92–7, 102, 103, 113, 114, 135–7, 144, 155, 158, 159, 165, 168, 172–4, 176–8
public service(s), 22, 32, 43, 59, 66, 70, 81, 82, 83, 86, 88, 92, 96, 123, 146

quality, 8, 16, 20, 23, 37, 39, 53, 55, 65, 68, 69, 71, 74, 81, 82, 83, 86, 95, 103, 105, 108, 126, 130, 143, 144, 159, 161, 166, 167, 174, 176

regulation, 3, 4, 7, 9, 10, 46, 48, 50, 58, 69, 89, 108, 109, 113, 124, 129, 136, 142, 143, 144, 151, 153, 154, 155, 156, 161, 164, 165, 166, 167, 168, 175, 176, 177
regulatory mechanisms, 113, 142, 151, 155
research, 4, 5, 11, 16, 21, 24, 31, 40, 50, 55, 56, 64–9, 70–7, 88, 98, 106, 139, 152, 157, 159, 166, 178
resistance, 11, 58, 90, 91, 109, 141
restratification, 83, 84, 141, 143, 146, 147
Rhoades, G., 19, 24, 29, 48, 62

Saks, M., 4, 10, 113, 114, 117, 133, 135, 136, 137, 138, 139, 140, 141, 142, 143, 144, 145, 147, 148, 149, 150, 151, 168, 170, 175, 176, 178
Santiago, R., 1, 4, 5, 8, 11, 12, 30, 32, 36, 37, 44, 47, 50, 53, 56, 60, 61, 62, 77, 172, 173, 177, 179
Serra, H., 10, 151, 152, 155, 161, 162, 164, 167, 171, 176, 178
social closure, 1, 6, 10, 33, 35, 135–9, 140, 143, 144, 145, 146, 147, 176
closure strategy, 109
social services, 8, 64, 65, 68
Stacey, M., 61, 123, 134, 138, 150
Stakeholder, 24, 64, 70, 71, 73, 143, 151, 152

State, 3, 4, 5, 6, 7, 8, 9, 10, 11, 15, 16, 20, 21, 22, 24–7, 30, 31, 33, 34, 35–8, 42, 44–7, 57, 58, 65, 66, 68, 71, 72, 76, 77, 81, 83, 85, 86, 87, 88, 89, 92, 93, 96, 97, 102, 104, 109, 110, 113, 114, 119, 122, 123, 135, 136, 138, 139, 140, 141, 142, 144, 145, 146, 147, 151, 152, 153, 154, 155, 156, 158, 161, 162, 164–8, 171–8
Status, 1, 16, 18, 19, 20, 27, 30, 34, 38, 42, 47, 64, 66, 77, 85, 86, 95, 109, 113, 114, 119, 120, 122, 136, 137, 138, 140, 141, 144, 152, 173, 175–7
Stoker, G., 125, 134
Student estate, 18, 22

teaching, 21, 24, 49, 55, 67, 69, 74, 75, 157, 166
technologisation, 81, 82, 89
Teichler, U., 67, 69, 70, 77, 78
Trow, M., 19, 23, 29, 48, 63
trust, 33, 82, 85, 86, 92, 93, 94, 96, 97, 98, 119, 141, 142, 144, 152, 155, 173
Twigg, J., 84, 87, 94, 95, 101

university, 15, 18, 19, 20, 21, 22, 24, 25, 27, 44, 47, 56, 58, 65, 66, 67, 68, 69, 70–6, 146, 175
users, 10, 11, 82, 85, 86, 90, 97, 110, 123, 135, 141, 144, 156, 157, 164, 167

Ward, S., 30, 63, 172, 180
Weber, M., 2, 10, 33, 34, 35, 42, 43, 135–9, 143, 144, 146, 147
welfare service, 83, 87, 95–7, 173
welfare state, 3, 6, 7, 9, 24, 25, 30, 31, 37, 77, 81, 83, 85, 86, 87, 89, 92, 97, 102, 122, 123, 146, 172, 173, 174, 175
welfare state reforms, 81, 96, 97

The manufacturer's authorised representative in the EU is Springer Nature Customer Service Centre GmbH, Europaplatz 3, 69115 Heidelberg, Germany. If you have any concerns regarding our products, please contact ProductSafety@springernature.com

Printed and bound by CPI Group (UK) Ltd, Croydon, CR0 4YY
23/03/2026
02076447-0017